OUR
CHANGING
WORLD-VIEW

Wits Press RE/PRESENTS

Wits University Press celebrates its centenary in 2022. Since its inception, the Press has been curating and publishing innovative research that informs debate to drive impactful change in society. Drawing on an extensive backlist dating from 1922, **Wits Press Re/Presents** is a new series that makes important research accessible to readers once again. While much of the content demonstrates its historical provenance, it remains of interest to researchers and students, and is re-published in e-book and print-on-demand formats.

OUR CHANGING WORLD-VIEW

TEN LECTURES

on Recent Movements of Thought in Science, Economics, Education, Literature and Philosophy

by

Lieut.-General the Right Honourable J. C. Smuts, P.C., M.P., F.R.S.
Dr. Robert Broom, F.R.S.
Professor J. P. Dalton, M.A., D.Sc.
Professor John F. V. Phillips, D.Sc., F.R.S.E.
Professor J. Y. T. Greig, M.A., D.Litt.
Professor T. J. Haarhoff, B.A., B.Litt., Litt.D.
Professor C. S. Richards, M.Com.
Professor H. S. Frankel, M.A., Ph.D.
Professor R. F. A. Hoernlé, M.A., B.Sc.
Mr. I. D. MacCrone, M.A.

WITS UNIVERSITY PRESS

Published in South Africa by:
Wits University Press
1 Jan Smuts Avenue
Johannesburg 2001

www.witspress.co.za

Published edition © Wits University Press 2021

First published 1932

http://dx.doi.org.10.18772/22021085553

978-1-77614-555-3 (Paperback)
978-1-77614-556-0 (Web PDF)
978-1-77614-557-7 (EPUB)

All rights reserved. No part of this publication may be reproduced, stored in a retrieval system, or transmitted in any form or by any means, electronic, mechanical, photocopying, recording or otherwise, without the written permission of the publisher, except in accordance with the provisions of the Copyright Act, Act 98 of 1978.

Cover design: Hybrid Creative
Typeset in 10.5 point Plantin

CONTENTS

Introduction: Saul Dubow — vii
Preface: H. R. Raikes — xvii

1. *Some Recent Scientific Advances in Their Bearing on Philosophy* — 1
   Lieut.-General the Right Honourable J. C. Smuts

2. *The Material World—Yesterday and Today* — 21
   Professor J. P. Dalton

3. *Evolution—Design or Accident?* — 47
   Dr. Robert Broom

4. *Man at the Crossroads* — 69
   Professor John F. V. Phillips

5. *Psychology in Perspective* — 101
   Mr. I. D. MacCrone

6. *Literature in the Machine Age* — 127
   Professor J. Y. T. Greig

7. *The Holistic Attitude in Education* — 147
   Professor T. J. Haarhoff

8. *Our Changing Economic World* — 167
   Professor C. S. Richards

9. *Africa in the Re-Making* — 197
   Professor S. H. Frankel

10. *Old Truths and New Discoveries* — 225
    Professor R. F. Alfred Hoernlé

INTRODUCTION

This remarkable volume, published in a handsome red cloth edition with gold lettering, can be read as a statement of aspiring confidence on the part of a young, civic university, asserting its maturation as a centre of serious and engaged scholarship. In 1932, Johannesburg was still a brash mining town, better known for the production of wealth than knowledge. Merely a decade had passed since the University of the Witwatersrand's incorporation, by parliamentary statute, as a university. In 1932 it had a student enrolment of just 1 782, taught by forty professors and forty-five permanent staff. The beginnings of a shift from investment in mining to investment in cultural capital was clearly underway.

On Christmas Eve, 1931, a fire entirely destroyed the university library and its invaluable Gubbins Africana collection, housed on top of a temporary wood and iron structure in the Central Block. There was no contents insurance to make good the damage. This book was in significant measure part of an ambitious programme of reconstruction. It was conceived as a way of raising public awareness of the need for rebuilding by demonstrating Wits' special role in the civic life of Johannesburg and its intellectual standing in the country. The fire was a baptism: notwithstanding the economic depression then engulfing the country (Wits suffered a 20 per cent cut in its state subsidy in 1932), substantial finance was raised by a special appeal fund. Progress was swift. A handsome new library, architecturally inspired by the Petit Trianon in the gardens of Versailles, was opened in 1934 by Prince George, Duke of Kent. The building was named after William Cullen, a Scottish chemist and metallurgist with interests in education, whose close links to the mining industry positioned him to spearhead the building campaign. Remarkably, half of the 60 000 volumes acquired by this time were donated.

Our Changing World-View: Ten Lectures on Recent Movements of Thought in Science, Economics, Education, Literature and Philosophy was therefore published in the midst of an interregnum. Four years after his appointment in 1928, the new principal, Humphrey Raikes, was yet to be confirmed in post by Council – a process that had been much delayed by internal political wrangling. Wits was in the midst of a major rebuilding on its Milner Park campus. The country was on the cusp of economic renewal, riding the wave of a mining-led boom occasioned by the country's abandonment of the gold-standard in December 1932. The politics of racial segregation were actively being debated at this time with the 'Native Bills', first introduced to parliament in 1926, midway through their decade-long parliamentary passage. Prime minister J.B.M Hertzog had recently been confirmed in power at the 1929 'black peril' election. Jan Smuts would soon return as deputy prime minister in the coalition 'fusion' government of 1933–1934.

For now, Smuts was leader of the opposition, a leading imperial statesman and intellectual, author of a widely discussed treatise on holism. He had just outlined this philosophy in a prestigious presidential address to the British Association for the Advancement of Science on the occasion of its 1931 centenary.

Firmly supportive of the Commonwealth idea, and fully committed to white 'South Africanism' – whose politics encompassed Anglo-Afrikaner 'racial' reconciliation and cautious moderation in respect of the 'native' or 'colour' question – Smuts was a hero to the Anglophone liberals and industrialists who constituted Johannesburg's cultural elite. It was therefore fitting that his chapter on recent scientific advances and their bearing on philosophy, in which he reprised his theories of holism, should open the lecture series. Most of the contributors to this volume engaged with his ideas. It was equally fitting that the closing chapter was written by Wits' leading public intellectual, Alfred Hoernlé, who conceived the plan to commission these ten lectures as part of the library appeal. If the review of *Our Changing World-View* in the scientific journal *Nature* is anything to go by, the slim volume proved successful in showcasing Wits as a vital intellectual centre at a time of dynamic societal change: The frank facing of realities in the South African situation in these lectures should give them an interest beyond South Africa itself, and their pragmatism as much as the holistic outlook give unity to the series. Furthermore, they indicate the high conception of educational work that Wits cherishes, and represent an attempt to encourage the spread of a wider culture among the people of South Africa as a whole.

That all ten contributors to the volume were white and male cannot today pass unnoticed. So, too, were the chairs and discussants who gave votes of thanks after each lecture (the sole exception was the writer Sarah Gertrude Millin who delivered the vote of thanks to John Greig's inaugural lecture on 'Literature in the Machine Age', chaired by Raikes). The selection of some of these government officials and politicians – including D.F. Malan and J.H. Hofmeyr – reveals a studied effort to introduce an element of bipartisan political representation. Yet, no black intellectual is represented here and, indeed, the politics of racial segregation bursts through the text only in a few of the contributions. For the most part, race is alluded to only in passing.

The chapter on psychology by I.D. MacCrone surveys contemporary trends in the discipline, from Wilhelm Wundt and Gestalt to Charles Spearman and Sigmund Freud. Although MacCrone is best known today for his pioneering study *Race Attitudes in South Africa: Historical, Experimental and Psychological Studies* (1937) there is no reference here to South African contexts. Similarly, palaeontologist Robert Broom, who along with Raymond Dart was the foremost expert on hominin development in South Africa, chose to lecture on evolution from the philosophical perspective of intelligent design and natural philosophy. No mention is made by Broom of his own discoveries, though examples from South African birdlife are adduced to make the point that Darwinism is insufficient to explain evolution: in Broom's view, only an underlying telos or guiding hand, closer to Smutsian holism or Bergsonian *élan vital*, can account for the development of molars in horses or the special beauty of birds and flowers.

The irrepressible subject of race emerges alarmingly in the chapter by John Phillips, not least because of the clumsy way in which it is bolted on to his chosen subject, botany. A devoted protégé of Smuts, Phillips was a self-styled 'ecologist' who was committed to studying the interrelations of all forms of life. Phillips's discussion of tsetse fly exemplifies his holistic ecological approach to the interlinked factors of plants, animals and humans in the 'biotic community'. Yet, this topic is prefaced by a fevered discussion of eugenics encompassing miscegenation, degeneration, and overpopulation, in tones that were insistent even by the standards of the day. Here, the dark side of ecology and preservationism is clearly on display. Phillips' fears extend also to the pace of modern life and the 'nervous strain' arising from telephones, machinery, and cinema. Even the 'horror' of television (a prospect that lay almost 50 years ahead for South Africans because of fears that it would corrupt society) is prophesied.

The perils and possibilities of the 'machine age' are addressed by several contributors, reflecting the aftermath of wartime destruction and the challenges of modernity. Johannesburg, the vibrant centre of South Africa's economy, was ideally placed to discourse on such matters. The dangerous thrill of the new is taken up by John Greig's lively contribution on 'Literature in the Machine Age'. Newly arrived at Wits from Vanderbilt University, Greig was born in Manchuria to a Scottish medical missionary and educated at Glasgow University. This broad experience provides the context for a breathy observation: 'In 1932 it is hardly an exaggeration to say that a hasty word dropped by some insignificant John Smith in a tiny dorp in the Northern Transvaal may affect the production of oil in Oklahoma or precipitate a revolution in Brazil. By means of the machine we have reduced the whole word to the dimensions of a village.' The insight anticipates Marshall McLuhan's 'global village' by a generation.

Greig appreciates the excitement and the dangers of interconnected speed. Notably, he takes issue with Phillips's catastrophism, arguing that science confers many benefits on society. For Greig (whose little-known biography of David Hume won the James Tait Black literary prize in 1931) there was more to fear by handing over increased power to men of scientific training – a common demand by eugenicists. This would amount to 'a calamity only a little less disastrous than a government composed exclusively of businessmen.' Greig was attuned to the spiritual dangers of the machine age, but his liberal humanism leads him to focus his fears, with a nod to Bertrand Russell, on the dangers of 'power wielded for the sake of power, not power wielded for the sake of genuine good.'

For the classicist, T.J. Haarhoff, classical Humanism 'is the parent of Holism' in the sense that it seeks 'significant connections' as well as 'harmony between man and man' and between 'man and nature' rather than uniformity. In education, this entailed bridging the gap between analytic and synthetic reading, between grammar and literature, between *philologos* and *philosophos*. In the South African context, it meant coping 'with the complex problems of race and nationality' and striving for 'fruitful diversity within a harmonious union', be this in relations between English and Afrikaans cultures or 'in our consideration of things like the Native Question'. Haarhoff was already a strong proponent of the Afrikaans language, yet he was opposed to narrow nationalism and he was a devoted liberal supporter of Smuts.

The philosophical dimensions of the machine age were taken up by Smuts in his discussion of new theories of space-time. The politician's remarkable capacity for synthesis is on full display here as he surveys approaches to relativity and quantum theory in the work of the German mathematician Hermann Minkowski and his student, Albert Einstein. Smuts touches, too, on the work of Max Planck and Werner Heisenberg. His own gloss on the 'new physics' emphasises its holistic character. Smuts likens knowledge to a prism 'which refracts or divides experience into a spectrum, dividing the real situation into the spectrum of certainty and uncertainty' and showing light to be both particle-like and wave-like. By analogy, Cartesian dualism was considered outdated as a result of new developments that 'release of the human spirit from the bondage of matter'; these held out the prospect of 'a still greater synthesis looming ahead, in which a spiritual view of the universe may not only be justified but may receive firm support from science itself.'

Mathematician J.P. Dalton's discussion of particle physics – building on his inspiring lecture series on Einstein and relativity delivered in 1921 – continues the line of argument opened up by Smuts. Dalton proceeds to argue against philosophical determinism. His survey of the wave-particle theory of matter, encompassing the work of Louis De Broglie, Erwin Schrödinger, Paul Dirac and Werner Heisenberg, focuses on phenomena such as the nature of the atom, x-rays, and radiation. In a clear, if oblique criticism of Smuts, Dalton concludes that the purpose of the mind is to interpret observed facts and not to attempt to 'squeeze Nature into a mould of its own contriving.' This leads him to the uncompromising view that 'of the ultimate structure of the material world we now know – precisely nothing.'

Two nicely counterposed contributions by economists bring us back to the problems of the society in a state of rapid transition. C.S. Richards, who went on to write a major study of state intervention in South Africa's iron and steel industry, here makes a case for laissez-faire economics, mindful of the fact that the First World War meant an end to an open world in which labour, capital and goods flowed unimpeded all over the globe. He rails against tariffs, quotas, and wage boards, all the while aware that there is no return to the status quo ante. Standing on the 'threshold of a new era', Richards maintains that there is no question more important than the choice between nationalism and internationalism in economic affairs. The tendency, he hopes, is towards greater worldwide economic integration, and a renewal of economic liberalism tempered by international machinery designed to preserve price stability and the settlement of global economic problems.

The influence of John Maynard Keynes on Richards' thinking is clearly evident here, as it is in S.H. Frankel's chapter on 'Africa in the Re-Making'. Notably, Frankel's argument is specifically focused on Africa; it anticipates in many ways the school of development economics which he later contributed to at the University of Oxford after the Second World War. While at Wits, Frankel placed great hope in the cautious liberalism of Hofmeyr. His economic thought drew on personal experience (his father was a grain merchant in Johannesburg and his brother developed the business to become Tiger Oats) as well as a keen awareness of history and anthropology, both liberal arts disciplines that were flourishing at Wits.

In this chapter, Frankel argues passionately against slavery and serfdom – both of which he sees as inimical to western civilisation. Yet, Frankel also sees progressive European civilisation as essential to African development. He is alive to the inherent exploitation of capitalist imperialism in South Africa in respect of the subjection of Afrikaner poor whites and poor blacks. At root, the causes of their subjection are linked. However, far from arguing against capitalism, Frankel maintains that in it 'economic development of the Native peoples lies the only hope for the future of this country'. Inspired by the thinking of the Dutch colonial A.D.A De Kat Angelino, as well as his British counterpart, Hilton Young, Frankel argues that the 'real problem of colonization' is a matter of creative destruction. 'Only that must be destroyed which it is in the real interests of the societies of the indigenous peoples themselves to destroy, and they themselves must be harnessed voluntarily to the task of transformation.'

The final chapter in this collection is by the German-schooled and Oxford-trained philosopher of idealism, Alfred Hoernlé, husband of the leading Wits anthropologist Winifred (née Tucker), and by now the éminence grise of South African liberalism. Hoernlé's deft discussion of Smuts and Dalton's treatment of physics raises the question as to whether nature is 'inherently indeterminate'. He also takes issue with Broom's view that there is a god-like 'directive power' in evolution. Turning to Greig's question about the capacity of art and literature to flourish in the machine age, Hoernlé expands on the problem of power by pointing to the 'most glaring paradox', brought home by the current economic depression, 'that we are poor in the midst of actual and potential plenty.' Part of the difficulty lies in determining in whose interest machines work. The optimistic view is that machines might offer the possibility of increased leisure without exacerbating unemployment.

By way of conclusion, Hoernlé meditates on the future of religion which, he argues, will not die out in the face of human progress. Nor will Christianity replace other religious beliefs like Islam. He is alive to the contradictions of Christian religion in a colonial context and the dilemma faced by non-Europeans in the face of its expansion. Which end of the dog to believe, he asks? 'The tail-wagging missionary end or the teeth-showing end of armed conquest and economic exploitation? It is the unsolved riddle still.'

Our Changing World-View invites comparison with a contemporaneous volume, *Coming of Age: Studies in South African Citizenship and Politics* (1930) timed to celebrate the 'twenty-first year of South Africa's life as a political unit'. Haarhoff and Frankel contributed to both volumes. But, whereas *Coming of Age* was overshadowed by policy choices reflecting immediate political and economic pressures, *Our Changing World-View* is more reflective and attuned to the life of the mind as it promotes Wits as a progressive, broad-based university. It should be remembered that Wits' origins lie in the Transvaal Technical Institute, created in 1904, with strong links to the mining industry and, before this, the South African School of Mines established at Kimberley in 1896. The absence of any contribution by engineers, geologists, or medical doctors to *Our Changing World-View* seems to signal the desire, on the part of a rising generation of thinkers, to demonstrate that utilitarian knowledge is not Wits' only concern or strength.

Much had been accomplished in a short space of time. In 1921, the settler colonial historian, George Cory, wrote sarcastically to fellow historian, W.M. Macmillan, about Wits' pretentions to be a university, joking that it would surely feature undergraduate courses in banking and bootlace-making with Yiddish as the medium of instruction. Just a decade later, Wits had survived a major fire as well as a divisive battle between Senate and the principal, Hofmeyr, over the forced resignation of anatomy professor Edward Philip Stibbe, who was accused of having had an extra-marital affair (three contributors to this volume, Dalton, Haarhoff, and Hoernlé, came out on the side of Stibbe). Scandals linked to morality and propriety were conspicuous in Wits' formative years.

Our Changing World-View was an occasion for Wits' leading faculty members to relaunch the university as a mature institution with a leadership role in public affairs. Above all, it was a means to project the university as a research as well as a teaching institution, led by a vigorous and ambitious cohort of liberal-minded intellectuals. This is partly explicable in terms of the need, as it was then perceived, to show Wits as fully worthy of university status: at one and the same time, a key institution in the life of Johannesburg, a valued South African national institution, and an enlightened educational outpost of the British world.

Saul Dubow
Smuts Professor of Commonwealth History,
University of Cambridge
17 March 2020

PREFACE

The educational work of a university is twofold: the actual teaching of its undergraduate students and the spread of culture among the people as a whole. The University of the Witwatersrand is still very young and with the limited resources at its disposal it has been compelled to restrict itself until recently to the first aspect of its work.

But the marked sympathy displayed towards the University as a result of the disastrous fire in the Central Block at the end of 1931 indicated that the citizens of the Rand were not unmindful of the value of the work which has so far been accomplished, and encouraged Professor Hoernlé to make a move in the development of the second aspect. The result has been the delivery of the public lectures printed in the following pages.

In offering the thanks of the University to the lecturers, I feel that I must single out for special mention the two who are not members of the staff. General Smuts and Dr. Broom are known the world over for their interest in the development of science and philosophy, but that they should have consented to spare the time which they must have spent on the preparation of their lectures indicates a very real sympathy with the aspirations of the University towards the development of a wider culture in South Africa.

It is also a pleasure to thank all those, many of them quite unconnected with the University, who presided at the lectures and proposed votes of thanks. More especially I wish to express the appreciation of the University to the Minister of Education, the Hon. Dr. D. F. Malan, who showed his interest in the University and in the Course by coming across from Pretoria to preside at the last lecture, and who encouraged us by the suggestion that similar courses of public lectures should be arranged in future years.

The order of the lectures, as published in this volume, differs in one respect from the order of delivery. Dr. Broom's lecture, although actually delivered sixth, now occupies its logical place as the third. Below, I give, for historical record, the programme of the lectures as actually delivered. It reveals that among the lecturers, chairmen and proposers of the votes of thanks all sections of the community were represented. The support thus given indicates, I feel, a real interest in, and a genuine willingness to co-operate for, the development of a true South African culture.

The lectures are printed substantially as they were delivered. The only exception is the addition, in Professor Hoernlé's lecture, of the last section, on "The Future of Religion," which had to be omitted in delivery owing to lack of time.

If there is one characteristic which marks the individuality of the thought of recent times, it is the overpowering belief in the dynamic character of the Universe. I refer not merely to physical motion, as exemplified by aeroplanes or the intra-atomic motions of electrons and protons, but also to that more philosophic sense of motion of which we generally speak as evolution—evolution in biology, philosophy, economics and even in education. Nothing fixed can any longer be considered stable.

This course of lectures was designed to give some insight into the changes in our world and in our theories of, and attitudes towards, our world. If it helps those who attended the lectures, or who now read them in book form, to formulate a philosophy of motion, it will, I maintain, have assisted in the development of a real culture for South Africa.

In conclusion, a special word of thanks is due to Professor Hoernlé, who conceived the plan of the lectures, and whose energy and enthusiasm have, through the mouths of the lecturers, produced an entrancing description of change and development.

H. R. RAIKES,
Principal.

Johannesburg,
14*th October*, 1932.

PROGRAMME OF LECTURES ON OUR CHANGING WORLD VIEW

Delivered under the auspices of the University Philosophical Society during the winter of 1932, in aid of the University Library Appeal Fund.

1. Monday, June 6th.
Subject: *Recent Advances in Science and Philosophy.*
    Lecturer: Lieut.-General the Right Honourable J. C. Smuts, P.C., M.P., F.R.S., Honorary Life President of the University Philosophical Society.
    Chairman: The Vice-Chancellor of the University, Mr. H. J. Hofmeyr.
    Vote of Thanks: Professor P. J. du Toit, President of the South African Association for the Advancement of Science.
    Professor R. F. A. Hoernlé, Department of Philosophy.

3. Monday, June 13th.
Subject: *The Material World—Yesterday and Today.*
    Lecturer: Professor J. P. Dalton, Department of Mathematics and Actuarial Science.
    Chairman: Professor R. F. A. Hoernlé (in the absence, through illness, of His Honour the Administrator of the Transvaal, Mr. J. S. Smit).
    Vote of Thanks: Dr. H. J. van der Byl, Chairman of the Electricity Commission.

4. Monday, June 20th.
Subject: *Man at the Crossroads.*
    Lecturer: Professor John F. V. Phillips, Department of Botany.
    Chairman: Dr. Pole-Evans, Chief of the Division of Plant Industry in the Department of Agriculture.
    Vote of Thanks: Dr. A. C. Leemann, Division of Plant Industry.

5. Monday, June 27th.
Subject: *Psychology in Perspective.*
    Lecturer: Mr. I. D. MacCrone, Senior Lecturer in Psychology.

Chairman: Professor J. T. Dunston, M.D., B.S., formerly Union Commissioner for Mental Hygiene.
Vote of Thanks: Dr. L. van Schalkwyk, Organising Secretary, Union Department of Education.

6. Friday, July 29th. Inaugural Lecture.
Subject: *Literature in the Machine Age.*
Lecturer: Professor J. Y. T. Greig, Department of English.
Chairman: The Principal of the University, Mr. H. R. Raikes.
Vote of Thanks: Mrs. Sarah Gertrude Millin.

7. Monday, August 8th.
Subject: *Evolution—Accident or Design?*
Lecturer: Dr. Robert Broom, F.R.S.
Chairman: Mr. J. H. Hofmeyr, M.P., M.A., D.Sc., former Principal and Vice-Chancellor of the University.
Vote of Thanks: Professor H. B. Fantham, Department of Zoology.
Professor R. A. Dart, Department of Anatomy.

8. Monday, August 15th.
Subject: *The Holistic Attitude in Education.*
Lecturer: Professor T. J. Haarhoff, Department of Classics.
Chairman: Dr. S. F. N. Gie, Union Secretary for Education.
Vote of Thanks: Dr. E. C. Malherbe, Union Department of Education.

9. Monday, August 22nd.
Subject: *Our Changing Economic World.*
Lecturer: Professor C. S. Richards, Department of Commerce.
Chairman: Mr. Samuel Evans, LL.D., D.Sc., Member of the University Council.
Vote of Thanks: His Worship the Mayor of Johannesburg, Councillor D. F. Corlett.

10. Monday, August 29th.
Subject: *Africa in the Re-Making.*
Lecturer: Professor S. H. Frankel, Department of Economics.

Chairman: Advocate F. A. W. Lucas, K.C., Chairman of the Wage Commission, Member of the Native Economic Commission.

Vote of Thanks: Professor Edgar H. Brookes, University of Pretoria.

11. Monday, September 5th.

Subject: *Old Truths and New Discoveries*.

Lecturer: Professor R. F. Alfred Hoernlé, Department of Philosophy.

Chairman: The Hon. Dr. D. F. Malan, Minister of the Interior and Education.

Vote of Thanks: Mr. A. H. Murray, M.A., D.Litt., Ph.D., Lecturer in Philosophy and President of the University Philosophical Society.

Some Recent Scientific Advances in Their Bearing on Philosophy

By
Lt.-General The Right Hon. J. C. SMUTS
P.C., LL.D., F.R.S.

Some Recent Scientific Advances in Their Bearing on Philosophy

In this paper I intend to discuss some recent changes in science and their probable effects on philosophy. These changes, so far as physics is concerned, amount to something like a revolution, and their repercussions on philosophy may yet be no less revolutionary. For the relations between science and philosophy have always been very close and intimate. Originally, they were the same thing, *Wissenschaft* in the broader sense, as the Germans call it. The early Greek philosophers were equally scientists, and Aristotle himself, in whom the movement of Greek thought culminated, was as much scientist as philosopher. We may say that a scientific advance has generally given a great impetus to philosophy. Thus, the coming of modern science in the seventeenth century also meant a philosophic revolution of a far-reaching character. The new philosophy began with the new science, and Galileo, Descartes and Newton—to mention only three names—had a profound influence not only in science but also in philosophy. Both the new empirical philosophy of Locke and the rationalist philosophy of Leibniz had their roots deep in the new science; and this is no less true of Kant's great philosophic synthesis. Coming to the nineteenth century, we find an equally strong influence of science on philosophy. This is seen not only in the general mechanistic tone which nineteenth-century science imparted to its philosophy, but also in the far-reaching influence of certain scientific concepts on philosophy. Thus, the new scientific principle of evolution has profoundly affected the whole outlook of philosophy, although philosophy had been acquainted with the vague idea of evolution at least since the time of Aristotle. But it is the recent advances in physics with which I shall be more particularly concerned. These are admittedly of a fundamental character and may therefore eventually have a correspondingly far-reaching effect on our philosophic outlook and ideas. It is admitted that Relativity and Quantum theory have between them made a greater change in physics than any other discoveries since the seventeenth century. They involve new viewpoints and a new technique which make it possible to re-survey accepted ideas and principles and to subject them to a far more searching scrutiny than was ever possible before. And this new fundamental critique of scientific concepts and principles has its bearing on philosophic concepts and principles as well. We have, however, to bear in mind that the new physical theories are still in a state of flux and far from having received a generally accepted formulation. The philosophic discussion must, therefore, be correspondingly uncertain. But even so it is probable that in philosophy no less than in science we are to-day passing the old frontiers and entering upon a strange new land, where surprising adventures may await us in future.

I shall begin the discussion with the two ideas of space and time—equally important for science and philosophy. They have the advantage of being well known to common sense, and thus lend themselves to easily understood treatment. I do not mean to say that they are free of snags and difficulties. Philosophy is full of profound discussions about their nature, their ontological status, and related problems. These need not trouble us here. We shall start with the plain common-sense meaning of space and time and gradually work our way into the new meanings opened up by recent discoveries. We all understand that events happen in space and in time—in space as the distance covered or traversed; in time as the interval which elapses between the beginning and the end of the event. An object travels a certain distance in a certain time, and its motion or speed depends on the time taken to cover the distance. This is plain common sense, as well as good science and philosophy. But behind this plain surface lurk many strange surprises, as we shall see. Apparently, space and time are quite clear and definite ideas; they are distinct and independent of each other; and they are ultimate or fundamental ideas—ultimates or indefinables both for science and philosophy. So far as science is concerned, we shall see that each of these three conclusions is incorrect, and it is the scientific realization of their incorrectness that has shaken the classical physics to its foundations. Let me briefly trace the steps by which this result has been reached.

The founders of modern science took the plain common-sense view of space and time just stated. Galileo and Descartes assumed them, and Newton explicitly formulated them in his laws of motion, which became the foundation of classical mechanics and physics. The vast body of modern science which thus arose rested on the common-sense space and time. Difficulty first arose in the second half of the nineteenth century when the identity of electromagnetism and light was discovered and Maxwell's equations of the electromagnetic field came to be applied to light. I need not here go into details, but the upshot of the matter was that in 1908 Minkowski came to the discovery that space and time were not independent of each other, that they had a joint operation in physical events, that they not only worked in combination but also varied jointly, and that in consequence time had to be added to the three dimensions of space in the exact determination of events. Henceforth, as he proudly pointed out, space and time separately were but abstractions and shadows, and the reality behind them was space-time. Since then space-time has become a commonplace in physical science, and the common-sense independence of space and time of each other (still accepted by the classical physics) has become a thing of the past. It is a departure so amazing that its real physical significance is even yet not fully realized.

Thus disappeared the separateness or independence of space and time in their merger in a greater whole. Meanwhile, a greater than Minkowski had dealt them a still heavier blow and destroyed their status as fundamental or ultimate concepts. In a rare stroke of genius, Einstein, in 1905, discovered that in one very important respect motion was not derived from space and time, as the classical mechanics taught, but space and time were both dependent on motion. Newton held, and we all believed, that motion or velocity depends on the time taken to cover the distance travelled: $v=s/t$. In other words, space and time are the basic factors, and motion is derived from them. So far as an outside observer of a moving body is concerned, this order was reversed by Einstein, who made their relative motion fundamental, while space and time became derivatives from it. From the point of view of an observer, space is not a fixed quantity but varies with velocity; similarly time. The faster an object moves, relatively to an observer, the smaller its space or volume becomes to him in the direction in which it travels. In other words, motion, in such a case, is not derived from space, but space from motion or velocity. Nay, more: velocity in such a case not only affects space, but also mass; the faster an object moves, relatively to an observer, the greater its mass or intrinsic substance becomes to him. Relative rate of motion thus becomes basic, and contracts or expands space, creates or annihilates mass, for the outside observer. So far as the volume and the physical substance of the world is observed from the outside, its motion becomes a strange creative factor. Such was Einstein's great insight of Relativity, and it has received the fullest confirmation in the minute world of the atom no less than in the immense range of astronomy—wherever, in fact, velocities of the order of light prevail, and their effects are thus big enough to be calculated. Minkowski discovered the greater whole of which both space and time are but parts or aspects; Einstein made the more fundamental discovery that not only space and time but also mass or physical reality, as they appear to an observer with a different frame of reference, are but aspects of something more basic, something curiously associated with velocity. The velocity of light has been shown to be a universal physical constant, and this may have something to do with the creative rôle which velocity plays in the Relativity theory.

These two discoveries are not mere speculations; they are physical insights which have been experimentally verified over and over again; they are theories which work and have proved fruitful in further physical discovery. They carry us far beyond the common-sense or classical view of space and time; indeed, they revolutionize our common-sense outlook. When once we realize that space and time are not separates or absolutes, but abstractions from a whole, functions of something deeper, co-ordinates or relations of things springing from a more fundamental physical reality, we begin to sense a very different world from that which superficially appears to our senses.

The next critique of space and time will carry us even further from the world of common sense and appearance. The space-time critique destroys their separateness and establishes their mutuality. The Relativity critique destroys their ultimate character and shows them to be derivatives or functions of relative velocity.

Both prove their interdependence. The Quantum critique which I am now going to mention establishes their interdependence in another and surprisingly novel way, and with consequences even more far-reaching than those of either space-time or Relativity theory. The Quantum theory, in its application to the concepts of space and time, may be roughly formulated as follows: When the position and velocity of very small units or ultimate particles are jointly considered, then the more accurately we can determine the one, the less accurately we can determine the other, the two inaccuracies being in a fixed ratio such that the two multiplied together always amount to the same universal constant. This constant is the quantum h, which was discovered by Planck in 1900 in quite another connection, but has now turned up in many fundamental physical determinations. The mutuality of time and space, which was proved by Minkowski in a general way, is now shown to be a close and fixed relation, capable of exact measurement, and coinciding with the mysterious quantum constant. Those acquainted with the subject will at once recognize that what I call the Quantum critique of space and time is nothing but Heisenberg's Law of Indeterminacy. Let me explain the law a little further.

When a comparatively large quantity or magnitude is measured, we can use a much smaller body as a unit measure and apply it repeatedly until the quantity or magnitude to be measured has been completely covered. Thus, where the length of a line is to be determined, we can take a small measure and place it continually end to end along this line until we have gone over the whole length of line and thus determined the number of times the unit covers it. This will give its length exactly in terms of the unit. But when the body to be measured is excessively small and the unit correspondingly smaller, when, *e.g.*, the distance between two atoms is measured by another atom, this process of superposition or juxtaposition becomes impossible for exact determination. The contact or proximity of the one slightly moves or displaces the other. The attempt to fix the position of the atom has altered its velocity and momentum. The measure affects the body to be measured and *vice versa*, and a certain unavoidable uncertainty arises in the determination. This can be mathematically determined. As the new physics deals with excessively small units, such as atoms, electrons, protons and photons, or radiations of the minutest wavelengths, this source of uncertainty has been repeatedly determined experimentally. And always the result is that the two uncertainties affecting the position and the velocity of the particle, when multiplied together, produce the quantum h—a quantity so small that expressed as a decimal it contains twenty-seven "0's," but still perfectly determinable and always the same. It is a fundamental uncertainty which inheres in the measurement of all ultimate units, and it applies not only to the position and the velocity of such units but also to their momentum and other measurable characters. This uncertainty involves that it is impossible to determine both the exact position and the velocity of a particle at any particular moment. The more accurately we locate a particle *here*, the more its velocity is altered and it becomes uncertain whether it is here *now*, and not rather in the immediate past or the immediate future. Similarly, if a change happens in such an ultimate particle *now*, or at a fixed moment, the chance increases that the place where it happens is *somewhere else* in the immediate neighbourhood. As the one becomes more certain and determined, the other becomes more uncertain, so that the product of the two uncertainties is always the same. This uncertainty h is as great a mystery of nature as the other absolute unit c or the velocity of light. Just now, when dealing with Relativity, we found the ultimate behind space and time associated with c; now, in the Quantum theory, we find it associated with h or an inherent uncertainty at the heart of things. Between h and c no relation has yet been worked out, as far as I know.

It is sometimes said that space and time relations are true of the macroscopic world, but do not apply to the microscopic world into which physics has recently penetrated. This would be a surprising result if it were true, for a physical state of affairs outside space and time would be really inconceivable. But it is an exaggeration which we are now in a position to correct, and the Quantum theory enables us to determine how the error has arisen. The uncertainty h is the price we pay for abstracting space and time from the underlying dynamic reality of which they are aspects or dimensions and for emphasizing them separately in our search for exact determination. Space and time, as abstractions, involve an uncertainty in the macroscopic, no less than in the microscopic, world; but the uncertainty can be exposed and determined in the microscopic world, whereas it is successfully covered up in the macroscopic world.[1] To go further and to speak of the breakdown of space and time either in the macroscopic or microscopic world would be a mistake. In the microscopic world of atoms, electrons, protons and photons, we deal with unit quantities whose actual determination in individual cases is possible. In such individual examination any particular flaw will be forced to the surface and will not be covered up in the mass or average. Quantum theory, therefore, discloses the true situation in physics as affecting the ultimate individuals which compose the world of matter. And, if there is any concealed flaw in our abstracted concepts of space and time, it will appear and does appear in Quantum physics. The abstracted or separated ideas tend to redintegrate themselves once more: they influence each other when brought together, they cohere in fixed ratios. Their mutuality and reciprocity involve that any emphasis on the one is at the expense of the other, any certainty about the one involves uncertainty about the other, so that the whole which they reflect is maintained throughout. The law of indeterminacy applying to physical units is simply this law of the whole. If we demand exact position, we pay in momentum; if we demand exact momentum, we expend our cash or certainty in position. The product h is an ultimate fact of nature. When, however, we come to the macroscopic world, the world as revealed to our senses, we no longer meet with individuals but with masses; the microscopic unities have disappeared and blended in the mass, and our observations pertain merely to the average. The small oscillations cancel each other out and only the broad effects are summed up and appear. In other words, the certainties of the individual cases add up and their oscillating uncertainties both ways cancel each other out. Only the one factor in h remains and the other disappears. We get a solid impression of space or of time, while the wavering uncertainties surrounding their correlative

---

1 This is well brought out in Prof. F. S. Lindemann's *The Physical Significance of the Quantum Theory*.

factor (time or space, as the case may be) have been swallowed up in the average. The determination of space and time is just as uncertain and faulty in the macroscopic as in the microscopic world, but the law of averages has eliminated the uncertainties and produced a final impression of certainty, permanence and inevitable order. Space and time are in neither case illusory, but merely faulty or defective. The first correction is space-time, which eliminates the grosser error, but even that is not sufficient, as space-time is itself an abstraction from the order of nature. The Quantum points to and actually measures a deeper element of error in our space-time approach to nature. Space and time separately are faulty and the measure of their error is determined by Relativity. But even space-time is faulty, though in a far more subtle way, and the measure of its error is determined by Quantum theory. Yet both space and time, though faulty, are not illusory but point to real features of the whole from which they have been abstracted.

The upshot of this discussion is that space and time are statistical averages, applying to the world of sense not with absolute correctness but only an extremely high degree of probability, which covers up the minute variations from the average disclosed by the Quantum theory. In coming to this conclusion we have reached a position of very great significance and it is, therefore, advisable to give it some further consideration. The consideration of space and time has led us to some of the deepest scientific and philosophic problems.

Sir Arthur Eddington has divided physical laws into two classes—primary law, which deals with the behaviour of individuals, and secondary law, which deals with the behaviour of masses or averages. As the macroscopic world consists of the innumerable physical individuals, its laws are secondary, while the laws of the Quantum and of Quantum physics—concerned with individual behaviour—are primary. This distinction applies not only to the laws of behaviour but also to the concepts of physics. Thus, time and space, energy, momentum, entropy, and the other concepts of the classical mechanics are all secondary or statistical. They are all the result of averaging, and their laws are laws of probability and not of absolute certainty. The apparently necessary connection between phenomena, the uniformity of nature which underlies it, the laws of motion and of energy are all in the last resort of this statistical character, as their apparent certainty nowhere amounts to more than a very high degree of probability. Induction itself, as the method of ascertaining scientific truth, has no other basis than the laws of probability. But, in the vast mass of particulars presented by the macroscopic world, the probability is so high as to exclude all practical doubt and to create the illusion of necessary connection and inevitable determination. In physics the law of entropy is such a statistical law, and similarly the law of cause and effect is a statistical law, based on so high a degree of probability as to produce the illusion of an inherently necessary connection.

In the case of primary law in physics the position is different, as we have seen. As it is concerned with individual behaviour, the averaging-out of variations in the mass is excluded. The uncertainties which exist and are inherent in the law of indeterminacy remain. The degree of certainty is lessened, the illusion of necessity is excluded, and prediction of results becomes more hazardous. The more intense the focus of certainty is, the more extended the fringe of uncertainty surrounding it becomes. Thus, at the *moment* that the quantum of radiation strikes its object, its *position* is quite uncertain, spread like a wave of uncertainty over the universe. Individual behaviour excludes all idea of necessity and inevitability and is in a large measure unpredictable. The past is the only certainty, the moment of action the only judge; the rest is in the nature of things largely undetermined. In fact, the law of indeterminacy draws the one clear physical distinction—apart from our consciousness—between the past and the future, and thus indicates the arrow of time. An individual event—apart from mass impressions—is not really settled before it has happened. Necessity, predetermination of physical happening, may be an illusion created by the mass, but the physical fact below it is the freedom or indetermination of the individual unit. That is to-day as indisputable a truth as any in the whole range of science.

This raises the issue between primary and secondary law in a very acute form. Even if it is conceded that the impression of necessity or necessary connection is an illusion, it will be asked whether there is no uniformity of Nature and no reliability on her procedure. How is the essential freedom which is claimed for the physical individual reconcilable with the immense regularity of Nature as a whole or with the power of scientific prediction which is based on that regularity? How is scientific prediction possible if individual happenings may or may not occur? The reply is that scientific prediction is of the same order as the expectation of an insurance company, whose calculations are likewise based on the law of averages and probability. In the individual case, complete uncertainty as to the date of death, in the mass a very high degree of knowledge as to the incidence of that event. Remember that every macroscopic event is the result of a statistical average, and not an individual case such as the law of indeterminacy covers. The impact of a bullet on a body is an average of an infinite number of electrons, protons and radiations colliding with that body, and in the result the uncertainties of primary law are averaged out and the gross macroscopic event becomes predictable. For practical purposes, therefore, primary law makes no difference and may be ignored, just as general Relativity is ignored in ordinary cases of gravitation. But it is of the deepest significance that physics itself has discovered this inner world of indetermination which exists as the true reality inside the massive regularity and ordered routine of the macroscopic world.

Our examination of space and time has shown that they are not clear and definite concepts, nor independent of each other, nor indefinables or ultimates. Their real status is that of statistical averages which make them apply with a very high degree of exactitude to the macroscopic world, but with much more uncertainty to the microscopic world or to individual physical units. This result may be generalized and applied to many other scientific concepts. Our senses are forms of mass action and their products are complex averages masquerading as simple things or qualities—such are sounds, lights, tastes, smells, and touch in all forms. Perception and conception are likewise forms of mass action or averaging. Our sensuous and mental apparatus is so constituted as to supply us with a number of statistical formulas for reading the events of the macroscopic world. Thus, not only time and space but mass, force, temperature, colour and many other physical percepts and concepts as well as cause and similar mental concepts are of a statistical character and have no higher ontological or metaphysical status. Scientific criticism and research have thus yielded very important results for philosophy as well.

The discovery of the statistical nature of our knowledge of the macroscopic world is of first-rate importance for both science and philosophy. Physical laws now cease to have the absolute character which they had in the nineteenth century. Instead, they are seen to be merely practical, pragmatic statistical formulas; and in particular their former iron necessity or determinism is now seen to amount to no more than a very high degree of probability. This has long been recognized to be the real character of the law of entropy, but we now see that this is also the true status of all macroscopic physical concepts and laws.

Even greater importance attaches to the other discovery referred to, which makes the macroscopic laws inapplicable to the ultimate constituent units of the physical world, and replaces them by the law of indeterminacy in this connection. The real issue raised is the inherent difference between primary and secondary law—the law of individuals and the law of averages. In the physical world the individual is of little practical importance and the average or mass is all-important; hence, the scientific laws of averages give us most of the knowledge we want, and physical science is inherently statistical. But in the world of life and still more of mind, the position is reversed; the individual takes precedence of the mass, and the physical or statistical laws are mostly out of place. We now see that even in physics the individual follows a different regime from the mass or the crowd, and we begin to understand that the sciences of life and especially of human behaviour may have to be very different both in categories and laws from the statistical physical sciences. Let us probe a little deeper into this matter, and let us in the first place stress the difference between an individual and an average.

From a practical point of view, an average can be usefully struck only where the resemblances markedly exceed the differences; where the units or individuals concerned have a fairly high degree of resemblance and their differences are small or negligible in comparison. The differences from the mean which constitutes the average must be practically unimportant. We may have an average horse or an average triangle; but an average of horses and triangles and other quite dissimilar things would be largely useless. Even in regard to apparently similar things, much will depend on our powers or technique of observation. Thus, things which appear similar to the naked eye may prove highly dissimilar under the telescope or microscope. If we could magnify microscopic particles to macroscopic proportions, their apparent similarity would largely disappear and the scope for useful averaging become correspondingly narrowed. The advance of technique in science is thus more and more emphasizing the characters of the individual. Even the simple filterable virus, if sufficiently highly magnified, might appear to be the complex structure it probably is. All macroscopic observation is thus a rough approximation, and in proportion as our fineness of perception is enhanced through technical appliances, the individual with its characteristics emerges more clearly from the mass or average of ordinary observation. The ultimate ideal of science would therefore appear to be to transcend secondary laws and to ascertain primary laws, to recognize the individual in the mass, and to see reality at closest range instead of at a distance and in a blur. In other words, science will tend in its own characteristic way and with its own experimental technique to approximate more closely to the standpoint of philosophy. For philosophy professes to study individual concrete reality, and not to confine itself to the conceptual world, the world of general concepts and universal laws which form the province of science. Philosophy emphasizes the principle of individuality in the world, and physical science is now approaching a similar standpoint and discovering that the advance involves a thorough revision of her own fundamental ideas. The physical law of indeterminacy which has thus been arrived at may carry far-reaching implications, even if it will not bear all the interpretations at present put upon it.

One particular implication which it seems difficult to avoid or deny is the involvement of what we call mind or knowledge in purely physical facts. The indeterminacy or uncertainty to which the law refers is not one merely of knowledge but really of physical happening. It is one thing to be unable to predict a result from want of the necessary knowledge; it is quite a different thing where the inability arises not from insufficient knowledge but from the uncertainty or indeterminacy of the event itself in the act of knowledge, and it is this latter indeterminacy to which the law refers. The act of knowledge, the act of observation or measurement which constitutes knowledge of the event, alters the event *ipso facto*. In ascertaining its position I have changed its time; in ascertaining its moment of happening I have shifted its position and rendered its position uncertain. Knowledge and fact, mind and matter, thus act in closest accord and affect each other and reciprocally determine each other. The act of observation (whatever physical means is adopted) shifts the position or the time of an event, as the case may be, and it is this physical shift which creates the uncertainty and makes prediction impossible. We know that events affect us through sense and so determine our knowledge. Here we see the reverse process. Knowledge or observation by way of indeterminacy affects events. But the effect is blurred in the mass and appears only in the individual case, when it also becomes accurately measurable according to the law of indeterminacy.

This measurable character of the uncertainty is another significant feature of the law of indeterminacy. The uncertainty created by the act of knowledge is not a vague, indefinite affair; it is a measurable quantity and is controlled by the product h, as we have seen. It is this definite amount of indeterminacy which makes this sort of physical uncertainty characterizing individual behaviour a matter of exact mathematical treatment, as recent developments in the Quantum mechanics have shown. The individual shift is not arbitrary; it is controlled by a norm or whole, such that the two factors of certain knowledge and uncertainty in regard to any particular event always yield the same product h. Knowledge acts like a prism, dividing the real situation into the spectrum of certainty and uncertainty; but the product of the two is ever the same, and reconstitutes the whole which knowledge has refracted and split. I come back to this holistic character of reality presently but wish to emphasize here the rôle of mind in material, physical nature.

If the above account of recent advances in physics is correct, it follows clearly that mind as it shows itself in observation and knowledge is a real factor, interacting with physical factors in the world as we know it. The idea of mind as something apart, as reading or interpreting a physical reality which is there unaffected by it, a reality which it can try to know and understand but which it cannot possibly affect or change in any way—this subjective view of mind is negatived by the recent physics. Mind in knowledge has commerce with matter; the physical situation is altered by the intervention of mind in the act of observation or knowledge; but this intervention is not disclosed by the coarse structure of macroscopic nature according to secondary law, and is only seen in the closer mesh of the primary laws and in individual behaviour in nature. So far as Quantum physics is concerned, this effective intervention of mind in matter, of knowledge in physics, is seen in a definite measure of physical disturbance or uncertainty which accompanies the movement of exact knowledge. The throwing of the stone of scientific certainty into the pool starts a measurable wave of uncertainty around it as its inevitable physical effect. But it is a definite ascertainable uncertainty, and Quantum law has actually measured it; it is the same fundamental unit which we find in many other connections in physics. There is no caprice about it; if we use the term freedom in this connection, it is a controlled freedom and always in a definite ratio to the factor of ascertained certainty and always in combination with it, producing the same result, h. The uncertainty is not outside the range of mathematical treatment. The indetermination or freedom which mind creates in nature is not lawless or capricious but is controlled by ascertainable laws of its own. In fact, both determination and indetermination are but elements of the whole dynamic activity or natural process which they describe in knowledge.

And this brings me to say a few words about the whole—this holistic character which meets us in so many connections in the world, in science and in philosophy. I have just now spoken of knowledge as a prism, which refracts or divides experience into a spectrum, where elements of experience are sorted out as separate things. It is part of the essential procedure of mind thus to analyze and discriminate and display a more or less discontinuous series in our knowledge of the world. But the question remains whether this spectrum truly reflects the nature of reality. We have a coarse spectrum of common sense, and a finer spectrum of science; but in both cases we have an analysis; the white light of the whole has been split up as a differential series, and the elements in this series tend to be considered as separate individuals apart from the whole. For practical purposes this view of the world as consisting of separate interacting things is quite necessary, and it is one of the greatest inventions of the mind. Even for macroscopic mechanistic science it serves well enough for all ordinary purposes. But during this century science has begun to see the limits of this common-sense worldview. I have already pointed out how science has found it impossible to continue to look upon space and time as separate things and has had to integrate them into space-time. And this integration is the climax of a long process during which a unification of practically all the forces of nature and forms of energy has been effected. The supposedly fundamental partitions between things have one after the other been pulled down, until to-day there remains only the partition between life and matter or, rather, let me say between mind and physics, as the great divide in knowledge. Quantum theory has, however, now carried us to a point from which the status of science and the laws of nature are seen in a new light, and has enabled us to get to a view of the physical individual and its behaviour which in some respects resembles the behaviour of the biological individual and thus helps to bridge the last great gap in our knowledge. Separatism is disappearing from natural knowledge and with it the foundations of mechanistic science are also disappearing. The world of reality is not the coarse macroscopic world of separate things depending on the secondary laws of averages, but the deeper world of the individual behaving according to primary law. The principle of individuality emerges as the true essence of this universe, in the physical no less than in the ethical or spiritual sphere. And in physics the law which determines the evolution of the universe as a whole is none other than that of the individual behaviour of its most primary units. Thus, Sir Arthur Eddington has, in a recent brilliant discovery, shown that the law which determines the wave motion of an electron is the same as that which regulates the expansion of this universe and the recession of the spiral nebulae. This universe is holistic through and through, with primary law as its foundation, with its parts not merely separately interacting but actually determining and shaping each other, and with whole and parts mutually shaping and determining each other. In a whole there is this pervasive fundamental mutuality of parts and whole which makes each a function of the other and negatives the absolute independence or separateness of the parts. The law of averages which implies separate, more or less similar and enduring units, mechanically and externally interacting with each other, does not apply to a whole, as such. Each whole is an individual, unique and as such not averageable in respect of its constituents. As a whole, as a real individual, the macroscopic laws do not apply to it, and it transcends the scientific principles of causation and determination.

Such a sweeping statement will come as a shock to scientists and will be immediately challenged by all those who attach value to science and to the light it has brought into the world. Let me, therefore, explain. And let me take the human individual as a case for discussion. The human individual can be viewed in two lights, and sustains two different rôles. In the first place, he is an assemblage of physical units and parts. As such, he is subject to the laws of averages and the ordinary principales of science. As a macroscopic entity the human body is on a par with all other bodies and obeys the same scientific laws whatever they may be—conservation, entropy, causation, determinism and the rest. So far we are agreed. But the human individual can also be viewed as an individual whole. A macroscopic assemblage may be a whole and individualized as such or it may not. Such an assemblage may be a mere mechanical aggregate, without organization, plan or cohesion of the parts *inter se*. In such a case it would be merely a matter for the application of the laws of average and entropy without any pretence to more. Again, it may be a highly organized machine, with parts arranged on a plan to subserve some manufacturing purpose. It would, in view of its organization and unity of plan, have some of the attributes of an individual or a whole, but not to such a degree as to prevent the application to it of the physical laws. Or it may be a highly complex chemical structure which would call for new categories of explanation and thus have even more of the character of a unity without, however, yet escaping the dominion of physical laws. Again, it may attain to a still higher form of organization and unity and may function as a living thing, with a system of internal physiological control, and with a wholeness such as no mere physical or chemical body ever possesses. Finally, it may become still more highly organized, with an intelligent internal self-control which can, within limits, initiate or inhibit the functioning of the body or its parts, with conscious purposes and ideals which determine the routine of behaviour; and it may thus possess a complex wholeness and centralized self-direction such as mere animals never attain to. We see in this rising scale of types a continually deepening character of individuality. The assemblage departs farther and farther from the character of an aggregate, a mere physical average, and develops a steadily increasing intensity of individual character. The factors of internal control and self-direction continually increase. From a physical assemblage we have now arrived at a unique individuality or whole. And here our trouble arises. As a physico-chemical assemblage, a material macroscopic phenomenon, the human individual is and remains subject to all the secondary physical laws. As a single whole or uniquely self-determined unity, quite outside the range of the law of average in respect of its internal parts, it is a subject of primary law. And it is also a subject of primary law in respect of its mental, moral and spiritual attributes which do not appear to fall within the province of secondary law. The human individual is therefore subject to the jurisdiction both of primary and secondary law. As a physical collection, he is a macroscopic thermo-dynamical system subject to the laws of energy. As a physiological unity, still more as a mental-spiritual unity, as a soul or personality, he is, within limits, a free agent, with power of initiative, of control, and of shaping his own destiny, regardless of physical causation and entropy. As a complex physical object, he cannot escape the fetters and the doom of matter. As a uniquely individualized whole or soul, he knows no such bonds and is master of his own fate.

There is nothing novel about this conclusion, which has been a commonplace of religion for some thousands of years. The dual nature of man is also the accepted view of common sense. But what is new is the process of reasoning by which this result is here reached. I have used no ethical, religious, or theological arguments. I have simply invoked the primary physical law of indeterminacy and another primary law which I have called holism, according to which evolution is a rising series of wholes, of which man is the highest, most complex, but most intensely individualized. If there is this increasing unity in organic and even inorganic nature, rising to personality in man, we are surely justified in arguing for an intensified application of primary law in biological wholes and especially in the human individual. The release of the human spirit from the bondage of matter and its macroscopic laws can, therefore, be properly based on the science and scientific philosophy of today and calls for no extraneous support. In view of the destructive effects of nineteenth-century science in this connection, the change is a most remarkable one. It shows that science leaves a clear opening for the intervention of other factors which may mould the spirit of man. Science is no longer covertly hostile; it is no longer indifferent or even neutral. And science will enter into the ethics and religion of the future to an extent which the nineteenth century would have thought incredible. It is only in proportion as a new synthesis is reached between science, art and philosophy that a new religion will arise in which the human spirit can once more rest with firm assurance. And the scientific and philosophic developments during the last quarter of a century afford us some hope that the movement towards this great consummation has already begun.

To sum up: Starting from certain vulgar errors in our conception of space and time and the progressive steps by which science has eliminated them, we have seen how their correction has opened up a new view of the nature of scientific knowledge and of the relation of mind to matter. And this relation points to a still greater synthesis looming ahead, in which a spiritual view of the universe may not only be justified but may receive firm support from science itself.

The Material World—
Yesterday and Today

By
J. P. DALTON
M.A., D.Sc.
Professor of Mathematics

The Material World—Yesterday and Today

"Of the Kosmos in the last resort, Science reports many doubtful things, and all of them appalling. There seems to be no substance to this solid globe on which we stamp; nothing but symbols and ratios . . . that way madness lies; Science carries us into zones of speculation where there is no habitable city for the mind of man.

"But take the Kosmos with a grosser faith, as our senses give it to us. We behold space sown with rotatory islands, suns and worlds and the shards and wrecks of systems; some, like the Sun, still blazing; some rotting like the Earth; others, like the Moon, stable in desolation. All of these we take to be made of something we call Matter, a thing which no analysis can help us to conceive, to whose incredible properties no familiarity can reconcile our minds."—*R. L. Stevenson*, "Pulvis et Umbra."

1.—*Introductory.*

The general idea underlying this course of lectures is that we should endeavour to give an account of the present-day position in certain branches of knowledge, and, when possible, contrast current views and theories with those in vogue a generation or more ago. In this scheme mine is the task to deal with the material world. You may wonder why this responsibility is entrusted to a mathematician, for it is surely evident that the world of concrete fact surrounding us can have little in common with the world of abstract symbolism in which a mathematician lives.

It is generally assumed that matter, as we know it, is a simple entity compared with humanity; it exhibits no caprice, no complexities, endures no loves or hates; it lies outside the domain of politics or of economics; it appears to be inherently stable, simple, dull. Perhaps in this dullness we may find the reason why Professor Hoernlé—to whose energy and enthusiasm are due the inception and successful inauguration of these lectures—deemed it probable that the subject would prove congenial to a mathematical mind.

However that may be, it has happened that my whole working life has been spent in intimate contact with physical theory, and that it has covered an epoch of astonishing fruitfulness in scientific discovery. I was still a schoolboy when Röntgen discovered X-rays. To indicate the general spirit of the times, I may add that the following year saw the abrogation in Britain of the law requiring every motor car to be preceded by a man with a red flag. In those days the gramophone was in its infancy—and exercised an infant's chief privilege in making frequent and appalling noise. There were then no airships or aeroplanes, no bioscopes or broadcasting, no talkies or television. In short, life was comparatively peaceful.

2.—*The Main Purpose of Physics.*

We have come to regard these mechanical achievements as desirable concomitants of progress; but, astonishing though they are, it is not of such that I intend to speak. They have, it is true, been given to us by physical science; they have been attained, however, not through conscious and directed effort, but rather as by-products issuing from the process of enquiry into the essence of material phenomena. During such enquiry the physicist encounters novel aspects of Nature; he investigates these and reveals their laws of operation. He is then content to hand them over to the technician for industrial and commercial development.

As he sees each new, and generally profitable, technique originate in his discoveries, the physicist turns again to his own proper function, which is to probe the mysteries of his environment and to examine the structure and behaviour of the material world. His unchanging quest carries him at times to the uttermost depths of space where giant nebulae whirl so far distant from the earth that it takes their light millions of years to reach us; and at times to the inmost recesses of the atom, where he numbers and arranges particles so minute that a hundred million million of them laid side by side would give a length of a few inches. In this search he appears in his true light as a natural philosopher who believes it possible to give a rational account of his surroundings, and seeks to find, in the regularities which he exposes, some dominant guiding principles.

3.—*Classical Mechanics and Causation.*

Our immediate knowledge of the material world is derived through our senses. We are conscious of the presence of gross matter because we see it, feel it, weigh it, move it. We set it in motion by the operation of agencies which we term forces. The relations between operating forces and resulting motions have been codified in a body of doctrine, due to Newton, to which we now refer as the Laws of Classical Mechanics. These relations were originally co-ordinating principles crystallized from an accretion of experimental observations; they brought within their scope the sweep of the planets, the ebb and flow of the tides, the flight of a projectile, the behaviour of a mechanism. Their power of accommodation was so vast that from statements of observed principle they were exalted into instruments of prediction. Our astronomical calendars give us, for years to come, times of sunrise and sunset, dates and times of eclipses of the sun and of the moon, of occultations of the stars. These are computations based upon the Newtonian laws, and the infallibility with which such predictions are fulfilled have hitherto justified our faith that these laws enshrine the major uniformities of Nature.

Underlying the system of classical mechanics are two important principles: (1) that every effect is due to some antecedent cause, or combination of causes, whose recurrence would guarantee a similar effect, and (2) that the linkage between cause and effect is necessarily continuous. For example, we press a trigger here and now; one second later a man 800 yards away drops dead. The primitive mind regards this as miraculous. We, more sophisticated, trace the chain of causation. Knowing the charge in the cartridge, we deduce its explosive force; knowing the weight and shape of the bullet and the rifling of the bore, we calculate the speed and spin with which the bullet emerges; knowing this initial motion and the state of the intervening air, we build up the bullet's path, and finally determine where and when it strikes its victim.

If we are unable to establish or, at least, to imagine a causal chain, we feel that our explanations are incomplete. The idea of "action at a distance" is so repugnant to us that we tend to deny the reality of phenomena rather than admit its possibility.

4.—*Determinism.*

The remarkable success which attended the laws of classical mechanics had its repercussions upon the philosophies of the latter half of the nineteenth century. Our bodies are material systems; they must therefore be subject to the same material laws. Now, if we know completely the state of a material system at any moment, the classical laws determine for us the state of that system at any subsequent time. If, therefore, human beings were material systems, *and nothing else*, there could be no possible escape from the conclusion that our actions are effects inevitably flowing from their antecedent causes; we should have no freedom of choice, for, granting the causes, the response would be inevitable. If only our knowledge of our own material systems were adequate, we could trace the irrefragable chain of causation from birth to death.

> Yesterday *This* Day's Madness did prepare:
> To-morrow's Silence, Triumph, or Despair:
>   Drink! for you know not whence you came, nor why:
> Drink! for you know not why you go, nor where.

Philosophical determinism was one of the chief bases underlying the conflict between religion and science which was a prominent feature of intellectual life in the latter half of the nineteenth century. For myself, I find it difficult to realize how any intellectual satisfaction or mental stimulus could have been associated with a denial of free-will. But it is not my function tonight to discuss questions of ethical values; I pass on, therefore, with the simple statement of fact that philosophical determinism is not founded upon any intrinsic properties of the mind itself; its assumptions are that we are but material systems, and that the material universe is itself deterministic. If either of these beliefs prove to be unsound, then determinism must seek its justification elsewhere.

5.—*Structure of Matter—Continuous or Granular?*

We are interested in aspects of matter other than its movements; the problem of its constitution, in particular, is as old as science itself. Take a piece of graphite, let us say, and break it into two pieces; each piece will exhibit all the properties of the original except its size and weight. Continue the process of sub-division as long as possible, and still the smallest speck obtainable will be as much carbon as the original. Sub-division alters the size, but not the nature of the fragments. There comes a stage when further fissure is impossible, even with the aid of a microscope; but our enquiring minds suggest the problem: if the process could be continued, would the recognizable properties of carbon persist indefinitely, or would we reach a stage when further sub-division would destroy the character of the particle and give us something which is no longer carbon?

The same fundamental question of structure arises in connection with every category of physical experience. Energy, radiation, electricity, space, time, are these, in their last analysis, continuous or discrete?

6.—*The Old Atomic Theory.*

In so far as the structure of matter is concerned, the chemist came to the aid of the physicist, for the chemist is able to command more powerful methods of sub-division. By heat, by solution, by chemical reactions, he is able to reduce matter to a degree of fineness long past the limits even of microscopic vision. For more than one hundred years chemists have insisted that matter is not infinitely sub-divisible. They have told us that every material substance is constructed from molecules, just as a house is built of bricks. Molecules are themselves divisible, but not without change of nature, so that the molecule is the ultimate constituent of a substance. The parts of molecules are atoms. When atoms of the same kind unite to form molecules, the resulting substance is called an element; when the constituent atoms are of different kinds, the substance is a compound. There are in all about ninety different kinds of atom.

It looked as if the premature boast of Lucretius, *Rerum primordia pandam*, had at last been fulfilled, for the chemists supported their theories with a wealth of experimental evidence that conferred upon their conclusions an irresistible strength.

7.—*Kinetic Theory of Matter.*

Atoms, like the Lucretian "first seeds of things," were pictured as hard, indestructible, eternal. The molecules of a substance were supposed to be in a state of constant agitation. In solids there is little scope for movement because they are tightly packed; solids are, therefore, but little compressible and very rigid. When the molecules are somewhat further apart the substance loses its rigidity, and becomes a liquid. In a gas the molecules are practically independent of each other; moving at random in all directions they collide with each other and with the walls of the container. Their impacts upon the walls account for the pressure of the gas, and the energy of their motions is correlated with the temperature.

8.—*Determinism Replaced by Statistics.*

In the physics of yesterday this kinetic molecular theory of matter seemed final. It was consistent, and it accounted at least qualitatively for such varied phenomena as vapour-pressure, viscosity, crystalline form. It had, however, one important consequence of a philosophical nature, for it effected a slight breach in the hitherto rigorously deterministic scheme of material law.

A cubic centimetre of a gas at ordinary temperature and pressure contains about thirty million million million molecules. A mathematician who took only one second to describe a single molecule would, therefore, require about a million million years to complete his description of all the molecules in that single cubic centimetre. Despite current beliefs to the contrary, mathematicians are no more foolish than other people, so it need not surprise us that the task will never be undertaken. But what the mathematician did was interesting. He said, in effect: "I cannot attempt to solve your deterministic system, but I can give you probabilities. I shall compute for you the chance in favour of a molecule having any specified velocity."

This was, I think, the first suspicion of failure of determinism in the material world.

9.—*Radiation.*

Our senses give us direct knowledge of things other than matter. Every morning when the sun climbs over the edge of the world we see his light, we feel his warmth. Although in this we daily witness one of the most marvellous mysteries of Nature, yet do we usually greet his advent with a yawn. Light and heat such as we receive from the sun we classify together with certain other phenomena as radiation. As they differ only in their methods of detection, I shall, for the moment, confine myself to light as typical of radiation in general.

Light originates in matter. It is transmitted across space with a speed that would carry it seven times round the earth in one second. It casts shadows, and from the general sharpness of those shadows we infer that it travels in straight lines. It possesses some characteristic capable of continuous variation, for our senses reveal to us a range of stimuli varying in colour from deep red to light violet.

10.—*Luminous Corpuscles or Vibrations.*

Rectilinear propagation at first suggested that light consisted of particles ejected by the luminous body. But it had been known since the middle of the seventeenth century that the nature of the shadow cast by an obstructed ray of light depended upon the size of the obstacle; if the obstacle were small, then the shadow would not have sharp edges. On the emission theory it was assumed that the edge of the obstacle attracted those particles of light that passed close by it; if this were correct, obstacles of the same shape but of different materials should cast different shadow patterns; and this inference was definitely disproved by experiment. Gradually, the theory gained acceptance that light is not a stream of particles, but a wave motion propagated through a medium that fills all space, and that the colour of the light is determined by the frequency of the associated periodic process.

11.—*The Aether.*

The wave theory of light accounted for numerous optical phenomena, but it necessitated the postulation of a purely hypothetical medium to support and transmit the vibrations. This medium—the aether—must have density and a kind of elasticity; it must be homogeneous and continuous; it must be able to percolate into the interstices of matter and yet it must not offer any resistance to the passage of matter through it. Despite these peculiarities, and despite the fact that the aether defied all attempts to detect the passage of the earth through it, by the end of the nineteenth century it was universally accepted as a reality.

How the vibrations of the aether were evoked by the luminous body remained thoroughly obscure; the final conclusion of the century was that the process must be electrical.

12.—*Electricity.*

We speak of two varieties of electricity, positive and negative but, at least at the time of which I now speak, this distinction was more a statement of behaviour than a supposition of separate existence; like charges repel each other, unlike charges attract. Owing to its property of flowing from a region of high to one of low electrical pressure, electricity was likened to a fluid. Whether we think of one or two fluids, is a matter of no importance at the moment, but we must ask our usual question: Is electricity atomic or continuous in its structure? Investigations by Faraday and his successors showed that in a conducting liquid a molecule splits into two portions, which are termed ions; the two ions arising from a molecule bear charges of electricity equal in magnitude but of opposite signs, and these charges are always simple integral multiples of a certain unit. These results suggested two ideas that have come to dominate all physical theory, viz., that there exists an ultimate indivisible unit of electricity, and that the binding forces which hold all matter together are of electrical origin. When a molecule is ionized this bond is ruptured, and the two ions separate, bearing individually the two charges in which the bond originated.

13.—*Electricity and Matter.*

Further evidence connecting electricity and matter was obtained from experiments upon the conduction of electricity through gases. When an electric current is driven through an evacuated tube, a torrent of negatively charged particles, all alike and far smaller than the smallest atom, issues from the negative terminal with speeds comparable with the speed of light. These particles are called electrons and the charge on each is the unit ionic charge. They travel in straight lines, just as light issues in straight lines from a luminous body, and they cast shadows. Unlike light, they are deflected by electric and magnetic forces, and they pass through thin sheets of opaque substances.

When electrons impinge upon an obstacle, the impact gives rise to a highly penetrating radiation called X-rays, a radiation that has since been shown to be an undulatory process, like light, but of frequency so high that it does not affect the eye.

While electrons pass along the tube from the negative terminal, a stream of positively charged particles moves in the opposite direction. These particles are more massive than the electron; the lightest of them is as heavy as a hydrogen atom, and they all bear charges which are integral multiples of the ionic unit.

14.—*Radioactivity: its Bearing upon Determinism.*

These and other facts fostered a suspicion that the atom could not be the indivisible unit hitherto assumed, a suspicion that was greatly strengthened by the discovery of radio-activity in 1896. Radium was found to give rise to three different kinds of ray, named α, β and γ, whose properties were practically identical with those of the positive and negative streams and the X-rays of the discharge tube. But whereas in the discharge tube these activities were artificially produced, in radium they were natural and spontaneous. In emitting these rays, radium disintegrates; it goes through a succession of transformations, appearing finally as helium and lead. That the energy changes accompanying these transformations are colossal is evident from the enormous speeds with which the α and β particles are ejected.

But neither in the realization of the alchemist's dream of transmutation, nor yet in the extraordinary vigour with which it takes place, lies the chief philosophical interest of the process. The transmutation has proved to be absolutely beyond human control;

neither heat, nor cold, nor chemical combination can interfere with this spontaneous disintegration, and it is subject to no deterministic law. Out of a large number of radium atoms, one in every two thousand ejects an α particle in the course of a year. The atoms are alike both in intrinsic properties and in external environment, and there is presumably no reason why one should die rather than another. Yet the Call of Destiny inevitably comes, and that call must be answered, but none can say how the victim is selected.

Our chain of causal connection is here definitely ruptured; we ascribe to each radium atom a certain chance of death. We deal again with probabilities, not because a deterministic scheme would be too laborious to work out, but because within the four corners of such a system there is no place to be found for the Call of Fate.

15.—*Nightmare.*

Such was the material world of yesterday. Between the sunset of yesterday and the dawn of today night must intervene, and night is not always a period of repose; it has its own doubts and fears, it brings its own dreams and phantasms.

I shall divide what I call the nightmare period of physical theory into three phases dealing respectively with (1) the space-time framework of material experience, (2) the interaction of matter and radiation, and (3) the microscopic structure of matter. Appropriately enough, these phases are not distinct; they overlap and confuse each other as dream episodes generally do; but they have this feature in common—each from its own particular angle launched an unexpected and vigorous attack upon the fortress of physical theory hitherto held to be impregnable.

16.—*Relativity.*

Of the first of these attacks I intend saying but little, for the topic is far too extensive for incidental treatment.

I have mentioned already that no experiment ever revealed the passage of the earth through the aether, although the delicacy of the tests applied was more than sufficient to confirm such motion.

Accordingly, Einstein, in 1905, rejected, if not the aether, then, at least, the properties which had hitherto been assigned to it. From his theory of relativity emerged the novel idea that the absolute space and time of the physicist are but conventional frameworks of description suited to terrestrial observers; there emerged, too, a theory of gravitation to which Newton's Law is but a first approximation; and there was established also a principle of considerable importance in atomic theories, viz., that the observed mass of a moving body is not an unvarying property of matter, but that its motion confers upon such a body an additional mass proportional to its kinetic energy relative to the observer. I may sum up the general influence of Einstein's theory by saying that it showed that classical mechanics applies to systems such as we normally encounter, but breaks down in the case of speeds comparable with the speed of light. The classical physicist consoled himself with the reflection that he never encounters such speeds except in the transmission of radiation and in the emission of α and β particles.

17.—*Quanta.*

The second attack upon the citadel of classical physics began in a very simple manner.

Radiation, whether visible, like light, or invisible, like radiant heat, may be sorted out according to its frequency; when this is done we speak of the ordered arrangement of frequencies as its spectrum. When you tune in to different stations at night you are exploring the spectrum of the electro-magnetic radiation in your neighbourhood. Different frequencies or wavelengths respond to different settings of your dials, while you recognize variations in the energy at different parts of the spectrum by the different strengths at which the stations come in.

Now, if you formed a theory of wireless reception that told you that on the same receiving set, with accurate tuning in each case, the local station should be practically inaudible, while Paris should come in at loud-speaker strength, you would promptly discard the theory as worse than useless. Yet classical physics gives for the heat spectrum of a radiating body an entirely wrong picture of the distribution of energy.

In 1901, Planck obtained a formula which reproduced exactly the experimental distribution of energy, but in deducing it he had to discard part of the classical system, and to assume that the processes of emitting and absorbing radiation are essentially discontinuous.

Planck's concept of quantized or atomized energy was supported by Einstein's later discussion of the photo-electric effect. For many years it had been known that a metal plate emits electrons, or becomes positively charged, when irradiated by light of suitable colour. In a loose kind of way this was attributed to an absorption of energy from the incident waves, but this idea could not account for the facts. Whether electrons are ejected or not from a given plate, and the speed with which they come off when they are ejected, depend solely upon the colour of the incident light. If weak light ejects no electrons, no increase in intensity of that light will do so. If weak light of a certain colour does expel electrons, then increasing its intensity merely increases the flow of electrons but does not influence the speed with which they emerge.

Now, according to classical theory, in which light is a wave propagation, feeble incident light would require an appreciable time to elapse before sufficient energy was stored up to effect the ejection of an electron, whereas experiment shows the response to be instantaneous.

Einstein claimed that the only possible explanation is that light energy is not spread out over an ever-expanding wave surface, but that light is atomic in structure. This concept of atomized light, or of light quanta, has received further strong experimental support, but I need hardly stress the fact that it is absolutely irreconcilable with the classical picture of energy transmission; and it leads us still further away from material determinism. We are forced to admit that while each atom in the metallic plate has the same chance of absorbing energy, only a few of them actually receive a quantum, nor have we any way of determining the actual recipients. And light seems to consist not of a transmission of energy by a uniform undulatory process, but of the propagation of a probability, a chance of receiving a quantum. The satisfying certitudes of classical physics now
> One by one creep silently to rest,

leaving us to deal with more modest probabilities.

18.—*The Nuclear Atom.*

In the meantime, searching investigations had been made into the structure of the atom.

His studies of radioactivity had suggested to Rutherford that in the α and β rays of radium he had a battery of artillery which, if he could but train them upon an atom, might yield some useful information about its inner composition. To his surprise, the particles generally shot right through the atom without change of course or of speed. Occasionally, an α particle was strongly deflected by some powerful repulsive force. From his experiments (1911–1914) emerged the nuclear theory of the atom, according to which the chief characteristic of the atom is not its solidity or compactness, but its emptiness. Atoms are built upon the lines of our solar system; at the centre is the nucleus, containing practically the whole mass of the atom, and yet extremely small even when measured upon the atomic scale. The nucleus is positively charged, the charge increasing with the weight of the atom to which it belongs. Surrounding the nucleus revolve planetary electrons in one or more rings. These are the familiar β particles of radium or of the discharge tube; they are the lightest entities known to science; in all atoms they are identical in mass and in charge.

The simplest and lightest nucleus is that of the hydrogen atom; it is called a proton, and it bears a unit positive charge. The neutral hydrogen atom consists of one proton with one planetary electron. Out of these two constituents, protons and electrons, all atoms are built; the weight of the atom depends upon the number of protons, and its chemical properties depend upon the number and the arrangement of its planetary electrons.

The atom next in weight to hydrogen is helium. Its weight tells us that the nucleus must contain four protons, and since the atom is electrically neutral there must be four balancing electrons. But a nucleus of protons only could not cohere, for they are all positively charged, and would therefore repel each other. In the helium atom, therefore, two of the electrons enter the nucleus to provide the necessary binding forces to hold that structure together, while the other two electrons remain in their orbit at a considerable distance from the nucleus.

19.—*Isotopes.*

As every neutral atom consists of an equal number of protons and electrons, one would naturally expect the weight of any atom to be an integral multiple of the weight of the hydrogen atom which contains one of each. This idea had indeed been suggested (for different reasons) in the early days of chemical theory, and had been rejected because chemical analysis shows beyond all possibility of doubt that the atomic weights of elements are not integral multiples of the atomic weight of hydrogen, and it was then considered unthinkable that atoms of the same element could differ in any way from each other. But on the nuclear theory it is at least conceivable that two atoms with different nuclear structure and the same outer planetary arrangement could exist. The chemist's atomic weight is the average weight of a large number of atoms, and cannot therefore reveal individual differences; but if it were possible to weigh individual atoms of a substance, then it would be possible to test the hypothesis. This has been done by the mass-spectograph of Aston, and the hypothesis has been fully confirmed. The element next to helium, for example, is lithium. Its position and its chemical properties tell us that its atom must have three planetary electrons. Its chemical atomic weight is 6·94. If its nucleus had seven protons and four binding electrons, the atom would be a little too heavy; if it had six protons and three binding electrons, the atom would be far too light. The actual substance must, therefore, be a mixture of these two atoms, the heavier atom preponderating, and this deduction has been amply verified by experiment. Such atoms of different weights, but of identical chemical properties, are called isotopes.

20.—*The Bohr Atom.*

With experimental victories such as this to its credit, one might have hoped that atomic theory was approaching finality. But if the radiation emitted by a luminous atom were due to the revolution of its planetary electrons, then, unfortunately, on the classical theory, the atom is dynamically unstable. To save the atom, Bohr, in 1913, rejected even more of the classical scheme than Planck had done twelve years before. On the classical basis a planet may revolve in an orbit of any size around its nucleus. Bohr, on the other hand, atomized or quantized the possible orbits. His rule for determining the possible orbits was perfectly arbitrary; and, moreover, in flat contradiction to the classical laws, he assumed that, while revolving in such an orbit, an electron emits no radiation. If an electron absorbs a quantum of energy, it jumps from its present orbit to another possible one of higher energy level; if, for any reason, it jumps to an orbit of lower energy level, in doing so it emits a quantum of energy which streams away as radiation. But it is only during such transitions from one orbit to another that energy can be emitted or absorbed.

21.—*The Conflict between the Two Theories.*

Bohr's theory, although it had no rational basis, gave some astonishing results; in particular, it accounted for the series of lines in the spectra of hydrogen and of ionized helium with an exactitude hitherto unattainable.

The two systems, classical and quantum, were incompatible, yet neither could be abandoned; both had to be applied to radiation, the former to account for its properties *qua* radiation, the latter to interpret the interaction of radiation and matter. Which set of rules should be applied in any particular case was settled on purely empirical grounds.

The conflict between the theories was merely the reflection of a conflict between two groups of experimental facts. Light, in passing through space, or around obstacles, or through lenses and prisms, behaves as if it were a train of waves; but on entering an atom it acts as if it were a particle. X-rays, on colliding with an electron, behave as if they were particles, but on reflection from a crystal surface they give a diffraction pattern just as if they were a train of waves. Admitting the facts, and there is no escape from that admission, there seems to be but one hope of avoiding the uncomfortable dualism, and that lies in assuming that waves and particles are but different aspects of some more fundamental entity.

This novel conception marks the dawn of the material outlook of today, but none can say what reality, if any, underlies such a bizarre synthesis. An entity that discloses itself to our experience only through some partial aspects must remain an abstraction, so that it need not surprise us that modern theories of matter are highly mathematical. Now and then they yield results which may be compared with the results of physical experience, but their foundations have not yet admitted any satisfactory concrete interpretation. I can only hope to give you a very crude and inaccurate account of a few of their main features.

22.—*De Broglie's Wave-Particle.*

Hitherto evidence of a dual nature has been confined to light and to X-rays, both of which we usually classify as radiation; their wave aspects were regarded as fundamental, their particle aspects as secondary. In 1924, De Broglie sought to investigate the consequences of assuming that an electron, till then regarded as a particle and nothing else, has also a wave nature. He started with the facts that according to Relativity, mass and energy are proportional, while according to the Quantum theory with every quantity of energy there is associated a periodicity whose frequency is proportional to the amount of energy. Combining these two principles it follows that with the mass of any material particle there must be associated a definite frequency of vibration characteristic of that particle. Premature interest in what it is that vibrates must be discouraged until the consequences of the hypothesis have been partially explored.

In the meantime you will find a very crude, but helpful, analogy in the motion of a centipede, one of the large round-bodied type with a large number of legs set closely together on each side. I cannot tell you exactly how many legs such a creature possesses, but you will admit that if all the legs on one side were raised simultaneously from the ground, then the creature would topple over. This disaster is averted by the provision that all the legs on one side are not in phase, or, as we would put it more colloquially, do not move in step. One result of this inconstancy of phase is that at one place the legs are widely spaced, while a little further on they are bunched together. As the creature progresses, a succession of light and dark bands passes across the array of legs, just like the ripples on the surface of a quiet pool. This wave, though easily visible, is not a concrete thing. It is not a part of the animal, for it moves with a different speed. It is a somewhat abstract phase-wave giving visible evidence of periodic variations of internal structure. And we can say, without imposing too severe a strain upon our language, that the creature is guided and controlled in its physical movements by its accompanying wave.

De Broglie's hypothesis is that every material particle is similarly accompanied by a periodic process that guides its passage through space and determines its behaviour.

The first success of this truly remarkable theory lay in the account it gave of the possible orbits of an electron in its atom. If, as seems reasonable, we assume that at each passage of the electron across some fixed point of its orbit, the state of the electron must recur exactly, and therefore with its guiding wave in the same phase as on its previous passage, then it is clear that the only permissible orbits are those which contain an exact number of wave-lengths. Calculation showed that these permissible orbits were precisely the quantized orbits of the Bohr atom.

This theoretical support was not, perhaps, particularly strong, as the Bohr orbits were purely hypothetical; but on the experimental side further verification was forthcoming which was all the more startling because it was derived from phenomena whose existence was predicted by the new theory, and had never before been suspected.

I have mentioned, incidentally, that the wave nature of X-rays had been established by reflecting them from the surface of a crystal, resulting in the production of a diffraction pattern. Now, if material particles have a wave aspect, and if suitable wavelengths could be found amongst them, they too should experience diffraction by a crystal. Calculations based upon De Broglie's theory suggested that electrons of moderate speeds should have a satisfactory wavelength for ordinary crystals. In 1927, Davisson and Germer, in America, reflected a beam of electrons from a crystal surface and found the predicted periodic structure in the reflected pattern. More striking still, Thomson of Aberdeen, in the following year, projected a beam of electrons through very thin films of metal, and photographed the resulting diffraction pattern, establishing visibly their identity of character with the diffraction patterns produced by X-rays and by light.

The argument now runs thus: electrons and X-rays are shown to produce identical results, therefore they are of identical nature. Electrons are known to be particles, therefore X-rays must be particles. X-rays are known to be waves, therefore electrons must be waves. Wave nature and particle nature must be united in each.

There is an obvious flaw in the logical arrangement, for isotopes are known to be differently constituted, and yet to give identical chemical results, so that it is dangerous to infer absolute identity from a special set of observed coincidences. Nevertheless, until some further basis of discrimination is established, the only reasonable working hypothesis seems to be to accept De Broglie's synthesis.

23.—*Schrödinger's Wave-mechanics.*

We now enter a shadowy land of theory, peopled by particles of doubtful character, by wandering waves, and by still more nebulous symbols—all mere ghosts of a vanished materialism. Two roads to this haunted region were surveyed in 1925, the first by Heisenberg entering through a forest of quanta, the other by Schrödinger struggling through a wilderness of waves. Strangely enough, when the two methods of approach came to be compared, it was found that their progress was step by step almost identical, identical both in distance and in direction. It looked as if quanta and waves were both screens of illusion raised before us to protect eyes that are not yet strong enough to withstand the glare of Truth. Of the two I shall mention Schrödinger's theory first, because, as Eddington has said, it is the only one simple enough to be misunderstood.

As a wave is essentially continuous and causally connected, we may regard Schrödinger's theory as a last effort to save the classical laws from complete extinction in the atomic field; for he regards the periodic aspects of Nature as fundamental, and her atomic aspects as purely derivative concepts.

Now, at first sight, it looks as if the general equation for wave propagation through space with which Schrödinger begins could not possibly lead to atomized features such as electrons, or discrete energy levels in an atom. A well-known analogy will show how this transition is achieved. You all know that many musical sounds, and many more that are only called musical, can be evoked from a vibrating string. Now, the general equation to wave propagation along a string gives as its solution all possible notes from all possible strings. If, however, you apply your equation to one particular string, you impose certain limitations upon the solutions, in particular, the two end points of the string are fixed and therefore fix its length. We speak of such limitations as boundary conditions. In the case of the string the boundary conditions limit the notes that can be emitted to those whose half-wave length is the length of the string, or one-half, one-third, one-quarter, etc., of that length. These are precisely the harmonics that the ear detects when the string vibrates. The boundary conditions quantize the frequencies; the harmonics are permitted, all other notes are ejected. In exactly similar fashion, Schrödinger found simple and reasonable boundary conditions which quantized his waves, and led naturally and inevitably to the discrete energy levels of the older theory, besides accommodating certain other experimental results that had hitherto proved refractory.

What is the vibrating entity in the Schrödinger wave? He himself gave it no physical interpretation, but in the course of his analysis certain combinations of symbols appeared which he translated into material existence. Born, however, suggested that the Schrödinger wave is a wave of probability. This may seem rather nonsensical at first, but it is in fact an everyday notion with us. We speak of a wave of crime passing over Johannesburg, or of a wave of malaria passing over certain coastal districts that prefer to remain anonymous only in that connection. We do not mean that every citizen is a criminal in the one case, or every inhabitant a victim of malaria in the other. We mean that during the passage of the wave the proportion of criminals or victims relative to the total population is appreciably enhanced; and relative proportion is exactly what we mean by a statistical probability. On this interpretation, what we call a material particle may be at any point of its wave, and the wave value at any point gives the probability that it is exactly there.

Now, the Schrödinger waves for a material particle are so arranged that they cancel out everywhere except over a limited region, so that the particle must be located somewhere within that region. Like ourselves, as these regions grow older, they spread, but the larger they are the smaller is their rate of spread. There is no difficulty in showing that in millions of years the spread of matter in bulk would be insignificant. But when the disturbed region is very small, as in the case of the electron, then the rate of spread is no longer inappreciable. An electron may be anywhere within its disturbed region. If that region is small, we know the position of the electron very precisely, but the rapid spread of its wave field renders it impossible to say where it is going except between very wide limits. On the other hand, if its wave field is extensive, it is spreading but slowly, and we know precisely the speed with which the whole field is travelling, but all we can say about the position of the electron is that it lies somewhere within this extensive field. This is the wave aspect of the Principle of Uncertainty of which General Smuts spoke to you last week—if we know where an electron is going we cannot say precisely where it is, and if we know precisely where it is, we cannot find out where it is going.

24.—*Quantum Mechanics.*

Heisenberg, who regarded the atomic aspects of Nature as primary, and its periodicities as derivative, was the first to announce the principle of uncertainty. He illustrated it by a very simple example. We wish to determine the position of an electron; to do this we must in some way manage to "see" it. Hence, we illuminate it with radiation of sufficiently short wavelength. The shorter the wavelength of the radiation we use, the greater is the energy of its quantum. When the radiation falls upon the electron, the impact causes the electron to recoil, and we can tell only within certain limits of probability where the electron was going at the instant of impact. To reduce this uncertainty, we must arrange for less vigorous collisions; we must, therefore, use radiation of longer wavelength. But the longer wave gives rise to a diffraction pattern, and all we can say about the position of the electron is that it lies somewhere within that pattern. The very arrangement that enables us to measure more precisely the velocity of the electron, automatically increases our uncertainty of its position.

This simple illustration illuminates for us one of the reasons why discrepancies between classical theory and experiment have arisen in the sub-atomic world, similar to some extent to those divergences in which the theory of Relativity originated.

25.—*Nature and Mind*.

With the passage of centuries, the capacity of the human race for abstract thought has shown practically no improvement, while its manipulative dexterity has increased with great rapidity. To allow for a low level of human intelligence, classical physics is compelled to deal with idealized systems. It is assumed that the systems under observation may be resolved into simple constituents to which may be assigned familiar properties in harmony with our normal experience; and it is further postulated that while under observation, the systems remain isolated from the rest of the universe. The constructed world of classical physics is therefore a hypothetical world; if it is to exhibit some degree of objective reality comparable with that of the world of sense-experience, then the natural philosopher must effect a synthesis from which verifiable entities emerge. If the hypothetical elements in terms of which he describes a particular experimental field are themselves macroscopic, the synthesis must be such that descriptions of the field given by different observers are reducible to identical terms which enshrine the underlying reality. The fixed aether of the nineteenth century, for example, served its purpose as long as its function was to accommodate the experience of a single observer, but it led to the possibility of discrepant accounts of the material world being given by different observers. For relative velocities small compared with that of light, the divergence was of insignificant amount, and the hypothetical aether caused no inconvenience; but for large relative velocities that hypothesis proved inadequate. A more satisfactory synthesis was made possible by Einstein's rejection of the fixed aether, and his formulation of the laws of motion in terms of entities which are essentially measurable.

The hypothetical elements of the world of matter—electrons and protons—are themselves microscopic, and therefore outside the world of sense; but their individual behaviour must be integrable into a macroscopic whole which is experimentally verifiable by any observer. Heisenberg's illustration of his principle of uncertainty suggests that the failure of the classical theory to complete this synthesis is due to the violation of the assumption of isolation. In dealing with particles so minute as the electron or proton, the influence of the instrument of observation is no longer negligible, and the position or speed of such a particle at any moment is not directly measurable. Hence the New Physics, inaugurated by Heisenberg, Born and Dirac, is endeavouring to achieve in the sub-atomic world a synthesis similar to that effected by Einstein for speeds comparable with that of light; its aim is so to formulate the laws of matter that their expression involves only entities which are experimentally verifiable. Neither electrons, nor their orbits, nor yet their jumps from one permitted orbit to another, can legitimately be termed sense-data, but frequencies and intensities of spectral lines are directly measurable. The latter, therefore, are amongst the chief variables in terms of which the New Physics describes the material world.

I confess that this is a very prosaic interpretation of the implications of the newer theories, much less attractive than a semi-mystical union of matter and mind. I cannot find in the principle of uncertainty any justification for assuming that the intervention of mind in an act of knowledge can modify in any way a physical situation. If, with Schrödinger, we postulate waves as the fundamental components of our microscopic world, then the uncertainty is an immediate consequence of the difference between the velocity of a group of waves and that of an individual of the group—a difference that can be demonstrated and measured on a macroscopic scale by purely mechanical means. If, on the other hand, we prefer to assume sub-atomic particles as our ideal elements, then the uncertainty originates in the purely mechanical difficulty of observing a particle and keeping it isolated at the same time. Instead, therefore, of a union of Matter and Mind, I see in the New Physics a deliberate attempt to compel Mind to perform its proper function as an interpreter of the observed facts, and to prohibit it from attempting any longer to squeeze Nature into a mould of its own contriving.

But it is high time that we emerged from our plunge beneath the surface of the material world. Gasping a little, perhaps, we come up, look at each other, and ask: "What do we now know about the ultimate nature of Matter, of Electricity, of Radiation?" A generation ago, the more modest amongst us might have said that "we know in part and we prophesy in part"; but passing years have found our knowledge false, have left our prophecies unfulfilled. I begin to suspect that we are chasing a will-o'-the-wisp, that we never *can* know a material entity otherwise than through its macroscopic attributes and manifestations. If, however, this suspicion is not well founded, then it seems to me that the question admits but one truthful answer. That answer is definite, it is concise, it may even be final. It is that of the ultimate structure of the material world we now know—*precisely nothing*.

Evolution—Design or Accident?

By
Dr. ROBERT BROOM
F.R.S

Evolution—Design or Accident?

All who have examined the evidence with an open mind admit that animals and plants have evolved from earlier types; but how the evolution has come about is a matter concerning which we know very, very little. Man is ever striving for certain knowledge, and when he thinks he has it he is very unwilling to have his faith shaken.

In the Early-Victorian period, to go no further back, the large majority were fully convinced that all forms of life had appeared on earth at the word of the Creator within a few days. Of course, it was manifest to anyone who studied the fossil shells and bones in the rocks that there was something wrong in this view, and endeavours were made to harmonize matters by regarding the "days" as indefinite periods of time. If the "days" were long enough—many millions of years—we might have a theory that would satisfy the geologist, and still be in keeping with the supposed divinely inspired account of Genesis. This was the view supported by Hugh Miller. He tried to show that the record of the rocks agreed with the Biblical account. It was rather a thankless task. The large majority of thinking people hated geologists for daring to upset the beliefs of their ancestors. They were spoken of as "infidels" and parsons fulminated against what they called their "horrid blasphemies." Poor Hugh Miller, shortly after he had given his elaborate theory to the world—perhaps seeing that it was unsatisfactory—died by his own hand.

Robert Chambers, in some respects bolder than Miller, published in 1844 his famous *Vestiges of the Natural History of Creation* and gave to the world one of the earliest and best accounts of the evolutions of the earth and its animals and plants. He tried to explain it all as directed by a Creative Providence. But he, too, was vehemently attacked. One review of his book says: "Prophetic of infidel times, and indicating the unsoundness of our general education, the *Vestiges* has started in public favour with a fair chance of poisoning the fountains of science, and sapping the foundations of religion."

Then came Darwin, with his wonderful wealth of facts, and gradually he converted the thinking world to the truth of evolution. He, too, was bitterly attacked by a large section, headed at times even by an able man like Bishop Wilberforce, of Oxford. Perhaps many felt like the silversmiths of Ephesus—"this our craft is in danger to be set at nought." Darwin, in addition to establishing the truth of evolution, gave a theory to try and explain how it had come about, how all living things tend to vary, and how in the struggle for existence Nature selected and bred from the most fitted.

For thirty years after Darwin published his *Origin of Species* the majority of biologists accepted his views. In addition to his theory of "Natural Selection," he proposed a second theory of "Sexual Selection" to explain many facts that did not seem to be the result of natural selection. A good many scientists, like Owen, were never satisfied with Darwinism, and the great American palaeontologist, Cope, published a book, entitled *The Origin of the Fittest*. Others went further than Darwin and considered that natural selection explained everything.

Curiously enough, just as in 1860 the *odium theologicum* persecuted those who accepted the new views, fifty years later the *odium scientificum* somewhat sneered at those who were unable to accept Darwinism.

A new school arose after Mendel's discoveries became widely known, and during the last thirty years hundreds have been working at the problems of heredity. Hunt Morgan and his pupils in America have been breeding and cross-breeding fruit flies, and have shown that most of the characters are associated with parts of the chromosomes which have been called "genes"; and they have been able to trace, not only in which chromosome certain genes are to be found, but in which part of the chromosome.

The geneticists hold that, as the characters are associated with the genes, changes taking place during the life of an animal owing to changes in habit cannot affect the next generation. They have shown, however, that very marked changes can be produced by the action of heat, electricity, or radium on the chromosomes and as a result of changes in the genes new characters are produced which breed true. So busy have they been with this new knowledge that little work has been done on the larger problems of evolution. Satisfied that they can produce new types, some have too readily assumed that they have got the clue to evolution.

Bateson, the greatest of the English geneticists, however, was not at all satisfied that he knew anything of how evolution had come about. He rejected all the theories. In 1914 he said: "We go to Darwin for his incomparable collection of facts. But to us he speaks no more with philosophical authority. We read his scheme of evolution as we would that of Lucretius, or of Lamarck, delighting in their simplicity and their courage." And in 1921 he wrote: "The many converging lines of evidence point so clearly to the central fact of the origin of the forms of life by an evolutionary process that we are compelled to accept this deduction, but as to almost all the essential features, whether of cause or mode, by which specific diversity has come to be what we perceive it to be, we have to confess an ignorance nearly total. . . . That particular and essential bit of the theory of evolution which is concerned with the origin and nature of species remains utterly mysterious."

Even J. B. S. Haldane, while supporting Darwinism, said in 1925: "We may justifiably adopt the working hypothesis that evolution has been due solely to fortuitous variations and the action of selection on its results. But we must remember that this is still only a working hypothesis."

Osborn recently said: "There is no evidence that minute individual variations, except immunity to disease, have been a cause of the origin or evolution of new characters," and "there is no reason to believe that minute rectigradations in their most rudimentary stages have sufficient survival value in competition with other bio-characters to affect the life of an organism." But he admits that "certain fluctuations of proportion may have distinct survival value, and tend to be accumulated through natural selection." Of course, natural selection plays a most important part in eliminating the unfit, but there is no evidence that it has ever had anything to do with the evolution of the fit.

The remarkable cases of mimicry in butterflies that used to be brought forward as affording such strong support for Darwinism are now looked upon by many as demanding some other explanation. Punnett, in his beautiful work on *Mimicry*, admits that it is difficult to see how some, at least, of the cases can have been brought about by natural selection.

And Watson, in his address to the British Association, when in Johannesburg three years ago, said: "We know as surely as we ever shall that evolution has occurred, but we do not know how this evolution has been brought about... The only two theories of evolution which have found any general currency, those of Lamarck and Darwin, rest on a most insecure basis; the validity of the assumptions on which they rest has never been seriously examined."

Still, Darwinism seems to satisfy many, and when, at the Zoological Section of the British Association in London in 1931, a series of papers was given in connection with the President's address on "A Hundred Years of Evolution," the majority supported Darwinism as the prime factor.

Some of the geneticists believe that all evolution is the result of saltations or mutations—moderate-sized jumps in some direction as the result of some agency acting on the chromosomes—but that these mutations are, nevertheless, purely fortuitous changes, and that, if the change is advantageous, natural selection favours it. Others prefer small mutations, and if small mutations do occur, natural selection might do the rest. Unfortunately we have no evidence of small mutations occurring in Nature, and the clearest evidence that evolution has not come about by mutations at all.

Lamarck, a little over a hundred years ago, propounded another theory which has had the support of many eminent scientists. His main point is that changes of structure are the result of changes of habit. The running limb becomes longer and more slender by the running, and each generation is born with a greater tendency to limbs adapted for running. During last century the greatest supporter of Lamarckism was the famous American, Cope, and to-day the chief supporter is Professor McBride, of London.

Kammerer and others have in quite recent years endeavoured to show by experiment that changes of habit or environment induce certain changes which are inherited. Some are satisfied that he has proved his case; others are as fully convinced that he has not.

Though I have for many years been much more inclined to favour Lamarckism than Darwinism, I have never had much hope that the matter could be proved by experiment. Evolution, as the palaeontologist sees it, goes on so slowly that he hardly expects to see any appreciable change in his lifetime. If it has taken, say, 10,000,000 years to change a *Merychippus* into a horse like *Equus*, we cannot expect to see any appreciable change in even 10,000 years.

But the case in favour of the loss, or reduction, of an organ from disuse seems very strong. Quite certainly, disuse is followed by reduction. We have thousands of cases. One of the most striking is the loss of the power of flight in birds that do not require to fly. It matters not whether the bird is a rail, or a pigeon, or a goose, or an eagle, or a parrot—if the wings are little used, they degenerate and the birds become flightless.

The most striking cases are the dodo of Mauritius and the extinct goose and eagle and large flightless rail of New Zealand. The living owl-parrot of New Zealand shows us perhaps the first stage in the evolution of flightlessness. Here is a parrot whose ancestors probably flew over from Australia, and it still has a wing that seems good enough to fly with if it wished to. But apparently for generations it has not thought it necessary to fly and now it cannot fly. The great extinct goose (*Cnemiornis*) was nearly allied to the living Australian goose, *Cereopsis*, and doubtless the ancestor flew over to New Zealand from Australia. Here it had no ground enemies and did not require to fly, and the wings became reduced and quite useless as flying organs. No doubt, the same was the history of the pigeons that gave rise to the dodo and the solitaire.

In all these cases, there is a clear connection between the change of habit which led to the disuse of the wing, and the degeneration. But whether the disuse was the cause of the degeneration is debated.

I do not remember having seen how the Darwinians explain the evolution of the dodo. The flightless beetles of islands, I know, are explained by the belief that flightlessness is an advantage—those with wings being blown out to sea by storms. Perhaps the same theory is held to explain the flightlessness of the dodo. Those ancestral dodos that could fly a little bit were blown away, and those that could not fly quite so well were left; and the process going on for hundreds of thousands of years resulted in the dodo. Such an explanation might be a plausible one for a flightless bird on, say, Ascension Island, but it would not meet the case of a flightless bird on either Mauritius or New Zealand.

Then we have the loss of eyes in moles. In the European *Talpa* and the South African *Georhychus*, we have small but functional eyes. The Darwinians explain the reduction of eye by the belief that those with larger eyes suffered from ophthalmia and thus the small eye was an advantage.

On the same principle, it is an advantage for the streets of Civita Vecchia to be so narrow, as Mark Twain pointed out. They are as full of bad odours as they can hold, and if they were wider they would hold more.

I do not know whether the ophthalmia theory is well founded on fact. It seems a little far-fetched; and in any case it will not explain the further degeneration of the eyes in the golden moles and in the Australian marsupial mole, *Notorhyctes*. In *Chrysochloris*, the eye is quite under the skin and probably functionless; in *Notorhyctes* it is merely represented by a rudiment which is certainly functionless. Then we have the loss of sight in the freshwater dolphins that inhabit muddy rivers. Perhaps, even here, the ophthalmia theory may be invoked, but what of the blind crustaceans in the Mammoth Caves of Kentucky—a crayfish, an amphipod and two isopods! The ophthalmia theory is a little too ingenious.

The reduction and loss of limbs in reptiles and amphibians burrowing underground is another most interesting case of degeneration. In quite a large number of different families of amphibians and lizards we find the same thing happening. The body elongates, the number of vertebrae increases, and the limbs become reduced and then lost. We can see all stages in the evolution among the lizards. The Darwinian explains the loss of the limbs by the quite plausible suggestion that even little limbs are a disadvantage and the lizard with no limbs will get down its hole to safety quicker than the one with even very small limbs. But, again, this fails to explain how the degeneration still goes on after the limbs have disappeared. In the underground snake, *Typhlops*, there is still a rudimentary shoulder girdle to be found though the limbs are lost; but in the higher snakes there is no longer any trace even of the shoulder girdle.

If there is some connection between disuse and degeneration, there is likely to be also some connection between increased use and greater development. The wing of the albatross seems to be a further development of such a wing as we see in the gull, and the ocean-going habit has doubtless been associated with the lengthening of the wing. This would be explained by the Darwinians as due to those with shorter wings being less able to survive in ocean flights. But, surely, the shorter-winged albatrosses could easily have survived by staying, like the gulls, a little nearer the shores. The ocean is very wide and does not seem to be overstocked.

The geneticists have shown that most of the little variations on which the Darwinians built do not breed true, and many hold, as Bateson did, that natural selection completely fails as an explanation of evolution. Other geneticists, however, have shown that mutations arise very frequently and hold that Nature can select the favourable mutations and thus give rise to new species or genera. But all the mutations that have been found experimentally are really pathological, and if they occurred in Nature could never survive. We have the well-known cases of "sports," or mutations, of the goldfish, formed by the Chinese and Japanese breeding carp in insanitary conditions. But what hope would there be of any of these fancy breeds surviving if liberated in the streams of China!

Others hold that there are probably small mutations constantly occurring in Nature and that some of these breed true; and if Nature selects the advantageous mutations we have a satisfactory explanation of evolution. Perhaps such mutations do occasionally occur in Nature and are selected, but it must be quite exceptional, and is certainly not the way in which most species have arisen.

Of course, if all horses had three toes, and a mutation arose of a horse with only one toe, and the one-toed horse could get over the ground more quickly and with more chance of escaping from its enemies, Nature would certainly favour this one-toed horse. And if similar mutations produced a few more one-toed horses, we might find the one-toed horse replacing the three-toed. But there seems very little difference between a mutation producing a one-toed horse and the creation of one. We are practically back to special creation and certainly we have conclusive evidence from palaeontology that one-toed horses did not arise in this way.

If acquired characters are inherited, Lamarckism would be a satisfactory explanation of the increase or degeneration of an organ, but it seems to me that it cannot explain the marvellous structure of the flowers in orchids or in *Strelitzia*, and many other plants with the wonderful adaptations for cross-fertilization or for the scattering of seeds.

Lamarckism has to bring in a psychic element to explain the origin of a new organ which could not be used before it is there. But, if this is the correct explanation of the origin of an organ, the same factor might just as well explain the further increase of the organ.

Darwinism, like Lamarckism, has always had difficulties in explaining the beginnings of organs. There is the old classical case of the electric organ in fishes. The electric organ is a transformed muscle. When it has developed so far as to be able to give a serious shock, it is manifestly a useful organ. But we have only to think of the countless generations in which it was neither a useful muscle nor a useful electric organ to see the difficulties of the Darwinian explanation.

Similar cases can be given by the hundred. The stings of the bees and the wasps are very useful in driving off enemies. But the sting is a modified ovipositor, and we have only to think of the perhaps hundreds of thousands of years during which the organ was neither a useful ovipositor nor a useful sting and was gradually developing into a sting, to see the difficulties of the Darwinian theory.

And a similar difficulty is seen in the development of the poison glands and fangs of the poisonous snakes. It seems, in the first place, so unnecessary for snakes to have poison at all. The harmless snakes are far more numerous in species, and in many regions more numerous in individuals than the venomous; so that the development of poison glands and grooved fangs seem unnecessary to preserve their lives. And then we have such marvellous specializations of the fangs. In the cobras and mambas the fangs are grooved; but in the vipers and pit vipers the fangs are hollow tubes, as beautifully developed as a hypodermic needle. Must we believe that the ancestral vipers which only had grooved fangs like the cobras, had to die out in competition with those snakes that had the margins of the grooves closing to form tubes? The grooved fangs are quite good enough for the cobras and the mambas, and one would fancy that what is good enough for the cobras should be good enough for the vipers.

Among lizards only one is known to be poisonous, the *Heloderma*, of Mexico. Of all orders of vertebrates the lizards appear to be about the most satisfactory. In all warm climates over the world they are abundant. There is a great variety in size and structure, but only this one is venomous. Must we believe that the fact that its bite is somewhat poisonous has saved it from perishing?

Then we might look at the flying phalangers and flying squirrels. The large flying phalanger of Australia only differs from the ring-tailed phalangers in having a fold of skin joining the fore and hind limbs. This is used for taking flying leaps from tree to tree and certainly looks as if it were a useful development that might have been evolved by Darwinism, those ring-tailed phalangers that could not stretch the lateral skin being more apt to perish than those better able to take flying leaps. It is all so very plausible till we look at the facts. The flying phalangers live in the same gum-tree forests as the ring-tailed phalangers and the vulpine phalangers, and the latter live just as satisfactorily as the flying variety. Nay, as they are more numerous, they are probably even better off without the lateral skin. If native cats stalked the phalangers along the branches the ability to fly might be an advantage. But the phalangers have no large carnivores to trouble them in the gum trees and almost certainly never had.

The struggle for existence, of which the Darwinians make so much, seems to me greatly overrated. Wallace pointed to the millions of eggs the codfish lays; yet the number of adult codfish apparently remains constant. Darwin showed that even in the slow-breeding elephant, if every female lived to ninety years and had no more than six young, a single pair would in 750 years have 19,000,000 descendants. And we are told we must admit that there is a terrible struggle for existence. Yes, in the immature eggs of the fish and in the baby elephants, but not necessarily between the adult codfish and the adult elephants. Wallace published a very striking chart which seems at first sight to be thoroughly convincing but the reasoning is quite unsound. We are told that there is a struggle for existence and that there is variation and heredity; therefore, there must be "survival of the fittest." But if a herring lays 20,000,000 eggs in a year and all are eaten by other fish except twenty, are we to assume that those twenty eggs were not eaten because they were fitter or that they would develop into fitter herrings?

But there is so much in Nature that cannot be explained by either Lamarckism or Darwinism. No one can surely believe that the remarkable development of the feathers and the wonderful colouring of the birds of paradise or the humming birds have been brought about by use or disuse of any parts of the animals, and it seems to me quite as impossible to believe that Darwinism had anything to do with the evolution. It is interesting to note how gorgeous colouring is principally met with in definite groups of birds—the birds of paradise, the hummingbirds, the kingfishers, the parrots and the pheasants. In many birds, the males are brightly coloured only in the breeding season and, doubtless, as is the case with the deer's antlers, the colouring is due to sexual endocrines. But the interesting point is that the gaudily coloured males do not seem in any danger of being exterminated. Almost all parrots are showily coloured, but they are remarkably well able to hold their own against all their enemies. The little drab-coloured birds are held to have been thus developed because their inconspicuousness is their safety. But a flock of parrots is as conspicuous as birds could well be. They ought theoretically to have been killed off by hawks, but they get along just as well as the inconspicuous sparrow. Or take the South African *muisvoël*. It is rather brightly coloured, and it has a long tail, both of which ought to be handicaps. But there seems to be no danger of the *muisvoëls* dying out. In the fruit season they are a pest.

Of course, as I have mentioned, Darwin brings in the theory of sexual selection to explain much of the gorgeous plumage of birds. The peacock gets its wonderful tail because the female has an eye for beauty and likes a partner with a fine tail. And the peahen has no grand tail because the peacock does not like his partner to be too attractive. It is wonderfully simple and ingenious, but very unconvincing. The domestic fowls are closely allied to the peacocks, and can be studied much more easily, but we do not find much sexual selection among them. It seems to make no difference to the hen whether the rooster has four nice feathers in his tail or only two.

Bateson says, "We no more look for utility in the details of a peacock's feather than in the iridescence of a Roman bottle"; and St. George Mivart once wrote: "Certainly the opal never gained its beauty by sexual selection."

And the glorious colouring of flowers has been evolved, the Darwinians hold, through those plants with the showier flowers being able to attract the insects that fertilize them, while the less showy flowers have to die unfertilized. Doubtless, the showy flower does attract the insects from a distance. But there are many flowers that are not showy and that are still able to get fertilized. And the red berries have been evolved because the redder ones attract the birds that eat them and scatter their seeds. But many berries and fruits are green and inconspicuous, while some that are bright red are poisonous. To attract the birds merely to poison them seems like killing the goose that lays the golden eggs. If only flowers and berries were bright coloured, one might believe that Darwinism had been the main factor, and that cross-fertilization and seed-scattering was at the bottom of it all; but some fishes are as brilliantly coloured as the birds of paradise, and sea anemones are often as gorgeous as the flowers of the forest. Even deep-sea fishes and crustaceans are often brightly coloured, while the tiny little copepods may be a brilliant scarlet.

The most satisfactory theory of the beauty of birds and flowers that has been advanced is that given by Smuts in one of the most beautiful passages in *Holism and Evolution*, which I feel I must quote:

"The song of birds, with its primary appeal to sex, but with so infinitely much more in it than the mere sex appeal; the glorious forms and colouring of birds and beasts and insects which, no doubt, rise in and from the struggle for existence, but finally rise above it and rob it of all its sordidness and drabness; above all, the wonder of plants and flowers which were meant for the eye of birds and insects, but contains so infinitely much more than the eye of bird or insect ever beheld or ever can behold—it is everywhere in Nature the same. Everywhere we see the great overplus of the whole. So little is asked; so much more is given. The female only asks for a sign to recognize the male and to help her to select him and stick to him in preference to others. And for answer she gets an overwhelming revelation of beauty out of all proportion to her modest request. The peahen has no discriminating understanding of the wondrous colouring of the peacock, which far transcends even our human powers; but in some inscrutable way something of an emotional nature in her takes it all in and is satisfied. It is deep calling unto deep; it is the whole appealing to the whole. There is evidently more in all this than the Darwinian factors can satisfactorily explain, and it would be both foolish and unscientific not to recognize this frankly. To me the conclusion of the matter is that the inexhaustible whole is itself at work, that Holism is an active factor interacting with the particular Darwinian factors, that not only its aim but also its output far exceed the immediate present utilities and needs of organic evolution, and that the bow is bent for the distant horizons, far beyond all human power of vision and understanding."

The evolution of the vertebrates is now fairly satisfactorily known. We can trace up from the fishes the lines by which evolution has travelled, and the steps by which reptiles arose from amphibians, and the mammals and birds from reptiles. Thus we know pretty fully the course of evolution in the mammals during the Tertiary period.

Most palaeontologists now incline, I think, to the view that whatever may have been the cause of evolution, it has not been quite a matter of accident.

It is very interesting to note that from Carboniferous times to Lower Eocene we can trace a line of small, very generalized types, from which are derived all the many branches that specialize in different ways. These small forms are, first, small amphibians; then small reptiles; then small mammal-like reptiles; and, lastly, small mammals. This line retains with little alteration the primitive hands and feet, and the evolution is largely a matter of greater brain development and whatever is required for more and more active habits. Most probably the forms throughout the whole line were omnivorous or insectivorous, and possibly the more active habits were associated with the evolution of more active types of insects. The crawling limbs became running limbs. The jaws became more powerful and the muscular mechanism more elaborate. The temporal muscle became enlarged and the temporal roof became fenestrated. The dentary bones became steadily larger. Powerful teeth were developed in the front of the maxillary bone, and corresponding large teeth in the lower jaw. One of these ultimately became the canine. With the steady evolution of the skull, teeth and limbs there was a steady development of the brain.

In Upper Jurassic times the active-limb, mammal-like reptiles gave rise to the first mammals. Doubtless the more active habits resulted in a very flexible skin, and scales developed into hairs, and a four-chambered heart evolved which resulted in the little form becoming warm-blooded. A new hinge to the jaw was formed between the dentary and the squemosal, and the little bones of the jaw became ear ossicles.

With probably comparatively little change except a still greater development of the brain, the little mammals lived through Jurassic and most of Cretaceous times. Then in Upper Cretaceous and Lower Eocene times all the limb-generalized mammals began to specialize in one way or another, and with the specialization nearly all increased in size. It was the time when flowering plants were first covering the earth and much of the land that before carried only a few gingkos or cycads or other gymnosperms became converted into grassy plains and here and there dense forests of trees. Many of the mammals took to the plains and evolved into a great variety of hoofed animals. Others became carnivores and fed on the ungulates. One little group took to forest life and became frugivorous or, at least, leaf-eaters. They specialized but little beyond the walking feet becoming clasping hands. The brain, however, for some reason, developed more than in any of the other mammals, the olfactory organs degenerated, and the eyes became better developed and, turning more to the front, stereoscopic vision arose and we had the important group of the apes. Then in Upper Miocene or Lower Pliocene from one of the higher apes man was developed.

All along, from Carboniferous to Eocene, branches were given off from the line of small generalized forms. All these branches became specialized in one way or another, and everyone, after flourishing for some thousands or millions of years, died out. It seems to be the invariable rule that forms that specialize in one direction can survive only so long as the specialization suits the environment, but that when the environment changes they can neither specialize nor go back to generalized types and must perish. The specialized forms nearly always increase in size, and all the giant animals of the world, past and present, have been greatly specialized.

If Darwinism were the main factor in evolution, we would expect that animals would be able to adapt themselves to new conditions, but they rarely seem able to.

In such sidelines as the Horse group and the Titanothere group, we know practically every step in the evolution. In the horse line we begin with a small four-toed whippet-like animal in the Lower Eocene, and ultimately come to the large one-toed horse of recent times. And the evolution has gone steadily on in one direction—in feet, limbs, teeth and skull. In Lower Eocene, for example, there are no molariform pre-molars. In the Middle Eocene every horse has one and only one molariform premolar in each lower jaw. In Upper Eocene every horse has two molariform pre-molars. In Oligocene every horse has three. This is not what we should expect if evolution were a matter of accident or if it were the result of mutation.

In the Titanotheres it is the same story. We begin with *Eotitanops*, an animal about the size of a mastiff in the Lower Eocene, and come steadily up to *Brontotherium*, a huge beast as large as a good-sized elephant, in the Lower Oligocene. In the Lower Eocene forms we have no more trace of horns than in horses. Then we find small wart-like growths, and finally in the Oligocene forms huge outgrowths of bone from the point of the head. Here, as in the horses also, we have a steady development in size, limbs and teeth.

It would almost appear, as has been held by some, that there was in the Eocene types some agency causing them gradually to develop into larger and more complex forms just as a chicken inevitably develops into a fowl. This probably is not the explanation, but clearly there is something directing the evolution, and that it has gone on in one direction seems to demand some other explanation than Darwinism.

As almost all branches of reptiles and the large majority of mammalian groups flourish for some millions of years and then perish, leaving nothing behind but their bones, we can hardly conclude that this evolution has been directed by an intelligent power. If directed by an outside spiritual power, we must conclude that the power either could not foresee the distant future, or that, at least, it was only interested in the present and the immediate future.

But one inclines to think that the line of small generalized forms may have been controlled by some other agency and that that agency had the distant future in view. That is, that the controlling power was an intelligence that had a definite end in view and could plan to bring it about. It is certainly extremely remarkable how the small generalized mammals live on till in Lower Eocene times the line of the Primates is initiated and then becomes extinct. It is strange that after Middle Eocene times no new mammalian order appears on earth. We have further developments going on along certain lines—like the evolution of the *Eohippus* into the horse, or *Systemodon* into the tapir or *Eotitanops* into *Brintotherium*, but no new lines start. Great evolution has shot its bolt, and only minor evolution is left, except in the one instance of man.

And the startling fact is that in every group evolution is practically finished. No new vertebrates can ever again arise, since no invertebrates are left that could possibly evolve into vertebrates. The fishes may modify and degenerate but no new groups can appear. The amphibians are played out. Only lizards, snakes, tortoises, crocodiles and *Sphenodon* are left among the reptiles and none of them could possibly start a new line of birds or mammals. Birds can never evolve into anything but slight modifications of existing birds. And the mammals are all now in highly specialized groups, and could never evolve into anything very different from those now alive.

But in quite recent geological times one striking new modification has arisen. It is probably only 10,000,000 years since an anthropoid ape allied to *Australopithecus* began to evolve into a primitive man by a remarkable development of the brain.

I am well aware that to suggest the possibility of an outside intelligence or power directing evolution is regarded by most as a dangerous scientific heresy. Everything in life must be explained in terms of physics or chemistry. Still, there are some eminent philosophers who hold that there is more in the universe than matter and energy. Bergson, in his delightful *Creative Evolution*, comes to conclusions somewhat different from mine, but still of a similar nature. And our great South African philosopher, General Smuts, expresses a somewhat similar idea. "Holism is a specific tendency, with a definite character, and creative of all characters in the universe." Perhaps my idea of evolution helps us to understand the *modus operandi* of Bergson's "Elan vital," and it may be it throws some light on the working of Holism.

The mechanist holds that there is no evidence in living matter of anything that cannot be interpreted in terms of physical laws. The vitalist holds that there is something else not found in dead matter, and this is the Entelechy of Driesch and others. Smuts, like many others, wishes if possible to avoid the appearance on the scene of a *deus ex machina* like Entelechy or Clerk Maxwell's demon. But whatever it is, there is reason to believe there is something in life which is not governed by laws of physics and chemistry.

Haldane has shown that in the ordinary physiological processes there are co-ordinating factors that cannot be explained by physics; and the work of the experimental zoologists also seems to show that there is something of a non-physical nature that controls development.

It has long been known that if in a developing tadpole the hind limb bud is cut off and the developing tail grafted on to its place, the developing tail will be converted into a limb. And if the limb bud be grafted on to the place from which the tail bud was cut off the developing limb will grow into a tail. When the growth is a little further advanced, the transformation no longer occurs. If a budding limb is cut off and fixed on upside down, what should have been the pulmar surface becomes the dorsal and the dorsal the pulmar. If we could experiment with a human foetus of, say, six weeks by rotating the budding hand, we could doubtless convert the thumb into the little finger. It would seem as if in development there is something controlling the growing organism.

But the experiments of Spemann are far more remarkable. If we look at a developing frog's egg we find at one stage a dark upper part and a light lower. The dark part may be looked upon as the growing body cells and the light lower part as the yolk cells. If we look at the egg a few hours later we find the dark part growing round the lighter, and ultimately leaving a little white plug at one point. If we make a section of the egg and examine it microscopically we find just above the white plug an invagination of the cells which forms a glove-finger-like opening into the cell mass. This opening is called the blastopore and the cavity becomes the alimentary canal. Above the cavity is a longitudinal row of developing cells which go to form the notochord—the foundation of the backbone. Above this, again, on the outside, is a longitudinal groove the edges of which afterwards close round and form the brain and spinal cord. This region, before it closes, is called the medullary plate.

Now, if a piece of medullary plate is cut out and grafted into the side, it does not become nervous tissue but ordinary skin, and a piece of the side grafted into the medullary plate becomes spinal cord, just as we should have expected from our knowledge of the experiments on the tadpole. From this it would seem that there was something controlling the development and able to mould any growing tissue to the requirements of the animal.

But if a piece of the lip of the blastopore is cut and grafted into the side, it does not form skin but a new medullary plate and ultimately grows into a nearly complete embryo, and it compels all the surrounding tissue to form the right parts of the new embryo. Apparently there is in the piece of the blastopore lip something that can organize the other tissue. Spemann calls it an "organizer."

It is generally held that in animals the vital processes are controlled by the nervous system—brain, spinal cord and nerves—but here we have something acting like a brain at a time when neither brain nor nerves have been developed. And the organism situated near the blastopore seems to control development at a distance, though there are no nerves.

Another interesting result of Spemann's experiments is that in the organism there is something like polarity. "Cells of the centre must have some longitudinal structure which determines partly the direction of the invagination and the orientation of the second embryo." Now here we have some rather remarkable agency that directs development, and the thought is forced on one—does this agency disappear after development has gone on at least as far as the brain, spinal cord and nerves? Perhaps—and perhaps not. There is much in life that is by no means clear. Many things that are not clear are put down to Instinct—as if saying something is instinct is any explanation. In fact, it seems to me that in life there is far less that is clear than there is that is mysterious.

The mysterious we are considering at present is—what is behind evolution? What is it, for example that leads to the increased molar in the evolution of the horse? Increased action, say the Lamarckians; the more likelihood of those with slightly larger molars surviving, say the Darwinians. To me neither explanation is satisfactory. Sudden mutations, say the geneticists. But all the evidence of palaeontology is dead against them.

Can it be that there is retained in the organism something like the "organizer," which we find in early ontogeny, that controls the whole economy and can increase and decrease the vitality of a part? Take the case of the flightless bird, may it not be that the organizer braces all the parts of the bird that are functionally active and partly at the expense of the unnecessary wings?

But how, it will be asked, can this affect the next generation? Perhaps this also may be explained on the analogy of the magnet. The ordinary bar magnet is theoretically supposed to be made up of a very large number of minute similarly magnetized particles. Perhaps the hypothetical "organizer" may, like the organizer of the developing embryo, have polarity, and perhaps a modification of the polarity in the adult may affect the polarity of every cell, including the germ cells.

In any case, it seems that the polarity of an organism can be affected—less vitality going to one part and more to another, and that somehow this affects the next generation. All the changes we find in evolution—Osborn's allometrons and rectigradations—are apparently due to gradual changes in polarity.

In the brachycephalic Titanotheres, the brachycephaly is not only seen in the change in the shape of the head but in the change in the shape of the molars, in the shortening of the snout, the reduction of the incisors and canines and in the development of the horn-like growths in the snout and of the wart-like growths on the jugals.

But whatever be behind evolution it seems quite manifest that neither Lamarckism nor Darwinism is a satisfactory explanation. And not only is there no evidence of evolution being the result of chance mutations, there is, in my opinion, the most conclusive evidence from palaeontology that evolution has not been by mutations. Evolution has certainly for long periods gone on by imperceptibly slight changes, and in one steady direction. There seems to me little doubt that in evolution we have two factors—one in association with the organism which can co-ordinate structures, and gradually modify parts to meet the needs of the animal. This force, able to deal only with the present, cannot be regarded as an intelligent force. And there is a second factor of quite a different nature. It is a power that can control the other, and modify the evolution towards a foreseen end. This power brought about the appearance on the earth almost simultaneously of two types of large-brained, warm-blooded animals—birds and mammals. And shortly after brought about the evolution of higher types of plant-life—plants with edible seeds and fruits, and often edible leaves. Nearly the whole earth became covered with grass and flowers and trees. Then when the stage was, as it were, prepared, and when all other mammals were evolving and specializing in different ways, one little line was kept generalized by living in forests, and in this little line a great development of brain took place.

And lastly among the higher members of this generalized group arose a line with a large brain and *we had the first man*. A brain development such as arose in this higher ape is quite unique in the evolution of the mammals. And the strange thing is that it arose in a group that had a useful manipulative hand, unspecialized molars, and stereoscopic vision, and in a higher ape where the hind foot had remained sufficiently plastic to develop into a walking foot which gave man his unique erect position.

The coincidences are far too remarkable to have been the result of accident, and to me it seems that there is no escape from the conclusion that man is a being whose evolution has been deliberately planned by an intelligent power.

The end of all evolution is probably the production of high types of human personality. The great power behind it all seems in no hurry and we have probably to evolve much further in the next ten hundred million years. If mankind could but realize the part he is playing in the great drama it might mean many changes.

Man at the Crossroads

By
JOHN F. V. PHILLIPS
D.Sc., F.R.S.E.
Professor of Botany

Man at the Crossroads

". . . Mankind is once more on the move. . . The tents have been struck, and the great caravan of humanity is once more on the march. . ."—General Smuts.

As a botanist is a student of plants, it could with justice be asked why I should select a theme obviously transgressing the barriers of the vegetable kingdom. Let me explain, therefore, that on this occasion I speak not as the *orthodox* botanist, but rather as the *ecologist*—one who sets himself the fascinating, if difficult, task of peering into the secrets of the interrelations of all forms of life, one with the other, and with the stage on which they have their being, the environment; one who tries to take the synoptic point of view as regards the implications and relations of knowledge won by specialists in biological and allied fields. To describe ecology as a sub-division of biology is to state a half-truth, is to miss the greater truth that ecology is an attitude towards facts and their meaning, a point of view aiming at combination and blending of rays from various facets, to produce a harmony of light and colour, a picture of life as a whole. In essence, the ecological attitude toward the material of biology is equivalent to Smuts' *holistic* attitude toward the evidences of matter, life and mind in the infinitely vaster field of the Universe.

Born first in the minds of students of plants, up to the present bearing its richest fruit in botanical investigations, ecology has commenced to play an ever-increasing part in the study of animal life, and more recently has attracted the attention of some of those concerned with problems in the health and in the sociology of man. Among statesmen, in his seeing the inherent value of ecological concepts and criteria in attempts to understand group, national and international relations, General Smuts has been exceptional. As an ecologist, then, I venture to lay before you some of man's troubles, and thereafter certain truths, certain suggestions emergent from ecological studies, attempting at the same time to show their bearing upon some of the weighty problems facing us.

Man at the Crossroads.[1]

Before dealing with the nature of the ways in which the ecological point of view would assist in making possible for mankind the spirit of progress and concord, let us consider the crossroads confronting man, and some of the difficulties of the way.

If we classify broadly the nature of the roads along which mankind may journey according to appreciation or disregard of certain basic tenets, we find the following:

Firstly, those leading toward increased insecurity, and a fruitless searching for harmony, reaching finally degeneration and chaos. Motive force along such roads is *Emotionalism*, controlled little, if at all, by the *True Spirit of Science*. Next, those proceeding to added efficiency in the material aspects of civilization, an efficiency unhallowed by a preservation—let alone a growth—of those transcendent values in man's nature, the humane, the ethical, those of reverence and the spirit. Such roads, destined to arrive at a coldly efficient, grimly material epoch in man's history, would have as motive force upon them science in her severely practical form, science lacking in her higher, nobler values because holding as her only aim the grasping of more and more power. Finally, those winding toward human betterment and concord. Motive force would be science practical, bringing material blessings to mankind, science in her correct attitude toward information, science aware of, and warring for, the true aims in the life of man, science calling forth the finest in human nature and working harmoniously with this her own offspring.

One or other class of road man must decide to follow, and the manner of his selection shall spell for him either advance or retrogression.

---

1 Since this lecture was delivered, Sir Josiah Stamp, in addressing students at the University of Edinburgh on 30th June, 1932, was emphatic that civilization is at the crossroads; it may go one way under the influence of mass desire and mass impression, or the other way under the influence of intellectual and moral leadership.—*Nature*, 9th July.

From a large number of obstacles facing man at the crossroads, I select a few of the most difficult, the most widespread, and, in their relations, the most important to surmount.

The Alteration of Man's Biotic and Environmental Relations.

As Clements (1931) and I (1931) have pointed out, man should be included in the biotic community constituted by plants and animals living as interdependent, co-acting members. Clements rightly stresses that under so-called natural conditions, and to some degree in rural ones, man is an intrinsic member of the biotic community, but through aggregation into cities, has there become a super-dominant, with plants and animals all but completely under his control, and the environment increasingly so. From Nature to city his changing relation to the biotic community and environment is so gradual, and yet so complete, as to warrant its being regarded as a single continuous ecological process—the usual distinction between *natural* and *artificial* being a matter of convenience only.

While man at earlier stages in this assumption of the rôle of a super-dominant member of the community is responsible for the disturbing of biotic and habitat conditions—as may be seen from the removal of forest for agricultural purposes and the snaring and hunting of the more readily capturable game by primitive man in Africa—it nevertheless is true that more civilized man under rural, village and city-development conditions produces very much more intensive and extensive disturbance. In some regions—for example, in South Africa—primitive man and his more civilized brother together act with alarming activity upon natural and rural community conditions, primitive man's action being accelerated and influenced by the example of more civilized man, or pressure of economic circumstances set by the latter.

While a corresponding array of agencies, differing in greater or lesser detail with the continent and region, doubtless could be assembled for any portion of the globe, suffice it for illustration to refer to some of the principal agencies of disturbance due to Native and European in biotic communities and natural environments in Africa; the influence of the European greatly overshadowing that of the Native. Vegetation, fauna, climatic and soil conditions, and hence conditions essential for human progress have altered appreciably, and for the worse, as the outcome of the interaction of such agencies as uncontrolled and intensified firing of vegetation of all kinds; reckless use of the axe in savanna, scrub, bush and forest; primitive and more advanced but wasteful agricultural practice; indiscriminate, heavy stocking of grazing and browsing lands; disruption of the biological relations (for example, in pollination, seed-dispersal, soil-development) of plants and animals; destruction of plants and decimation or extinction of animals; introduction of alien plants and animals, such sometimes creating biological and habitat problems of the greatest economic importance; wrongly designed public works—such as roads, railways, drains, irrigation schemes—responsible for unnecessarily accelerated run-off of water and consequent soil erosion. In a word, plants, animals, aerial conditions, soil factors, and important associated conditions, such as water and soil fertility conservation, are disturbed by man, to his own ultimate detriment.

If we turn to an apparently different but really related matter, the problem of treatment of subject races, we have yet another instance of man's alteration of biotic and habitat relations due to his not seeing things as a whole.

It is felt in informed circles that the problem of just treatment of subject races is of greater importance as regards the future of the world's race relations than any other with which international policy is concerned—in such regions as Africa and Asia.

Since the war, the concept of the brotherhood of man has been extended at a somewhat rapid rate to subject races, chiefly in the continents named. If we consider the sequence of events, we see three distinct stages in the attitude of ruling to subject races, today some countries experiencing the second, others the third. Oppression, interference with tribal traditions, institutions, ceremonies and laws were embraced in the early, often inconsistent rule of the conqueror. At a later stage, determined attempts to graft Western ideas on primitive or more advanced civilizations (*e.g.*, Africa and India respectively) were made, with the object of completely "Westernizing" the Natives.

A tendency to make up for the evils of the past is the latest development, but to make up for such far too rapidly, to grant complete freedom of action, within the Empire or on an entirely national basis, to races largely not ready for such privileges. Many of those genuinely sympathetic with the subject races appear to forget that the granting of freedom too suddenly, too fully, may do much harm to both receiver and giver. Not only from the political aspect are portions of Africa and of Asia likely to provide storm centres of serious trouble, unless greater firmness be shown in the granting of greater or lesser autonomy, unless more time be taken in the granting of tribal freedom, but such countries are unlikely to advance economically and socially at the rate and to the degree possible, unless firm and enlightened measures be taken to help the Native to help himself.

An instance of the lack of an attitude of sufficient paternal discipline on the part of the ruling races is seen in Africa, in the absence of enforced, properly regulated measures regarding the sale of *surplus* stock by Native tribes gauging individual and tribal prestige not by the quality, but the quantity of stock possessed. Failure to dispose of stock in excess of the grazing and browsing capacity of the territory available, results in cumulative and serious depreciation in quality and extent of pasturage, wastage of soil, and degeneration in size and quality of the stock. An associated factor operating in the direction of degeneration of stock is the non-enforcement of regulated emasculation, overproduction of miserable offspring by overtaxed mothers being the outcome. Another African example is the non-enforcement, on fair and systematic lines, of tribal action against the vectors of human sleeping sickness, nagana in stock and malaria. As regards measures against tsetse, vectors of human and animal trypanosomiasis, the outcome of large-scale, well-planned work on the part of the Natives would spell ultimate destruction of the fly, the winning of much pasturage, and the removal of one of the greatest scourges of the continent.

When we turn to countries—and South Africa is one of these—wherein occurs avowed or subconscious oppression of

Native races emergent from the fear of subjugation of ruler by ruled, we find much that is not only unjust but also unwise, economically and socially, so much fuel cast to the smouldering embers of discord that later will kindle a very holocaust of misery. Such countries fail to realize that, without embarking upon miscegenation, they must be prepared to accept the Native as an integral factor in their economics, social structure and politics.

Connected with the relationships of ruling and ruled races is another mighty problem—miscegenation. Black, brown, yellow and white races are coming into ever-closer contact, particularly in Asia and Africa; miscegenation is on the increase, especially in the lower European strata. There are, of course, two widely divergent views regarding miscegenation; the one that crossing produces an inferior type physically, or mentally, or morally, resulting in a lowering of the standard of culture and life; the other that crossing is not unsound biologically, instances being cited from high achievements of mulatto and negro with varying proportions of white blood. From the results of intermixture of the Levantine peoples with Natives of South America and Africa, I feel that miscegenation is distinctly undesirable from family and national standpoints—these, after all, being psychological-biological factors demanding most serious consideration. At present we cannot dogmatize, but until scientifically unassailable data are adduced in its favour, we who live among coloured races should realize the need for reducing to the minimum legitimate miscegenation, as well as its counterpart.

On examining, quantitatively, class composition of the European populations in the old and the new world, and on attempting to envisage the position in the coming years, we cannot but be impressed with the gravity of the situation. We are breeding from the lowest strata in our social organism, whereas there is over-stringent control of family-size—due either to sense of responsibility or to desire for "freedom" on the part of women—on the part of those classes likely to produce men and women of achievement, intellectual, social and otherwise. Such classes are being eliminated "unobtrusively but fatally," as aptly put by Ruggles Gates. Investigations, such as those by Raymond Pearl, in America, demonstrate that while the labouring classes and the unemployed show a higher proportion of fertile families per unit of population, a much larger average number of children per family, and are reproducing in excess of their representation, the professional-clerical-civil-service classes are not reproducing to maintain the present status of representation. While it is perfectly true that in some occupations—notably, the industrial—human units "wear out" more rapidly than in others, and must be replaced faster, and while there has had to be, and probably will continue to be, an ever-increasing production of labourers to meet the demands of development, it remains a nightmarish fact that birth-control in the higher classes is disturbing the proportions of the classes. Furthermore, it must be remembered that the physically, mentally, morally unsound in all classes, but overwhelmingly so in the lower classes, are free to reproduce with little let or hindrance.

A point that cannot be overlooked in connection with this problem—the solution of which is vital to the progress of mankind—is that while research and scientific propaganda have received relatively little support from our leaders, absence of a scientific attitude on part of the parliaments of man, of rational behaviour by religious sects, of enlightenment regarding biological principles in social groups and movements and in the individual of lesser education, has confused the issue and impeded advance. Admittedly, there are now signs of co-operation on the part of certain governments and religious sects.

Directly associated with the problem of rational birth-control is that of our attitude toward the socially undesirable—habitual criminals, perverts and the like. In earlier times, while the immoral and amoral flourished for a space, they ultimately were destroyed, often their offspring with them. Today they are housed, fed, protected at the nation's expense and, after a season, are loosed again upon the people. Promiscuous and free propagation on the part of such undesirables often entails their unfortunate progeny becoming in turn a tax upon the State.

Our present strongly emotional attitude of "save all," intimately associated as it is with religious dogma, is biologically and economically unsound. The additional burden due to undesirables has to be borne by the already overladen worker in various classes.

A more rational attitude toward the sterilization of undesirables, after careful personal and family investigations in each instance by capable workers, still waits to be adopted, to the discredit long overdue of unscientific emotionalism, root cause of our present dilemma.

Man's Changing Habits.

Down the ages of man's history, he has evolved habits to suit his particular need, but none so rapidly and none so effective as those of the past quarter-century; habits due to the tremendous technical, industrial and transport developments following in the wake of victories of science in physico-chemical fields.

Obviously, a cursory treatment of several examples only of change in man's habits can be attempted.

Owing to the remarkable achievements in the world of mechanical transport, there is a growing decrease in our desire and in our ability to walk—a state of affairs not in any way compensated for by the sharpening of wits springing from our having to operate, catch, alight from and avoid rapidly moving vehicles. Although exhibited widely by the older generation, this tendency to avoid walking any but the shortest distances is becoming all too strongly marked in young Europeans, particularly in those living in tropical, sub-tropical and warm-temperate regions. Are we commencing to forget how to walk rapidly and for long distances? Judging from observations made in South Africa, at least, I should say that we are in danger of so doing, and this despite the influence of such movements as the Boy Scouts, Girl Guides, and "hiking." Be it remembered that whatever the position might be in the higher classes, the effects of reduced need for walking in the industrial classes are not altogether counteracted by increased opportunities for sport, as the masses do not partake in such, being content to act as spectators, or to obtain "recreation" in a cinema.

Nervous strain and defective hearing springing from the use of, or association with, the thousand-and-one pieces of noise-creating apparatus—ranging from the telephone to road-breaking machinery—cursing our civilization, must be on the increase in our cities. Our nerves are too frequently at "tense" by day and for part of the night. With television the horror will be increased, destroying what little privacy the city dweller still possesses; ostrich-like, we shall try to hide our heads, seeking a protection we cannot find.

As an outcome of excessive lighting in our cities, cinemas by day and by night, and fast travel, the strain upon the eye of city-dwellers has become much aggravated, a condition to which the abundance of cheap, small-printed reading matter doubtless is contributing. Use and disuse probably have had profound influences, down the ages, in the development and degeneration of organs in plants and animals. Due to the taking of soft, preserved and synthetic foods, civilized man is using his teeth less and less, hence decay in the teeth of children and adolescents is on the increase. It is conceivable that under existing conditions the loss of functional teeth at an increasingly rapid rate may take place, with evil effects upon the general system. Although the average civilized man in good employment eats too much, too often, too fast and often the wrong food, I agree with Dale (1931) that, as regards qualitative and quantitative dietary needs of men of various races and in various climates, it is very probable that a large proportion of the human race is living at a nutritional level preventing it from full achievement, physically and mentally.

Following the extension of European settlement in regions hitherto occupied by Native races has been the growing tendency for Native garb to be replaced by European clothing. Progressive as this may be in the instance of more highly developed individuals and tribes, it is suggestive that primitive races so often commence showing signs of deterioration in physical well-being, on assuming European clothing. Probably better by far would it be to encourage a modified form of Native costume, than to try to convert the Native to the wearing of European garments which he cannot or will not keep clean, which he in all probability is not in any case fitted to wear with the maximum of benefit to his powers of disease resistance, and which are neither suited to his conditions of life nor to his psychological make-up.

One of the most urgent problems of our time is the steady stream of mankind from rural areas to cities—a stream accelerated in its rate by economic depression. While, as will be mentioned later, ecological work shows that organisms under certain conditions grow and reproduce better if given optimum conditions of crowding than if isolated, it has been demonstrated even more clearly for organisms ranging from protozoa to man that overcrowding is responsible for retardation in growth and in reproduction, and for increased mortality. Non-regulated crowding in cities—especially in Europe, where pollution of the atmosphere by smoke involves a very definite decrease in direct sunlight and in anti-rachitic short waves, such as the ultra-violet—demands more attention paid to it than ever before, attention upon a more scientific basis, combining knowledge from the fields of physics, physiology, public health, domestic and communal engineering. Under present circumstances, no regulation of influx is attempted, and little of a really basic and extensive nature along the line of provision of wider streets, more open spaces and more generous provision of domestic room.

Not only does such overcrowding spell decreased individual and national physical vigour, but what is intimately associated therewith, and perhaps of even more importance, the evolution of a dreary, hopeless uniformity of outlook, notable for its almost complete lack of interest in any pursuit but the obtaining of food, shelter and the pleasures of the taproom and the picture-palace.

Man's mistaking Knowledge for Wisdom.

Within the past fifty years, great advances in education, lower and higher, have been achieved. But increasingly the results testify that much of this so-called "education" does not educate, does not satisfactorily add to the sum of knowledge, does not give sufficiency of wisdom. Education systems have added to knowledge while paying far less tribute than desirable to wisdom; wisdom being understood in the sense of Gough as "knowledge made our own and properly applied," the use of the best means for attaining the best ends, and the true conception of the objects of life. In the sense of the possession of wisdom so defined, the great majority of schooled humanity may be said to be uneducated—it possesses merely a greater or lesser knowledge of facts without understanding their relations and significance.

Education authorities the world over—with important exceptions here and there—pride themselves on the number of students within school or university, and more especially upon the number and "quality" of the passes in examinations, paying little if any attention to the far more important issue whether those within their gates are being educated or merely "crammed." In part due to syllabus and examination fetishes, this attitude is more largely traceable to the failure on the part of many teachers to appreciate the true meaning of education, and to *deductive* and "cram" methods being easier to apply than those heuristic or *inductive*. It therefore is not surprising to find that the results of such an attitude are passes, degrees, prizes, but absence of background of general knowledge, width and depth of understanding, ability of adjustment to particular problems on the part of the great "schooled but uneducated."

So much for general education; if we turn to instruction in the methods of science, we find that during the past twenty-five years, "science," as generally taught in schools, on the whole has been a pale shadow of the real substance. Often taught in theory only, by ill-informed teachers, often as physical science without reference to biology, or as an insipid form of botany in no way linked with either physical science or life, this drab material has failed either to educate or to inspire. In far too many university departments the sciences have been taught as so many isolated subjects without correlation and without setting, and without any attempt to arouse interest in the contemplative, philosophical, cultural values contrasted with the purely schematic, technical and practical ones. It largely has not been realized that science is an integrated body of knowledge and wisdom, and that to be scientific in outlook entails understanding how to make as complete a use as possible of existing knowledge.

To this long-continued lack of vision in the teaching of science, the attitude of many otherwise cultured people, who do not understand that science is as much concerned with philosophic and spiritual values as any other branch of intellectual activity, is largely due. On the other hand, the Humanists have not been conspicuous in making advances regarding the exposition of the truth that there are, in fact, no natural sciences and no humanities; every branch of intellectual activity being as natural and as humane as its savants make it. This divergence in outlook between the so-called Humanists—the men of letters, the historians, the philosophers—and votaries of science is one of the most disturbing of our generation and augurs poorly for future advance.

Despite our material welfare being so greatly due to and dependent upon advances in biological science, pure or in its applied forms, the astounding fact is that an elementary, but intelligent, understanding of the general principles of biology is not yet demanded of persons otherwise educated, and even highly educated. Indeed, as Dale recently pointed out, even an eminent physicist may be ignorant of biological knowledge to a degree quite impossible in the normally educated biologist with reference to physics and chemistry. Because he does not yet know sufficient respecting the nature, the life, the relations of harmful and useful plants and animals, and because he in the aggregate lacks an intelligent attitude toward his own place and rôle in Nature, man to-day is suffering not only in material aspects but also in the aesthetic and philosophical.

Finally, our problems in general education and in the understanding of facts and their relations, are not likely to be solved satisfactorily unless we attempt more seriously to interlink the information won for us by specialists. Essential as specialization is, even more so is the correlation of the fruits of such studies. One of the gravest lacks of the present time is a flair for synthesis and correlation on the part of a sufficiently large number of educated people, in the various fields of intellectual activity—hence in the words of the poet, "knowledge comes but wisdom lingers."

Man's Tardiness in Applying the Scientific Attitude to Economics.

Little need is there to stress the troubles of the present economic situation. Most of the economic landmarks are either gone or going. Rightly has Armstrong said that money-making, as the aim and end of life, is being made impossible by over-running the machinery which has made such a doctrine possible. Costs of living, wages and interest, in being jostled out of their proper relations one to the other, have been responsible for unemployment.

Unemployment has spelt the misery of millions and the putting back of the clock of economic and social progress. Labourer, capitalist and public have made equally strong and widely divergent claims, and we await a satisfactory formula for their investigation and settlement. Regulation of production of primary products, notably in agriculture, has been applied all too spasmodically, consequently the present evils of flooding of markets, sharp and unpredictable fluctuations in prices, needless competition harmful to both producer and consumer, and cruelly unequal distribution of essential food materials. Emergent from our experiences of the past two years is the somewhat startling realization that men of business and banking appear to have no scientific basis in their relations, their beliefs, their outlook; they appear to lack in empirical formulae; they vouchsafe few signs of ability for unravelling the cross-tangled skein in which the finances, the business, the commercial confidence, the credit of the nations are tied today.

When we consider agricultural economics, we find that of the basically important factors involved—production, marketing, research into problems in pure and applied science, and the guidance of the farming community—the factor most urgently demanding organization and rational regulation is production. The situation in the wheat market alone is indicative of the dire need for gauging the requirements of the world and for international co-operation among administrators, business men, producers, and agricultural experts, so that contract systems based on the fruits of wide vision, commercial, technical and scientific knowledge might be brought about. Despite a reduced production in all the principal wheat exporting countries, except Canada and Russia, during the past ten years, and a present reduction rendering the current year's crops insufficient to meet the demands of consumption and necessitating a drawing upon accumulated stocks, it is estimated by the International Institute of Agriculture that these stocks will remain heavy at the end of the current crop year. Sisal, sugar, maize, rubber, wool and other important raw materials show the same unsatisfactory features; they do not pay the cost of production, and in virtue of their being produced in excess of demands, their prices have sunk sharply and to a lower level than wages. A cause of overproduction operating unobtrusively but surely during the past fifty years, has been the advance in agricultural science and practice, ranging from improvement of strains to development of highly efficient agricultural machinery; advance with which agricultural and general economics have not kept pace. Hence it is that while our granaries, ranches, warehouses are overloaded, in 1932 hunger itself stalks throughout the world.

In the past, and indeed to almost similar extent in our present dilemma, scientific investigation of the world's problems in general and agricultural economics and industry has been in the nature of a last, almost a forlorn hope, has not been an integral part of economic production, a fixed charge, an abiding faith. Our captains of industry, our leaders in commerce, all too seldom have been familiar with the methods of science, all too rarely have possessed at the same time properly organized knowledge regarding economic and industrial aspects of their business, with few exceptions have been incapable of a rôle making possible intimate contact between practice and laboratory or study.

As the argument of Pearl and his associates that the human environment in all its complexity, has as perhaps the most significant factor in it the economic situation, cannot fail to be true in most circumstances, the economic uncertainty and policy of drift must be viewed today with the gravest apprehension.

To us living in new lands such as Africa, one of the most persistent, one of the outstanding uncertainties is the attitude that should be taken toward the development of virgin territory. Sound development of country belonging to primitive peoples, for their own welfare, by axiom is a sacred trust of civilization. But would such development—until production is rationalized—in the long run spell further over-production, and in this way quite unnecessary, and at present largely non-existent, distress among aboriginal peoples, or would it mean that all peoples of whatever race, colour, creed could find food and raiment sufficient for their needs and within their capacity of attainment? Herein lies our problem.

Man's Inability to Govern Himself.

"Statesmen are not enough; we want today the scientific spirit in human affairs."—*General Smuts* (1930).

Thorny and hard-baked as is the ground of discussion concerning the problem of human government, it has to some extent been broken on various occasions, and notably in his Sidgwick lecture on "Democracy," by our philosopher-statesman, General Smuts.

Greatly daring, but daring only because I feel that biological studies support so firmly the General's outlook, I venture to touch upon this controversial subject, a solution of which is germane to all studies aimed at making possible the whole progress of man.

Existing systems of government have failed, or show every sign of failing. Party politics have aggravated rather than improved matters; national governments, even, seem incapable of evolving effective working policies in our international economic and political impasse. Equally impotent are proving republics and dictatorships. National socialism of the kind growing up in Russia—while apparently temporarily successful—depends too much upon a wholly selfish outlook, on an undesirable scientific attitude negligent of humane and ethical values, and repudiating one of the tenets intrinsic in the true scientific spirit—internationalism.

Truly our "times are out of joint." Our present social world is one in which prevail lack of policy, confusion, insecurity, pointing—unless matters alter radically—to the disruption of the foundations of our civilization. International, national, communal, group confidence and trust are passing, if, indeed, they still exist. Lacking all too greatly in intellect and outlook of that high order likely to bestow the blessings of wholesomeness, wholeness and concord, the governments of man, for the greater part, struggle in a morass simultaneously a maze.

Scientific knowledge, the methods of science, the wisdom of science, either are not called in at all, or are called in partially or too late. Notably, is this the position in our Empire, but even in countries supposedly more capable of taking the scientific outlook than ourselves—notably Germany, America and, more recently, Russia—the general truth holds. Traceable as this is to lack of appreciation in high places of the values of scientific wisdom and the need for combined knowledge and leadership, and to parliamentary and public obscurantism, it must be realized clearly that an almost equally potent cause has been the individualism, prejudice and lack of interest in public affairs on the part of most representatives of science. Certainly in the Empire alone, there has been a neglect of opportunity for extending the viewpoints of science and of assuring that her more eminent savants served upon important commissions with various terms of reference, impinging on or included within the field of science. In this attitude of apathy and absence of organization, the average worker in science truly is at the crossroads. His own course must be decided and charted before he can aid in piloting governments. Whether he shoulders his responsibilities or whether he continues to seek seclusion from public affairs will influence for better or for worse the international social problem.

While we still dedicate too much attention to trying to solve our national and international problems on the basis of political scheming and money, we have still to grasp the truth, that satisfactory answer to our cry for healing can come only from organization, thought, knowledge and wisdom derived from sound scientific and technical knowledge, owing its inspiration to "the cool, serious, gentle spirit of science."

Where the influence of science in government has been in the direction of the purely materialistic—and such an influence does exist and may grow more rapidly than the inspiration of science in her aesthetic, ethical and spiritual attributes—another problem faces us: that of growth of materialism at the expense of true culture, idealism and love in human nature. As I mention later, this dark outlook can be made bright by the radiant torch of science holistic.

Truths and Suggestions Emergent From Ecological Studies and Having A General Bearing on the Problems Facing Man at the Crossroads.

For the sake of showing how biological investigation, employing, along with specialist methods, those of ecology and prosecuted with the ecological outlook, may throw light upon fundamental relations in Nature, I give a condensed account of the interrelations of environment, plants, animals and man in the life and the home economy of one of Africa's most deadly insects, *Glossina morsitans* Westw., one of the tsetse-flies. Therefrom, and from other investigations by my colleagues and myself, I shall draw in the sequel certain truths and suggestions having a general bearing on the problems facing man at the crossroads.

The Tsetse-fly and the Web of Nature.

Within the limits of its distribution in the sub-tropics and tropics, *G. morsitans* generally occurs within regions showing undulating plains and hills.

Growing upon the plains are extensive vegetation types falling into the following classes: Open Grassland, often on alluvial soil, with or without a scattering of trees and shrubs, these being checked in development by ever-recurring grass fires; *Acacia* Open Woodland with grass, short or long; *Combretum* Open Woodland with grass, short or long; deciduous or largely deciduous Scrub, either very dense, or as islands of variable density in other types, and with little or no grass.

Upon the hills is the very extensive "Miombo" or *Berlinia-Brachystegia* Woodland, made up of widely spaced grey-barked trees, with a moderate to poor grass stratum. It is possible, indeed, probable, that these types are related stages of the plant succession having as its ultimate expression the deciduous Scrub, but kept "open" by agency of fire.

Here and there, in sites above 4,500-5,000ft., flourishes the *Brachystegia microphylla-Berlinia* Upland Woodland with larger trees than the *Berlinia* Woodland, and variable height and density of grass and prevented by fire from developing—probably to evergreen sub-tropical Scrub.

As the *Berlinia* Woodland is left for the opener types, more especially during the dry season when the foliage has fallen, the severity of the aerial and soil conditions increases. Discounting the Scrub, which is highly unattractive to game on account of its tangles, thorns and poverty in grass, the *Berlinia* Woodland provides aerial conditions somewhat less bright, hot and dry than the opener types, but somewhat more severe than those in the *Brachystegia* Upland Woodland.

In the region under description, Central Tanganyika, the game is generally distributed during the rainy season (December-May) throughout the opener types, largely finding its home in the open grass. During the dry season, however, when water remains either in a few perennial streams or holes chiefly in opener types upon alluvial soil, the game and the important associates, such as lion and leopard, aggregate within short distance of the watering places. Within such sites the grazing usually is attractive. Although game exists to some extent during both dry and rainy season in the *Berlinia* Woodland and in the *Brachystegia* Upland Woodland, it is found to much greater number in the open communities, this being due to more abundant grass and water, and to better visibility enabling it the more effectively to avoid beasts of prey.

For the reason that the tsetse, so far as we are able to judge from field and laboratory observations, and from the absence of carbohydrate-digesting enzymes, is entirely blood-taking in Nature, it is not surprising that the movements of game have a profound influence upon its habits. Investigations by my colleagues, Dr. Nash and Dr. Jackson, have demonstrated points of interest given below, information that their later work probably will refine.

In territory where the opener types or grazing areas are extensive, the game population great, its seasonal movements on a grand scale, and tsetse abundant, it seems that a game concentration causes a striking increase in the fly density-activity in the *surrounding* country; and that when the game disperses the density-activity again decreases. A marked rise in the proportion of female tsetse accompanies the game concentration. Around waterholes where game collects, dense fly "centres" form, and may continue for a period after the game disperses.

In territory where the grazing is limited to small glades in a mass of denser vegetation, where the game is relatively sparse, and tsetse numbers medium to low, somewhat different relations appear. According to Dr. Jackson, such local glades, showing perhaps waterholes for part of the year at least, are highly attractive to game. Much less attractive are the *Berlinia* and *Brachystegia microphylla* Woodlands ascending the slopes and covering the tops of surrounding hills, and the *Combretum*-Open Woodland interspersed with deciduous Scrub. At the grazing-drinking sites, therefore, are formed centres of fly, showing a much higher proportion of females than the fly of the vegetation types adjacent, and a high proportion of young fly. A very high proportion of males, however, is seen in the population of the *Berlinia* Woodland, females scarcely showing themselves. And now comes the point of importance—the fly of the centres in the open glades are *hungry* fly; this is determined from an external examination of abdomens, from the fact that young, therefore hungry, fly are present, and from the large proportions of females, which normally do not show themselves unless they are either hungry or desire to mate. *Replete*, or not yet sufficiently hungry as to desire to proceed to the glades, however, are the fly of the *Berlinia* Woodland. Furthermore, it seems as if the fly of the vegetation transitional between open glades and the *Berlinia* Woodland is a mixture of *hungry* fly proceeding from woodland to glade, and of *replete* fly moving from glade to woodland.

Although Dr. Nash's observations in a region rich in game during the dry season suggest that the physical rigours induce the fly to leave the opener, severer types for the less severe woodland, from which it sallies from time to time to the opener types for game, Dr. Jackson's observations in a region in which game is very sparse in the late dry season, suggest that the fly has to spend more of its time in the opener types, searching for game.

So important a rôle in the ecology of game and fly is played by vegetation, acting through habitat, that it has been possible, on the basis of critical quantitative sampling over a long period, to classify the types in fly-belts in Central Tanganyika, in accordance with their relative density-activity of *G. morsitans*.

In addition to the relationships of vegetation, game and fly must be mentioned other interrelations of animals and vegetation, such as the influence on plants of selective and seasonal grazing and browsing by game, large and small, and selective destruction of grass, herbs and woody plants by termites; the indirect influences upon vegetation through medium of soil-trampling by large game, excavation by delvers and burrowers, and aeration by earthworms; pollination of flowers by insects and birds; dispersal and destruction of fruits and seeds by animals ranging from elephant to carnivores and insects; the action of man not only through the practice of shifting cultivation, setting train to new successions in plants and animals, but also through the agency of grass fires, now a definite feature of the dry season, and holding in check the young of animals and the development of denser vegetation in open types. As the foregoing biotic relations affect the nature of the habitat, as the habitat regulates the nature of the vegetation, as the vegetation canopy controls the degree of light and insolation within the types, and as these factors are correlated with grazing quality, game abundance and responses of *G. morsitans* in terms of density and activity, it is clear that they are strongly influential in the home economy of the fly.

In other connections, man comes into the picture from time to time. He is driven from his villages by advancing human or stock trypanosomiasis, with the result that woody vegetation rapidly develops upon his gardens and pastures, game advances, and with it the fly.

Conversely, he may be living within a vegetation-cleared area sufficiently great to prevent the advance of fly—which cannot traverse or live in large open areas—but may be inhibited from grazing his increasing stock in the adjacent woodland on account of the presence therein of fly. Over-grazing accompanied by sheet and gully erosion results, this process setting in action new stages in plant and animal successions. Finally, he may remove vegetation, drive out the game, and thus upset the equilibria for the existence of tsetse.

Reviewing the story of the inter-relations in the ecology of *G. morsitans*, it is seen that there is a wonderful web linking and interlinking the physical factors, the plants, the animals, the tsetse and man himself, a web of the most intricate spinning of woof and warp. Alteration in the tension of any single strand is immediately transmitted to a magnified degree throughout the web.

From contemplation of the conditions existing within webs of relationships similar to the biotic community just described, and from more detailed investigations of the behaviours of individual species in response to habitat and biotic interrelations, there emerge truths and suggestions of the nature of those to be discussed. These are the relations of cause and effect, integration, the relations of the whole and its parts, competition and co-operation as basic biological principles, optimum association of organisms and the existence of cycles in Nature.

Cause and Effect.

From first principles, we are aware that cause produces effect, but it is not sufficiently recognized, either in biology or in the affairs of man, that while cause is responsible for effect, effect in many instances becomes cause, and cause effect. That such is the relation is evidenced by the interrelations of environment and organisms. Environment either as an integration of factors of aerial and soil nature, or in instances working through one or more directly acting especially powerful factors—for example, water-aeration of the soil and the light-heat-humidity complex of the air—*acts* upon the organism, producing in it a response in a single vital process or in general behaviour. In virtue of this response of lesser or greater complexity, the organism in turn *reacts* upon the factor or the complex of the environment, influencing it in accordance with the nature and intensity of the response produced, in the first place by the environment itself. Such alteration in the environment in turn calls forth perhaps a greater intensity of response, or perhaps an entirely new response in the organism; and so continues the process of effect becoming cause and cause effect.

A second feature demonstrable by ecological analysis of cause and effect is that a major cause may consist of a very large number of constituent causes intrinsically and intricately related, forming in their integrated influence a whole or total cause differing in greater or lesser degree from its component causes, and according to the nature and distribution of these, producing a major effect differing in greater or lesser degree from the effects of its constituent causes. Examples of this are to be seen in the sometimes almost innumerable sub-divisions of the environment—the *microhabitats*, as they are called—making up a general environment, and differing one from the other in some factor or factors or in varying intensity of a factor, and forming a whole environment somewhat different from any of its parts. Dependent on the differences, the size, the distribution of the micro-habitats within a general habitat are the differences between the effects of the micro-habitats and the general habitat, in terms of responses of organisms of dominant nature or larger size.

Another matter of the widest application in the study of life and its problems, is the realization yearly being made clearer by ecological work, and plant-pathology with an ecological outlook, that well-being of the organism and the provision of well-being by means of assistance, are much more dependent upon an understanding of the cause-effect, the action-response-reaction relations of environment and individual organism or community, than upon a knowledge of the minute details of pathology. In the growing and management of plants, at all events, this change in outlook has focussed attention upon the need of granting the plant or plant community those habitat and associational conditions most conducive to well-being. Its wider application in economic botany and its extension in the realm of human medicine would do much to alleviate some of the pressing problems alluded to already.

As regards ultimate causes in biological behaviour, it is noteworthy that it seems increasingly clear that the ultimate cause is the environment, physical and biotic; the logical sequence of relation studies being factor, function, form, phylogenetic history. That this seems to be the case in the study of plants is suggestive as regards investigation of problems connected with man as an individual and in his social relations. Add to this the truth that the environment, as result of its inherent physical nature and the influences of organisms within it, is dynamic, that is, for ever changing, and it is plain that cause-effect problems in human life and border fields are likely to be elucidated the more readily, the more clearly it is appreciated that the setting of life so largely determines its responses, its reactions.

Integration.

Ecological research—particularly that aimed at obtaining information concerning fundamental interrelations of organisms of all kinds and the stage on which they play their parts—has shown that in addition to there being a cause-effect relation of some complexity between environment and organisms, there are numerous examples of beneficial or harmful interrelations or *co-actions* among the organisms themselves. Thus, there are *co-actions* between plant and plant, plant and animal, and animal and animal, the outcome of which are modifications in responses, and in reactions on the environment, by the particular organisms concerned. In the example given from the ecology of the tsetse, it is seen that there is a wonderful web linking and interlinking environment, plants, animals, tsetse and man himself; a web of the most intricate and delicate spinning. Stimulation of any single strand sooner or later is transmitted to a magnified degree throughout the web. Such linkage of action, reaction, *co-action*, serves to illustrate what is understood by integration, and teaches the necessary lesson that man lives in a world of the most complex physical and biotic interrelations; that he constantly incurs the risk of throwing out of equilibrium other components in the web of relations which he helps to form; that it behoves him to know more than he does about the world of matter and life around him; that he must avoid the temptation, the danger, of overstressing the importance of any factor, process or agent in problems impeding his advance in biological and allied fields. Lastly, there emerges plain for the acceptance, that analysis is not enough—that analysis and co-ordination must work hand in hand; that facts are not enough—the meaning and the relations of the facts, too, must be known.

The Relations of the Whole and its Parts.

Since the giving to the world of "emergent evolution" by Lloyd Morgan (1923) and of "holism" by Smuts (1926), there has been a slight tendency among certain biologists and students of social science to accept the concept that the whole is more than the sum of its parts. It is not without interest that Clements (1931) should mention that the intimate relation of the concept to a certain tenet of the positivist philosophy of Comte (1832) has been a recent discovery, it being realized for some time that Spencer, too, closely approached the same point of view. What is, perhaps, of more direct interest to the botanist, however, is the fact that Clements, on the basis of his ecological researches, came to this conclusion with reference to plant communities as early as 1901, and referred to his views in various papers between that year and 1920, to meet with ridicule in most biological quarters and partial support only in a few.

As I have stated elsewhere (1931), from my investigations in the Knysna forests and in the savannas of Tanganyika, as well as from what I have observed in other spheres, I see that this concept holds true in biotic communities in which plants, animals and man are associated. The reactions of the biotic community are more than the sum of the reactions and *co-actions* of the constituent plants and animals. This *something more* is represented *inter alia* by the aggregate shading, alteration in temperature and rate of evaporation, the improvement of the soil, and the responses of the plants and animals themselves. A biotic community in many respects behaves as a complex or multi-organism, in its origin, growth, development, common response, common reaction and its reproduction. In accordance with the holistic concept of Smuts, the biotic community is something more than the mere sum of its parts: it possesses a special identity—it is, indeed, a mass-entity with a destiny peculiar to itself.

Further support is given when the courses of succession in plants and animals are studied; when it is seen that from widely divergent primitive habitats, such as bare rock, shifting sand, free water, there can be built up from the most diverse successive stages of plant and animal population a biotic community or whole, essentially similar on the three altered habitats, but as regards the numerous constituent stages, something very different from the mere sum of the innumerable stages.

That this concept receiving so much detailed support from ecological work—for other examples could be cited—has wide application in the troubled field of human aspirations, striving and co-operation, is evident to any thinker. Never more urgent than today is the demand that man should see things as wholes, should see the wood as well as the trees, and should focus the enhanced vision that would come from such a holistic view, upon the construction on a sound, co-ordinated foundation, of the improvement of affairs and of society.

Personally, I find that this concept of the *something more*—applicable, as several philosophers have taught us, to such wholes as harmony in music, a poem, a picture—leads me to experience when studying a natural community or a splendid scene in Nature, the spiritual inspiration of science. Combined with the sobering of emotionalism and the blessing of the view dispassionate, is the birth of a fuller, more humane outlook on life, the rising within—shall we say, for sake of a better name, the soul—of a feeling of a mighty reverence.

Competition and Co-operation.

Descriptions of Nature "red in tooth and claw" for too long have overemphasized the stress of competition among organisms, have neglected both fundamental quantitative study of competition and the truth that there is inseparably associated with competition co-operation among organisms.

Clements (1929) and his associates and myself have attempted within recent years to obtain more information regarding competition and co-operation among plants. As regards co-operation among animals, Empedocles (495–435 B.C.), according to Allee (1931), foreshadowed it, while recently several workers, principally Wheeler (1923), have studied the phenomenon in social animals; Allee doing outstanding work with non-social lower forms. From the work done in various fields, it certainly seems that co-operation as well as competition is a fundamental biological principle. Competition, or a joint demand in excess of supply available, having to do with all reactions connected with supply of energy and material in the environment, is a cardinal and universal function of biotic communities, and, as such, tends to obscure co-operation—at least, as regards plants. Co-operation does take place among plants in communities—for example, the mutual benefit derived from proximity, this being of great significance in protection against severe transpiration due to insolation; species dependent upon the same bird or insect pollinators or fruit-dispersers may flower and fruit at different seasons, or at the same seasons but in different years; plants of the same general size and habit may be rooted at quite different depths.

Allee has demonstrated experimentally that unconscious co-operation due to tropistic response to environment exists in a wide range of lower animals, and results in protection, improved growth and reproduction and the like.

Among social organisms, it appears from the work of Wheeler that not only is there competition for food, mates, safety, but also co-operation to insure to one another these same conditions indispensable for development and survival. As Elton (1929) points out, each deer competes with its fellows, yet co-operates with them to form the herd—a more efficient unit. So far as co-operation among plants and animals is concerned, numerous examples could be cited, but it must suffice to instance here co-operation among pollinating, fruit-dispersing, germination-assisting and pest-destructive animals and plants.

Among higher animals, such as baboon, there are distinct signs of group co-operation. When we consider the case of man, we find group co-operation working up to national co-operation, and in the instance of enlightened individuals and groups in some nations, a tendency toward international co-operation.

Co-operation, at first automatic and unconscious in lower forms of life, therefore, develops more and more until it becomes conscious in higher forms; according to Allee, it begins humbly with its roots in the fundamental properties of living matter, working gradually upward through tropisms, senses, sex and the survival values centring about a developing social appetite.

All this being so, and it being true that one of the most significant factors in the human environment is the economic one, does it not seem logical that in human society more and more conscious, organized effort should be exerted to place competition and co-operation in their proper relative settings, that efficiency and the "milk of human kindness" may march side by side?

Optimum Association.

While retardation of growth due to overcrowding has been recorded in organisms ranging from bacteria and protozoa to higher plants and man, it has remained for Allee to demonstrate that this is not the whole story; that under certain conditions simpler non-social animals, *e.g.*, protozoa, sea-urchin eggs and larvae, tadpole tails, fishes and *Tribolium* (the flour beetle)—grow and reproduce better if given optimum crowding than if isolated or overcrowded. Such increased growth and reproduction are due, *inter alia*, to mass protection from extremes of light, water and temperature, poisons and the like. Studies by myself in biotic communities support in a general way the argument of Allee: optimum espacement of plants and optimum density-activity of animals responsible for pollination, fruit-dispersal, soil-improvement, result in better conditions of growth, regeneration, and general vigour than do under-stocking or over-stocking of plants, and superabundant or insufficient representation of important animal associates.

A bearing upon human problems is seen here. Overcrowding is one condition, optimum crowding another. Optimum crowding in human communities is to be aimed at, for the sake of the development of the spirit of conscious group co-operation, resulting in optimum conditions of health, economic progress and social enlightenment.

Cyclic Phenomena.

Careful observations indicate that cyclic phenomena are a feature in Nature. It is plain from the work of Douglass on growth-rings in trees and sun-spot cycles, that there is an interesting correlation among sunspot phenomena, physical conditions and growth response in plants. Studies aimed at gathering information upon flowering, fruiting, regeneration phenomena, as regards the appearance of fungus and insect pests, and arrival in large numbers of fruit-dispersing birds, indicate the existence of biological cycles regulated to greater or lesser degree by climatic cycles. Elton has thrown much light upon cyclic change in animal numbers.

The investigation of the interrelations of natural cycles and the occurrence of particularly favourable or unfavourable health and economic factors in human society has only just been begun. That climatic factors through their influence upon crop and food conditions, and effects of the rigours of cold upon the labouring classes, may play an important rôle in deciding political agitation and social upheaval, is not to be doubted.

Careful forecasting, correlated with information as to agricultural conditions and the outlook of the masses, will still prove of the first importance to administrators.

There is much more that might be said respecting the truths and suggestions provided by the ecological outlook, but enough has been adduced, in my opinion, to warrant my belief that such an outlook more widely applied to the affairs of man would help to ease the way for torn feet and weary spirit.

Conclusion.

I have told of our troubles and of my views as to the potential of the ecological attitude and the spirit of science holistic for putting things in order. I have mentioned, too, my personal belief that spiritual experience is an emergent from a study of the *whole* in Nature. Lest I be held ignorant of the issues between the materialism of science and human nature in its aspirations and its spiritual values, I venture a final thought on the all-important matter of the relations of these; what Julian Huxley recently termed "the chief unresolved antimony of the present stage of our civilization."

With Russell and with Huxley, I view with the gravest misgivings the possibility of a world based on the purely *practical* aspects of science. A world no matter how efficient as to control of environment, no matter how rich in food, clothes, comforts, transports, pleasures, physical and intellectual, must be materialistic, cruel, depressing, because lacking in wisdom of the true aims of life, of the right application of the mighty power given it by science.

It has been argued by the writers mentioned that science in her "power" impulse has far outstripped science in her "love" impulse—hence the clash of Science with human nature, hence the strange, confused barring of the progress of both. Continued development of the "power" of science at the expense of human values undoubtedly would produce a world of horror; for example, a world warring with weapons all too effectively forged by science.

Personally, I do not share the pessimism of these and some other thinkers, for I am convinced that there is a rising tide of thought in favour of enthroning the true science—science in her holistic form. By this I mean science practical and ethical, cognizant of and providing for the continued growth of the highest spiritual aspirations in human nature, her applications directed by the self-same spiritual values she herself engenders.

A function of trouble is to make us think. If our world trouble increases and our desire and our ability for serious and co-ordinated thought, then it will have served as purging flame and inspiring stimulus.

From this story of the problems facing man at the crossroads, it is to me clear that man must set his foot upon that road having as its goal science in her holistic form—practical, philosophical and rich in idealism. This road I feel he will take, for, like Tawney, I believe "it is more contemptible to be intimidated by distrust of human nature than to be duped by believing in it." For, after all, "To the solid ground of Nature trusts the mind that builds for aye" (Wordsworth). And does not Goethe sing of Nature: "Her Crown is Love"?

REFERENCES.

ALLEE, W., 1931: *Animal Aggregations.*
CLEMENTS, F., WEAVER J. and HANSON, H., 1929: *Plant Competition.* CLEMENTS, F., 1931: *Carnegie Inst. Wash. Year Book.*
DALE, H. H., 1931: Lockyer Lecture: Biology and Civilization.
ELTON, C., 1929: *Animal Ecology and Evolution.*
MORGAN, C. LLOYD, 1923: *Emergent Evolution,*
PHILLIPS, JOHN F. V., 1931: The Biotic Community, *Journ. Ecol.*
SMUTS, General the Rt. Hon. J. C., 1926: *Holism and Evolution.*
SMUTS, General the Rt. Hon. J. C, 1930: *Africa and Some World Problems.*
WHEELER, W. M., 1923: *Social Life among the Insects.*

Psychology in Perspective

By
I. D. MacCRONE
M.A.
Senior Lecturer in Psychology

Psychology in Perspective

1.—*The Background.*

THE aim of this lecture is to give an account of contemporary psychology so that it may be seen in its proper perspective. Certain recent developments in psychology have excited so much widespread interest that there is a real danger of overlooking the wood for some of the trees; and it is in order to supply a corrective to this rather unfortunate tendency that I wish, first of all, to fill in some of the background without which contemporary psychology, its aims, achievements and problems, cannot be properly appreciated. Psychology in one sense is very old, for it can claim, in common with several other intellectual disciplines, Aristotle as its original founder; in another sense, however, it is very young, for as an independent scientific study relying upon experimental method it goes back no further than about the middle of the last century. For that reason it has been said that psychology "has a long past but a short history," and fortunately for us we are only concerned with the history. By common consent the name of Wundt (1832-1920) is pre-eminent in that history, for it was he who, more than any other single individual, founded modern psychology as an independent experimental science and whose influence dominated it up to the close of the 19th century. Contemporary psychology, it is true, has completely overflowed and even obliterated the lines laid down by the Wundtian or "classical" psychology of the last century, but its significance can only be fully understood if we bear in mind the main source from which it derives.

Briefly put, the achievement of Wundt consisted in establishing psychology as an experimental science upon its own feet. Before that time the experimental investigation of psychological and near-psychological problems had been in the hands of physicists and more particularly physiologists. Men like Weber and Fechner, Helmholtz and Hering, Wundt's immediate predecessors and contemporaries, were by training and profession physicists and physiologists who had become interested in psychophysical and psychophysiological problems with which they dealt by means of the experimental techniques already established in physics and in physiology. Thus in 1860 we find Fechner publishing his *Elements of Psycho-physics*, in 1866 Helmholtz publishing his *Physiological Optics*, and in 1868 Hering publishing his *Binocular Vision*—all of which contained material, both factual and methodological, that was of outstanding importance for an experimental psychology. In this connection the earlier work of J. Müller on sense-physiology, more particularly on the sensori-motor arc or reflex, had laid down a basis for the study of sensory experience which at the time provided, and still does provide, a common meeting ground for physicist, physiologist and psychologist (*vide* a joint discussion on vision held in June this year at the Imperial College of Science and Technology and attended by leading British and foreign physicists, physiologists and psychologists).

Wundt, who had received part of his training in a physiological laboratory and who had been for a time an assistant to Helmholtz, succeeded in making explicit the psychological implications of these border-line activities. In 1873–74 appeared the first edition of his *Principles of Physiological Psychology* in one volume—the sixth and last edition appeared in 1908–11 in three volumes—which supplied the "new" or experimental psychology not merely with a solid foundation but also with a good deal of its superstructure. For Wundt the distinguishing feature of the new science was its systematic use of introspection, *the* psychological method, but this method could only yield data that were of any scientific value when combined with physiological, that is, experimental technique. Thus, for example, by controlling the stimulus it becomes possible to carry out systematic introspection or observation of the subjective sensory phenomena and obtain comparable results for a number of subjects. Psychologists had always employed introspection but in an unsystematic and often superficial manner; it was Wundt's great service to erect it into a systematic, precise and reliable method applied under carefully controlled and experimental conditions and often with the aid of elaborate apparatus. Perhaps the best summary of what Wundt actually did for the new science is given by Boring in his *History of Experimental Psychology.* "So Wundt took the nervous system from the physiologist, vision and audition from Helmholtz, certain fragments of experimental physiological psychology from Weber, psychophysics and Weber's law from Fechner, the reaction experiment from the astronomers, associationism from the British psychological philosophers; he bound them together with a systematic logic that he himself contributed, and he made the new psychology" (p. 656).

In 1879, Wundt, who had in the meantime been appointed to a chair at the University of Leipzig, established the first psychological laboratory, and for upwards of fifty years played a predominant part as an indefatigable worker, writer and leader in the science which owed so much to his genius. The successive editions of his constantly revised *Principles* served as a source book, while the steady stream of research publications embodied in the *Philosophische Studien* issued by the Leipzig laboratory provided a stimulus to, and a guide for, an increasing number of workers in the new field, many of whom had received their training in Wundt's own laboratory. His pupils, both German and American, carried the new science to other university centres, and by the end of the century the new science, complete with laboratories, had been firmly established on the Continent and in America. First, work both qualitative and quantitative upon the simpler mental and sensory phenomena, upon reaction time and association, upon monocular and binocular perception and the perception of depth, upon feeling and attention, was pursued, and later the higher mental processes, memory, thought and volition, were fruitfully investigated by the new methods and with a thoroughness and attention to detail that were truly Teutonic. The work of men like G. E. Müller, Stumpf, Ebbinghaus, Külpe and, above all, Titchener, who became the leader of the new psychology in America and its most typical representative in that country, immeasurably raised the status of the rapidly growing science, and of its kind still remains unsurpassed; and all considered themselves experimental psychologists in the Wundtian sense of that term.

In order to prepare the way for a discussion of the more recent developments in psychology, it may be as well to review briefly some of the characteristic features of this psychology that occupied so much of the stage during the last two decades of the nineteenth century and the opening decade of the present century. It was, in the first place, a highly self-conscious psychology with a logic of its own that sharply distinguished it from the current philosophical or "schreibtisch" psychology, on the one hand, and from the physiology out of which it had arisen, on the other. In the second place, it confined itself exclusively to the investigation of the adult mind or consciousness to which alone its method of introspection could be applied. In the third place, in order to secure the highest degree of accuracy and precision, it aimed at the greatest refinement of the method of introspection. Finally, and most important of all, it confined itself within a very narrow conceptual framework—mind was consciousness, psychology was the science of the contents of consciousness and the ultimate elements of consciousness were sensations, images and feelings. As a psychology, it was atomistic, associationistic, intellectualistic, to the last degree. These characteristics become more significant when we bear in mind the exclusive reliance upon the introspective method and the way in which it was applied. Thus, from the point of view of introspective analysis mind can only present itself as a succession of mental states or states of consciousness—compare James's analogy of a "stream of consciousness"—which, by introspection, are reduced to a congeries of further unanalysable mental elements. The life or activity of the stream itself is lost, since introspection, like a photographic camera, can only reveal successive "positions" of elements within the "stream," but never the "streaming" itself. But, somehow or other, a return from the mental elements to the immediate experience from which the analysis began, must be made and so recourse is had to some or other variation of the doctrine of association, for example, in the form of "mental chemistry," creative synthesis or synthetic acts of attention. Again, an introspective psychology is necessarily dualistic and intellectualistic, since it confines itself by implication to the mind or mental state "as it is," without reference to what "it is for," and in the mental state nothing more can be found by introspection than the mental elements—sensations, images and feelings—into which it is analyzed. Finally, and perhaps most significant of all in the light of contemporary psychology, the scope of introspective psychology was confined to the study of the "generalized, human, adult mind or consciousness," while the high standard demanded for success in introspection gave it an almost esoteric quality. Child psychology, animal psychology, abnormal psychology, together with any form of applied psychology, were simply all ruled out, since these could never form part of a science of psychology which relied mainly, if not exclusively, upon the method of introspection for obtaining its data. It was this feature, perhaps more than any other, that led to revolts against the Wundtian psychology and finally brought about its dissolution.

To understand the more positive factors that brought about a change of front in the development of psychology, we must turn to follow some of the directions which the new psychology took when it reached America. That psychology, as we have seen, had received its first impulse in Germany. The American psychologists who introduced it into America had all been trained in Germany, since at the time they could go nowhere else to be trained. Titchener, for example, an Englishman by birth, had left Oxford for Leipzig, where he was one of Wundt's pupils. In due course he became professor at Cornell in 1892, where he remained until his death in 1927. Of all the American protagonists of the Wundtian psychology, he was perhaps the only one that remained faithful to it up to the very end. For most of the others, as well as for those who had not been so strongly under its influence, or who belonged to the younger generation that had not been trained in Germany, the Wundtian framework became too narrow and too rigid; in fact, not sufficiently psychological. William James, for example, who had no great regard for what he described as "brass-instrument psychology," refused to abandon life for the laboratory. His great work, though it added little to the principles of psychology, did provide an orientation that was far more congenial to the temper of American psychology and which finally found expression in the "functional" psychology of Angell and of Dewey, as contrasted with the "structural" psychology of Titchener. According to the latter, the study of mind should be conducted from the point of view that prevailed in the physical sciences; according to the former, the study of mind was to be regarded as an extension of the wider study of biology. Functional psychology, in other words, was not interested in mental states but in mental operations, not interested in consciousness but in performance, not interested in the sensations, images and feelings of the mind but in the responses of the psychophysical organism to its environment. Thus, the mind was squarely placed in a biological setting, where its rôle or function was to maintain an equilibrium between the organism and the environment. Every mental act was a reaction and the stimulus-response formula applied without exception to all psychological phenomena. Functional psychology justified child psychology, animal psychology, abnormal psychology, differential and applied psychology, as the emphasis came to be shifted on to problems of performance, adaptation, learning, habit-formation and individual differences. Some of these problems were, as a matter of fact, already being investigated by British psychologists who had been totally unaffected by the contemporary development of experimental psychology on the Continent. This insularity of British psychology left it free to develop its own characteristic interests, which were, thanks to the influence of Darwin, largely evolutionary and comparative. Galton, for example, who was interested in the problem of mental inheritance, initiated the study of individual differences and devised its peculiar device, the mental test. He was the first to realize the importance for this study of statistical technique, and more particularly of methods of correlation which today play so important a part in the scientific study of mental abilities and of problems of mental measurement in general. Animal psychology, again, was first placed on a scientific footing by the work of Lloyd Morgan and of Hobhouse, whose *Mind in Evolution* anticipated later developments in experimentation upon intelligence in animals. Finally, academic psychology with its emphasis upon striving as a fundamental category, culminated in the hormic psychology of McDougall, who emphasized the continuity of behaviour in man and in animals in terms of an underlying identity of instincts. Thus, on the whole, the angle of approach and the kinds of problems that were characteristic of British psychology found ready acceptance in America; and, in turn, the problems of individual differences, of mental measurement, of animal behaviour, were "captured" and vigorously developed by American psychologists. Their great success was based upon an ever-increasing extension of, and reliance upon, experimental and quantitative techniques—a lesson that had been learned from German experimentalism—to problems that were no longer confined to the study of the adult mind; and American psychology at its best may be regarded as a happy combination of German method and thoroughness with an outlook that had more in common with British psychology.

2.—*Behaviourism, Gestaltism, Noegenesis.*

So much for the perspective, since it is high time that we turn to some of the more important systematic developments in contemporary psychology—the so-called "schools of psychology" that have come into prominence in recent years. The first of these, which began as a revolt that never settled down to a development, is usually known by its American name of "Behaviorism," but has long since ceased to be of any importance in the original and extravagant form in which it was first presented. Psychology as a study of behaviour or the responses made by the organism to its environment is clearly in line with the development of a functional psychology and, in fact, McDougall, quite independently of the "behavioristic" revolt, and with no sympathy whatever for its point of view, had so described psychology before "Behaviorism" came into prominence. But the new movement was a much more radical departure from psychological orthodoxy, and under the leadership of Watson, with whose name it will always be associated, it proceeded to challenge one by one the most strongly held psychological presuppositions. Watson, who had devoted himself to animal psychology, first of all rejected introspection on the ground that it was quite useless as a method in the scientific study of animal behaviour and substituted for it the method of objective observation such as might be practised, for example, in astronomy. Having rejected the method, the next step of rejecting consciousness upon which that method was based seemed a perfectly natural development and, as such, excited little opposition so long as the rejection was made on the ground that consciousness was irrelevant to the study of animal behaviour, even though to the psychologist who was not a student of animal behaviour, the practice of ignoring some of the data might not appear strictly scientific. But when Watson took the final step and announced that human behaviour also could only be scientifically studied in the same way as animal behaviour, he soon found himself in conflict with the great bulk of his fellow psychologists, and out of the conflict "Behaviorism" was born. Watson certainly had the courage of his convictions, and he expressed them in no uncertain voice. Consciousness was not merely, not relevant to the study of behaviour, but it did not exist and "psychology which had first of all lost its soul and then its mind, was now in danger of losing its consciousness." In fact, according to Watson, it had no consciousness to lose. Behaviour, both human and animal, is nothing but a series of reflex movements excited by external and internal stimuli and the organism nothing but an elaborate responding mechanism controlled by environmental forces. Learning is nothing but the retention of successful responses and the elimination of unsuccessful responses which are made to a succession of stimuli, though the terms successful and unsuccessful are, strictly speaking, meaningless in any mechanistic interpretation of behaviour. Language or vocal activity is nothing but a substitution for bodily activity, although, as a matter of fact, there is a profound psychological difference between genuine language or verbal activity, on the one hand, and vocal activity on the other. Thinking is nothing but sub-vocal activity involving more particularly laryngeal movement, as well as any other form of short-circuited or implicit muscular movement that may be available. The nursery has nothing to say about instincts, for there are none, while the relative claims of heredity and of environment, of nature and of nurture, are disposed of in the following quotation: "Give me a dozen healthy infants, well formed, and my own specified world to bring them up in, and I'll guarantee to take any one at random and train him to become any type of specialist I might select—a doctor, lawyer, artist, merchant-chief, and, yes, even into beggarman and thief, regardless of his talents, penchants, tendencies, abilities, vocations and race of his ancestors." These are some of the positive contributions of a radical or mechanistic behaviourism, most of which would be rejected to-day by psychologists who have no objection to describing themselves as students of behaviour. But Watson's revolt has on the whole served a very useful purpose, and psychology as a science has greatly profited by his excursions. Negatively, it has cleared away a lot of useless accretions and sheer verbiage and has obliged psychologists to re-think and re-formulate their presuppositions, while positively it has opened new avenues of approach to old problems and made important contributions to the study of child behaviour and the unlearned behaviour of man. Fresh attempts of a much more original nature, such as those now being made by Holt, to trace the continuity in development of behaviour from below upwards so as to include, by giving a new interpretation to, what are usually called conscious processes, have no doubt profited by the mistakes of a too simple "Behaviorism." Holt, whose attempt frankly aims at an explanation of the total behaviour of the organism according to principles that are the result of the most recent physiological research, does not begin by begging the question whether consciousness does or does not exist. Instead he tries to show how, for the conventional interpretation of the facts of consciousness, another interpretation may be substituted which does justice to the psychological phenomena while at the same time remaining within the physiological limits laid down. How significant for psychology this enlightened behaviourism is likely to be, we cannot tell, but it does bring out the importance for psychology of the contributions made in recent years from the side of physiology. Of these, the most familiar is Pavlov's work on the conditioned reflex, which fitted in so well with the point of view of mechanistic behaviourism. The technique of conditioning was in fact applied by Watson himself to the emotional behaviour of young children as early as 1919, and as a psychological theory the principle of conditioning is being applied to such problems as learning, habit-formation, and the nature and development of the unconscious. We seem to be approaching the stage when once again the psychological outlook is being profoundly affected by developments in physiology.

While "Behaviorism" was fluttering the psychological dovecotes in America, another revolt had begun, this time in Germany, which has since become familiar in English-speaking countries under the name of "Gestalt-psychology." The two movements had nothing in common with one another except that they both came into prominence at about the same time just shortly before the Great War. The initiation of the new movement in Germany is usually ascribed to Wertheimer, but closely associated with him were two other psychologists, Koffka and Köhler, who have both played a conspicuous part in developing the new ideas and in making them familiar to English-speaking psychologists. The concept of the "Gestalt" or "Gestalt-Qualität," the form-quality, had been introduced into German psychology as early as 1890 as a supplementary concept, but the name Gestalt-psychology is now usually applied to the Wertheimer-Koffka-Köhler or Berlin school of psychology, which claims to have been the first to take the concept of the *gestalt* seriously as a fundamental mental hypothesis and to have given it a new and revolutionary interpretation; in fact, the Gestalt-psychology or configurational psychology, is regarded by its authors as a "neue Psychologie." To appreciate this claim on behalf of Gestalt-psychology, we must bear in mind that it had come to be taken for granted in much of current psychological theory and practice that the aim of introspection was the reduction of mental contents to their ultimate elements, and that this assumption had been but confirmed by the general procedure of physical science and by the influence, more particularly, of sense-physiology, which led to an emphasis on, and a search for, a one-to-one correlation between stimulus and sensation—the so-called "constancy-hypothesis." It was against this introduction of an "Atomismus" and a "Physikalismus" from without into a psychology whose data were thereby distorted that the Gestalt-psychologists first raised their protest, especially with regard to their effect upon data within the field of perception. Thus, for example, Wertheimer, by a series of ingenious experiments, showed that since the perception of apparent movement when two stationary stimuli are successively exposed with a suitable interval of time is phenomenally indistinguishable from, and psychologically as real as, the perception of actual movement, a satisfactory psychological explanation would have to account for both phenomena in identical terms. This, however, was just what current psychological theory, couched in terms of individual stimuli, sensational elements and subjective acts failed to do, and as a result these hypotheses were one and all rejected by Wertheimer. Instead, he put forward the hypothesis that the movement as perceived is itself a primary *gestalt* or configuration, an organized whole in experience that cannot itself be analyzed into anything psychologically simpler or more ultimate without destroying it *qua* movement, and that in the last resort its immediate substratum is a physiological process in the brain field. The persistent bias displayed by introspective analysis in favour of atomistic sensations each correlated with a specific stimulus simply led to losing sight of the wood for the trees; in other words, the presence in the field of perception of segregated wholes, of configurations, of patterns, was systematically overlooked or neglected, although from the standpoint of naïve experience they are its most conspicuous feature. The *gestalt* is, of course, more than the sum of its constituent parts, as is illustrated by the case of a melody that can be transposed from one key to another with a change in every one of its single notes but which is still perceived as the same melody. On the other hand, if the results of introspective analysis are regarded as the primary psychological data, then the perceptual wholes or *gestalten* can only be accounted for by the introduction of the *ad hoc* hypotheses, such as subjective acts, acts of attention, creative synthesis and the like, which do not explain the *gestalt* but explain it away. Hence, the only way out of the impasse is to dethrone the sensation as the primary psychological datum and to regard it as an unreal abstraction which has been hypostatized as the result of correlation with the corresponding stimulus. In its stead we have the perceptual *gestalt* whose local properties are supra-locally determined, an organized and segregated whole whose parts are in dynamic interrelation. Moreover, the *gestalt* itself is always perceived as a figure against a background—the figure being defined, structured and standing out against the ground which perceptually is vague, unorganized and at a lower level. Since the perceptual *gestalt* is the primary and immediate psychological datum, its genesis must lie outside the experience of the individual and can, therefore, only be accounted for in terms of some physiological hypothesis. As Köhler has tried to show, the *gestalt* as a mode of organization is not peculiar to psychological phenomena but is also a characteristic of physiological and physical processes. This holistic character, as displayed at the physiological level, provides the immediate substratum of the psychological *gestalt* and so "explains" its appearance within the field of perceptual experience. Such an explanation, however, appears open to the objection that the psychological phenomenon which is being explained is merely translated into physiological terms and that this physiological *gestalt* conceived on the analogy of the psychological *gestalt* is then itself made use of as a hypothesis to explain the psychological phenomenon. In other words, the *gestalt* which itself to begin with poses the problem, comes to be made use of as the very means of disposing of that problem by converting a formal resemblance into a real, underlying identity.

Gestalt-psychology has not confined itself to demonstrating the reality of the *gestalt* in perceptual experience. Thus, it has sharply challenged the behaviouristic interpretation of animal learning, which holds that all such learning is blind and unintelligent, a mere sequence of random responses that leads through a succession of trials to a gradual improvement by the elimination of the unnecessary or unsuccessful responses. Such an interpretation, the Gestalt-psychologists contend, implies that the animal itself does not participate in the learning process, and could only have arisen as the result of confronting the animal with situations which were either too difficult or too remote from its experience to provide it with an opportunity of behaving intelligently. Hence, the significance of Köhler's experiments on the mentality of apes, for these animals, placed in situations in which the successful responses could not have been achieved by a process of blind trial and error, however prolonged, nevertheless succeeded in finding the correct solutions to a number of problems. Thus, while Watson and Thorndike had observed the behaviour of rats learning to find their way through a maze, or cats learning to find their way out of a problem-box, and had come to the conclusion that the whole activity could be accounted for in terms of specific responses made to a series of specific stimuli, each response occurring in sequence like beads upon a string, they overlooked the fact that such random behaviour was forced upon the animal by the very conditions of the experiment; and, further, they overlooked the fact that sooner or later, provided the animal persisted, the correct response would inevitably be made but not necessarily with any appreciation on the part of the animal of the relevance of the response; that is, the response would be purely accidental from the point of view of the animal. In Köhler's experiments, on the other hand, the animal, however persistent, could not achieve the correct response by random trial and error but only by what normally would be called "insight," and its behaviour in such cases would quite rightly be interpreted as intelligent. Thus, the chimpanzee, who, after vainly trying to seize fruit dangling beyond its reach, drags up a box on which it mounts and so secures the prize, has solved its problem but not by aimless and haphazard bodily activity; while the same chimpanzee once again shows insight when it makes use of a stick to roll within reach fruit lying outside the bars of its cage, and even achieves the feat of slipping one stick into the socket provided by the other in order to secure the fruit which lies beyond the reach of either stick taken singly. The behaviouristic theory is obviously inadequate to explain such cases of learning, since it cannot provide for the fact of solution, for the novelty and originality of response, which is so characteristic of the animals in these situations. From the point of view of Gestalt-psychology, the solution is the result of insight, and insight consists in seeing relevant things together—that is, in the perception of a *gestalt*. In learning, however, the *gestalt* is not provided ready-made, as we find in the case of sensory perception, but it has to be achieved. The mere sensory stimulus of the box, for example, is not by itself sufficient to evoke the appropriate responses of dragging the box towards the fruit—it might, for that matter, just as readily evoke responses of sitting down—but it is only when the box comes to be perceived in relation to the fruit and both in relation to the baffled animal itself, as all mutually interdependent members of the same *gestalt*, that the appropriate responses are made to the box which is now perceived in an entirely new context as something to stand on. The insight, when it comes, is as a rule immediate, a sort of "a-ha" affair—hence the sudden drop in the curve of learning as compared with the gradual improvement in the curve of practice or habit-formation to which all learning is reduced when it is regarded as nothing but the retention of correct, and the elimination of incorrect, responses. Gestalt-psychology, as contrasted with radical behaviourism, does strive to save appearances in the field of behaviour and at the same time to avoid the pseudo-scientific hypotheses against which so much of behaviourism is rightly in revolt. But compared with the rather naïve theories of certain forms of behaviourism, Gestalt-psychology is undoubtedly much more subtle and profound, much more truly radical. Its greatest merit lies in the fact that it has not only raised new problems but that it has also provided a new angle of approach to old problems even in the field of perception. It has given a fresh impetus to psychology in almost every direction.

Psychology in Great Britain has never been characterized to anything like the same extent as in Germany or in America by systems or movements. It has been an affair of individuals, a Ward, a Stout or a McDougall, rather than of schools—a Leipzig school, a Wurzburg school or a Berlin school. In recent years, however, there has steadily developed under the leadership of Spearman, professor of psychology at the University of London, a school of psychology now generally known by the name of the Noegenetic psychology or, simply, Noegenesis. It is essentially a psychology for psychologists and for that matter, with regard to some of its aspects, confined to those who have had a mathematical and, more particularly, a statistical training. Noegenesis embraces within itself two quite clearly distinguishable though mutually supplementary aspects—a quantitative and a qualitative aspect. It is a psychology characterized by a high degree of originality and a truly extraordinary combination of first principles with meticulous attention to details. In no other psychology are theory and practice so closely wedded to one another.

On its quantitative side, Noegenesis sets itself the task of introducing order into the welter of human abilities and their interrelations. The measurement of abilities by means of the test device had been introduced into psychology by Galton and had taken root in America but without producing much fruit. Revived by Binet in the form of the measurement of intelligence, it had had a spectacular practical success, but the practice had far outstripped the theory and once more the test movement seemed threatened with a collapse. The superstructure had no secure foundation and it was this that Spearman set himself to supply. Confining himself to an analysis of the quantitative results of a large variety of tests, and making use of more and more refined statistical methods in the absence of which the mere multiplication of results seemed to lead to an ever-increasing confusion of interpretation, Spearman claimed to show that every ability, every intellectual operation, could be divided into, or be regarded as, the joint result of two factors—the one, a general factor that was common to every ability whatever; the other, a specific factor (or factors) that varied from ability to ability. This is the famous Two-Factor Theory which at one stroke gave a clear-cut theoretical interpretation to the mass of empirical data and justified the practice of the intelligence test. The general quantitative factor or "g," which is common to all abilities, accounts for their intercorrelation, and it is this "g," the acceptance or rejection of whose existence is purely a matter of statistical argument, that is measured by any reliable intelligence test. It may, therefore, be equated, though it is not identical, with what is popularly known as an individual's "intelligence" or general mental ability.

On the qualitative side, Noegenesis seeks to analyze the nature of intelligence and to discover the ultimate laws of cognition. In this quest the influence of an older, more academic and even scholastic tradition which seems so incongruous when contrasted with the general drift of contemporary psychological thought, is strongly marked. Intelligence is the intellect in action and all intellectual operations which give rise to new knowledge fall under one of three laws or principles. These are: (1) the Apprehension of Experience, which reads: "Any lived experience tends to evoke immediately a knowing of its characters and experiencer"; (2) the Eduction of Relations, which reads: "The mentally presenting of any two or more items tends to evoke immediately a knowing of relation between them"; and (3) the Eduction of Correlates, which reads: "The presenting of any character together with any relation tends to evoke immediately a knowing of the correlative character." These three laws govern all noetic activity or generation of new knowledge and hence they are known as laws of noegenetic activity. They are as fundamental for the psychology of cognition as are the three laws of motion for physics. All this seems too good to be true and somehow or other the doctrine of noegenesis has had little influence outside the circle of those who have worked directly under Spearman's influence. There may be several reasons for this fact. In the first place, the psychology of pure cognition is at the present time not a problem about which the majority of psychologists are exercising themselves; in the second place, the doctrine places in the forefront the concepts of the mental state and of the mental act, neither of which finds ready acceptance in present-day psychology; in the third place, the formulation of the three fundamental laws of noegenesis appears to be nothing more than the "psychologising" of the results of the logical analysis of a proposition into its two terms and the relation between them. Thus, according to the first law, we have first the apprehension of A followed by the apprehension of B; according to the second law, we have the eduction of a relation between them, that is, A-B; according to the third law, we have the eduction of a correlate, that is, given A: B:: C: x, we find the unknown term that satisfies the relation. Now if we take such a well-known test of intelligence as the analogies test and analyze the formal steps of the process from premiss to conclusion, we find that it falls neatly and logically into three steps corresponding to the three noegenetic laws. Convert the results of the analysis into psychological operations and we have the three laws themselves.

Some of the finest and most penetrative work of Spearman and his school has been upon the interrelation of abilities and upon the specificity or generality (overlapping) of individual abilities. We have already dealt with the former and the development of the Two-Factor Theory as its solution, but the importance of the latter for general psychological theory compels a brief reference. In popular psychology there is a widespread belief in mental faculties, such as attention, discrimination, memory, imagination, etc. So long as these terms are regarded as mere class-concepts which indicate no more than a formal resemblance between the abilities grouped together under each term, they serve a very useful purpose as classificatory devices which enable the psychologist to reduce his data to some kind of descriptive order. But unfortunately, this restricted and only legitimate use of these terms is consistently disregarded in popular psychology and even to a certain extent in scientific psychology, though in theory the fallacies of a faculty-psychology have been exposed time and again. Of these the most persistent is the conversion of the name into an entity followed by the reference of all the acts that go by the same name to that entity regarded as a unitary function. By saying that an individual has a good memory we imply that all his acts of remembering are expressions of one and the same faculty of memory to which they are due, and that having a good memory he will be able to remember names, faces, instructions, mathematical formulae or what not, with equal success. Even if we reject the former use of the term as utterly unscientific, there still remains the problem of the relations of the individual abilities classed together under the same name. Is each ability specific and, if not, what is its spread or to what extent does it overlap with the other abilities? Is the ability to discriminate between differences in weight the same as the ability to discriminate between differences in pitch or are they two specific abilities, independent of one another? The answers to these questions are provided by the Two-Factor Theory, for the same criterion which leads to the division of each ability into a general and a specific factor will also determine whether the specific factors of any two abilities overlap or are independent of one another. The importance of the Two-Factor Theory can thus hardly be overestimated, for it provides a basis for a unified science of human abilities; in the words of its author: "it found a chaos and left a science."

3.—*Psychoanalysis and Social Psychology.*

No review of contemporary movements in psychology, however summary, which did not make some reference to Psychoanalysis could possibly be regarded as complete. A few years ago any such reference in a lecture like this would very likely have been one of two kinds—either frankly damnatory (the more likely) or mildly favourable with a strongly marked tendency to wait and see (the less likely). Psychologists, like any other class of men, are after all also human and it is therefore not surprising that they shared, and still do share, with others those prejudices that make an impartial and objective survey of Psychoanalysis almost impossible. Apart from any such emotional difficulties of a general kind, which, from a psychoanalytic point of view, appear perfectly natural and whose absence would indeed give rise to a very serious problem, there are certain difficulties of a professional kind that are felt more particularly by psychologists. Psychoanalysis, among other things, is also a psychological theory and its terminology, therefore, is a matter of some concern. Now psychoanalysts have not, as a rule, paid much attention to questions of terminology and have for that reason invited criticism which has for the most part dealt with the shadow rather than with the substance, but which has also at times drawn attention to what are real confusions of thought concealed by an elaborate use of metaphor. Thus, the question whether mental processes are or are not unconscious is not a matter that can be disposed of on terminological grounds as some psychologists seem to think; on the other hand, to speak of a "repressed idea" is to jar every nerve in a psychologist's body, for the phrase is, to take it at its face value, nothing more than a meaningless noise. There is this to be said, however, on behalf of the psychoanalyst, that he is struggling to formulate concepts for which the ordinary working psychological vocabulary is at times quite inadequate, since that vocabulary is more properly fitted to recognize only those phenomena that occur at the conscious level of mind. Again, Psychoanalysis is, above all things, a dynamic or conative psychology and hence the standing temptation to indulge in a crude hypostatization and a multiplication of entities as a means of providing obvious explanations. Psychoanalysts are not as a body distinguished by a highly developed critical sense or a burning desire to analyze their own concepts, while those who might undertake this task are usually handicapped by lack of a first-hand knowledge of the relevant facts, so that their analysis often becomes a purely verbal exercise. The point I am trying to make is this: there is a philosophical distinction which is sometimes made between knowledge by acquaintance and knowledge by description, between the knowledge which an individual acquires by looking at a thing—say, a landscape—and the knowledge that same individual acquires by merely having the thing described to him by another. In the same way, we may acquire a first-hand knowledge of the psychoanalytical landscape by actually undergoing an analysis, or we may acquire our knowledge at second-hand by reading psychoanalytic literature. A knowledge by description, however intensive or extensive, can never be equivalent to a knowledge by acquaintance and hence criticism informed solely by the former kind of knowledge is handicapped; on the other hand, the theory should not be a caricature of the facts, it should be able to tolerate logical analysis—if not, so much the worse for the theory. Now I very much doubt whether psychoanalytic theory would succeed in withstanding such analysis without undergoing considerable reformulation; whether, in other words, not the facts themselves but our interpretation of them would not have to be considerably revised. There appears at present to be a gap between general psychological theory and psychoanalytic theory which in the interests of both should not be allowed to persist.

As every schoolboy knows, Freud of Vienna first devised the psychoanalytic technique as a therapeutic method for the treatment of psychoneurotic disorders. The outstanding feature of that technique is the use of free association on the part of the patient, who is required to do no more than simply relate what he finds present in his consciousness. In theory this appears simple but in practice it proves very difficult to follow the rule without constant evasion. Psychoanalytic technique, apart from its use as a therapeutic method, can also be used for exploring the mind, more particularly the unconscious mind, of so-called normal individuals and revealing to the individual himself the significance of his personality traits and attitudes. The practical and the scientific uses of the method are, however, so closely bound up with one another that it becomes impossible to separate the two—to undergo an analysis is to live through an experience which not merely enlarges one's knowledge of the self but which at the same time must also bring about profound changes in that self.

The development of the psychoanalytic technique is an interesting illustration of the way in which most scientific discoveries come to be made. It was not a sudden, happy inspiration on Freud's part but the result of a slow process of groping and feeling the way step by step illuminated by occasional flashes of insight. In the last resort the proof of the pudding lies in the eating and Freud's method worked—it did get rid of the psychoneurotic symptoms effectively and permanently where other methods such as suggestion and hypnotism failed. In the same way the psychoanalytic theory, with its basic concepts of psychical determinism, libido, infantile sexuality, repression and the Unconscious, was not an *a priori* construction but an induction which grew step by step as the only possible interpretation of the facts which were being brought to light by the method. And that process is still going on as more facts are brought to light and further elaboration of theory is required. Both the practice and the theory were in the beginning the results of Freud's own single-handed efforts maintained with a truly heroic persistence in the face of a hostility such as only members of the medical profession appear to be capable of. Apart from the personal aspect of the matter, however, there was this to be said from the psychoanalytic point of view, namely, that psychoanalytic theory might still conceivably have been true in spite of the hostility, while if there had been no hostility the theory must necessarily have been false.

Let us briefly review some of the main concepts of the theory. From the dynamic point of view there is the concept of a mental conflict at the unconscious level between incompatible and fundamental "wishes" or impulses which sooner or later gives rise to a state of tension which is dealt with either by sublimation, that is, a displacement of the incompatible wish accompanied by inhibition of its aim, or by repression. Both sublimation and repression are unconscious processes—the former following what is called the reality-principle since it leads to a more adequate adaptation to the demands of reality, while the latter follows the pleasure-principle since the original aim of the wish is not abandoned but finds gratification in disguised and distorted forms that frequently lead to symptom-formation or social maladjustment. Psychoneurotic symptoms are one expression of this disguised gratification, dreams another—hence the formulae: every symptom is a compromise-formation in which both the repressed and the repressing forces are represented; every dream is a disguised wish-fulfilment. The concept of repression is, according to Freud, the cornerstone of psychoanalytic theory, for from it follow all the consequences in the way of the conscious and unconscious development of the psyche; in fact, human nature as it reveals itself in every unique personality may be regarded as the result of the reaction of man's original nature to repression. Recent developments of theory present a very systematic account of the psychical structure. At birth the psyche is constituted by two groups of impulses: (1) nutritive and libidinal, and (2) aggressive—the so-called Life and Death Instincts. To the psyche in this form the term "Id" is applied to indicate the fact that it is, and remains, unconscious, non-personal or impersonal, out of touch with the external world. The Id is that something within us, the source of all our fundamental impulses, which, nevertheless, can never form part of us, of our conscious selves. Out of the Id come to be differentiated as the result of the pressure of the environment, including the social environment, those two mental structures, the Ego and the Super-Ego, whose interrelations with one another and with the Id are exceedingly intricate. The Id is, as we have seen, unconscious, but it is also non-moral and alogical and can only wish, that is, strive for gratification. An organism at the mercy of Id-impulses would soon be annihilated; therefore, as a purely utilitarian device there comes to be differentiated out of it a psychical organ, the Ego or consciousness, the rôle of which is to establish contact with the external world and to restrain the Id-impulses according to the demands of the environment. At a later stage of development we find yet a further differentiation, namely, the Super-Ego which represents, from within the psyche itself, the demands of the social environment as originally represented by the parental authority. The conditions which give rise to the development of the Super-Ego are difficult to unravel. Briefly, however, it appears that the Oedipus complex is abandoned or partially abandoned as the only way of getting rid of the increasing anxiety due to the threat of genital punishment or loss of genital gratification which constitutes the castration complex. When the Oedipus complex is abandoned, there follows a reaction formation leading to identification with the parent or parental authority which, as a result, becomes incorporated within the psyche in the form of the Super-Ego. In the picturesque metaphor of Freud, the Oedipus complex is shattered by the castration complex and the Super-Ego is its heir. The consequences for the future development of the individual are momentous. In the first place, since the Super-Ego is predominantly unconscious, the individual's conscience or the conscious part of the Super-Ego plays a relatively minor rôle in the inhibition of impulse. In the second place, in so far as it is unconscious the Super-Ego can undergo little or no modification as the result of later experience. Hence at the adult stage the Super-Ego represents a primitive or archaic standard of morality—it is unnecessarily severe, tyrannical and intolerant and makes no distinction, for example, between the mere existence of an unconscious wish and its overt realization. Thus we have the paradoxical position that the individual is not only much more immoral than he believes himself to be because of his repressed wishes but that he is also much more moral than he knows because of his unconscious Super-Ego. In the third place, the chief function of the Super-Ego is criticism of the Ego, which it holds responsible for the wish even though that wish may appear quite harmless and innocent from the point of view of the more enlightened conscience. Hence the creation of an unconscious sense of guilt within the individual which is regarded as one of the most important discoveries in recent psychoanalytic investigation. The Ego is indeed in a most unfortunate position, for it has to satisfy the demands of no less than three irreconcilable powers, namely, the Id, the Super-Ego and the external world—a feat which is manifestly impossible for any Ego even when assisted by sublimation, rationalization, projection and other mental mechanisms.

Psychoanalysis has been applied to a wide range of phenomena. The psychopathology of everyday life, such as slips of the tongue, of the pen, etc., wit, dreams, myths, symbolism, literature and art, religion, culture, education, crime and delinquency, and even the choice of profession and of love-object, have all had some fresh light thrown on them from a psychoanalytic point of view. One of the most significant developments of Psychoanalysis has been its application to the study of personality and the obscure origins of many of our personality traits. Freud's most recent contribution has been a study of personality types in terms of the distinctions between the Id, Super-Ego and Ego. Thus we have the pure "erotic" type which represents the claims of the Id. Persons belonging to this type have their main interest centred in love. "Loving, but above all being loved, is for them the most important thing in life. They are governed by the dread of loss of love, and this makes them peculiarly dependent on those who may withhold their love from them." The second type is the "obsessional," characterized by the supremacy of the Super-Ego. "Persons of this type are governed by anxiety of conscience instead of by the dread of losing love; they exhibit an inner instead of an outer dependence; they develop a high degree of self-reliance." The third type is the "narcissistic," whose characteristics are in the main negatively described. "There is no tension between Ego and Super-Ego; there is no preponderance of erotic needs; the main interest is focused on self-preservation; the type is independent and not easily overawed. . . Persons of this type impress others as being 'personalities'; it is on them that their fellow-men are specially likely to lean; they readily assume the rôle of leader."

Psychoanalysis with its emphasis upon the individual and his adjustments to the social environment may be regarded as a part of the wider study of social psychology which is one of the latest and most promising offshoots of psychology. It was not so very long ago that social psychology was identified with the study of the behaviour of crowds and mobs; and still more recently with the study of the development of instincts and their operation in the social behaviour of man. Today the central problem of social psychology, that which gives it a unity which it has hitherto lacked, is the study of the nature and development of the individual personality and its interaction with other personalities who constitute its social environment. For a long time psychology has fought shy of the problem of personality—it has always seemed too vague and too complex to serve as a topic for scientific treatment. But agreement upon definition and upon method is gradually clarifying the situation and the very recent introduction of experimental and quantitative techniques is providing social psychology with an equipment of objective and verifiable data. Tests and scales for the measurement of personality traits and social attitudes which have always been regarded as beyond the reach of any kind of objective measurement (compare the similar attitude towards the measurement of intelligence) are being extensively devised and though a great deal of the activity is still at an admittedly tentative stage, results obtained have already shed a great deal of light upon problems of great theoretical interest such as the interrelation of traits, the generality or specificity of individual traits, the existence of personality types. Scales for the measurement of inter-racial attitudes, of political and economic attitudes, to mention only a few, have also been devised with a sufficient degree of validity and reliability to justify their being put to practical use.

If the study of personality is interpreted in a sufficiently broad sense, then social psychology is in the happy position of being able to bring to a focus the contributions derived from many different sources. Thus it can draw on biology and gland-physiology for their contributions to the influence of inherited and innate factors upon the development of personality; it can draw on behaviourism and objective psychology for their contributions to the influence of habit-formation and conditioning upon the development of personality; it can draw on psychoanalysis and psychopathology for their contributions to the influence of unconscious and abnormal factors upon the development of personality; it can even draw on social anthropology and the study of primitive cultures for their contributions to the influence of particular cultural backgrounds upon the development of personality. To all these social psychology can supply a logic of its own by its emphasis upon the behaving individual as some sort of integrated whole (*gestalt*) or personality in interaction with other personalities at the psychological level. This emphasis upon the individual personality as the terminus *a quo* and the terminus *ad quem* combined with an experimental, quantitative and statistical approach, wherever possible, to its problems, should serve to mark off for social psychology an ample and highly promising field for investigation.

Literature in the Machine Age

By
J. Y. T. GREIG
M.A., D.Litt.
Professor of English

Literature in the Machine Age

When we look back over the course of English literature from about the year 1800 until the present time, and compare the work of the major writers with that of major writers in any earlier period, two facts emerge. The first is this: nearly all the major writers of the nineteenth and twentieth centuries, and many of the minor writers too, are ill at ease. They are not all ill at ease about the same things, and many of them are quite unable to define the causes of their discontent; but they are alike in having no firm foothold, no assured place, within the society of their own time. And the second fact is this: as the nineteenth century passes into the twentieth, literary discontent seems to increase rather than diminish, the gulf between writers and society, instead of being bridged, widens.

Some of the earlier writers of the period—those we are wont to call the Romantics—allay their uneasiness by taking refuge in some fairyland of the fancy that bears very little relation to the life of every day, or in some remote period of time the life of which appears more congenial to their troubled spirits. Coleridge flees to Xanadu or achieves a dream-like serenity with his Ancient Mariner—

> Alone, alone, all, all alone,
> Alone on a wide, wide sea;

or, driven back to Highgate, escapes once more into the fog of German metaphysics. Byron is for ever stridently running away; Childe Harold's Pilgrimage may not lead to anywhere in particular, but it leads very definitely away from what was troubling Byron, namely, himself, and the men and women of his time. Keats the Cockney, had he lived longer, might have achieved an almost perfect synthesis of the Greek spirit and the spirit of the English Elizabethans; but never, so far as we can tell, would he have proved the poet of his own age. Shelley has no abiding place on earth, no home except amid the clouds. Scott, less sensitive perhaps than any of the others, a man whom we might have expected to find tolerably at ease in the Zion of early nineteenth-century Edinburgh, is none the less driven to seek a spiritual refuge in the Middle Ages and in the eighteenth-century Scotland that had virtually passed away before he grew to manhood; what was Scott's so-called Toryism but a continual protest against the political, social and economic tendencies of his day? Wordsworth, after an initial period of revolutionary fervour, renounces the world of affairs, to enter into a mystical, satisfying, but somewhat ill-defined communion with Nature. Charles Lamb is an Elizabethan, Hazlitt a malcontent in most things, Leigh Hunt a malcontent in politics and at the same time a somewhat sugary regressionist in literature.

So again later in the century. Tennyson, that mellifluous technician and delayed adolescent, is obviously perplexed and puzzled by contemporary life: he flees in the flesh to a hedge-concealed fastness in the Isle of Wight and in the spirit to the castles and tourneys, chivalry and frailties of Lyonesse and Camelot. And after him, stepping daintily lest they soil their shoes, follow the Pre-Raphaelites, painters and poets. Even Browning, that "robustious, periwig-pated fellow," though he sighs to be in England now that April's there, sighs from Italy, his spiritual home. I choose only a few examples from the poets.

As for the prose writers (those, at least, outside the ranks of the scientists), it is enough to mention names. Was Carlyle ever at ease for long in the England of the nineteenth century? Was Arnold? Was Ruskin? Was Cardinal Newman? Was Samuel Butler?

The novel, by its very nature, is closer to contemporary life and thought than any other form of literature. Yet even the novelists illustrate the point. We are all aware of the social reformism that sometimes blessed and sometimes cursed the work of Dickens and George Eliot. Of those unhappy, untamed, rebellious sisters, the Brontës (and especially Emily) what need be said? As for Thackeray, he appears to me the best example of them all. He is at the same time one of the greatest and one of the weakest and most pathetic of English writers. The genuine passion that informs his best work is hatred, hatred of shams, of meanness and hypocrisy; and looking about him in the world, he discerns only too many shams to be exposed. But alas, though a good hater and clear-sighted, he is frightened too, and insecure, timid about coming into the open, always glancing over his shoulder to make certain that his line of retreat is still intact. He is valiant and cowardly by turns, nonconformist by conviction, conformist out of fear. An unhappy figure, always ill at ease.

There are, of course, exceptions, real or apparent. Jane Austen seems to be a real exception, but isn't. For though some of her work was done within the nineteenth century, it all belongs unmistakably to the eighteenth in manner and spirit. A better exception is to be found in Trollope, a novelist thoroughly comfortable in the station and society to which it has pleased God to call him. Hence perhaps Trollope's recent vogue in post-War England. His work is a kind of narcotic, not a stimulant.

My first contention, therefore, comes to this: that the main current of life in nineteenth-century England flows in one direction and the bulk of the writers who count go in other directions; they do not draw upon and participate in a "current of ideas in the highest degree animating and nourishing to the creative power," they do not derive their inspiration from such a "national glow of life and thought," as Sophocles, Shakespeare, Racine, Dryden, even Milton, could enjoy.[1] That, I think, distinguishes the English literature of their time from the literature of any earlier time. Shakespeare belonged to his own age, accepted his own age, expressed his own age; so did Milton, though with reservations; so did Sir Thomas Browne; so did Dryden and Congreve; so did Pope, Addison and Fielding; so did Swift, though again with reservations; so did Hume and Samuel Johnson. But with the passing of the eighteenth century the greater of the men of letters no longer accept and express their own age; they either revolt against it with some violence or turn away from it to the less disturbing regions of romance. In a word, we discover a new cleavage between literature and society.

And as time goes on the breach enlarges. The writers of to-day, in England and America, may call themselves by various

---

1 The phrases are Matthew Arnold's, though he applied them only to the writers at the beginning of the nineteenth century.

names, attach themselves to various schools—realist, classicist, romantic, imagist, symbolist, vorticist, naturalist, or what not. But whatever the label they tie round their necks, they are nearly all romantics in this sense, that they are forced either to escape from the atmosphere of to-day into a more serene, untroubled atmosphere in which their souls can breathe, or, seizing such weapons as lie to hand, to pitch themselves into a struggle against the very civilization that has nurtured them. From the multiplicity of current literature it is difficult to choose examples without suggesting that I have found only what I am looking for. But let me risk the accusation. When we think of English literature between 1900 and 1914, which are the first names that come to mind? Mr. Shaw, Mr. Galsworthy and, perhaps, Stanley Houghton in drama; Mr. Masefield, Mr. A. E. Housman and Robert Bridges in poetry; Mr. Wells, Arnold Bennett, Joseph Conrad and Mr. Galsworthy in prose fiction. I don't wish to imply that these were the only good writers, or even that they were the best; and I have deliberately omitted the Irish school of poets and dramatists, lest you should say that Irishmen are always "agin' the government," anyhow, so what does it signify? But the authors I have selected were typical, and each in his own way eminent. Now the three dramatists are all social rebels, all hostile critics of contemporary life. Mr. Wells, for all his skipping about and turning back upon his own tracks, has always been a social rebel too. Mr. Housman's poetry is traditional in manner but explosive in content, like Hardy's: no one would call him a conformist. Conrad is easy to classify—too easy, perhaps: he stands or falls as a romantic of romantics, at home only in conditions remote from the workaday and industrial world of to-day, the memorialist of that last relic of the pre-Machine Age, the sailing ship. Bridges, for all his classical manner, might properly be called a romantic too; he deliberately shut himself away from the world. There remain the late Arnold Bennett and the present Poet Laureate. If both are counted as conformist, we have still only two exceptions in a list of nine.

I hardly need to dwell at length on the post-War writers of England and America. Everyone is conscious that nearly all their work is literature either of escape or of rebellion. Hence the dissatisfaction that so many of us feel with it. It tends to become precious and insignificant in escape, or violent and without balance in rebellion. Even its occasional obscurity is a form of protest against the age, though I think an ineffective one. One can understand and to some extent sympathize with the desire to withdraw into a coterie. It is not all vanity and mutual back-scratching. It is a method of showing your contempt for the world as it exists. But the world is commonly apt to reciprocate your contempt, and leave you to wither in your own aesthetic parlour. It is more effective, surely, as well as more courageous, to tell the world bluntly, even brutally, how contemptible it is—and take your chance with the censor.

I have spoken only of a single art, the art of literature. I believe illuminating parallels might be found in other arts, in painting and sculpture especially, and in music to a less extent. By the nature of their media these arts are kept more remote from everyday affairs. Not even the musician, however, can go his own way untouched by the fall of empires and the rise of industrial millionaires.

Throughout the nineteenth century, then, English men of letters have been more or less openly at variance with the ethos of their own age; and in the twentieth this antagonism between literature and society is intensified rather than diminished. What conclusion shall we draw? That the men of letters are wrong, and the other members of society, in so far as they hold common ideas and common ideals, right? Or that the men of letters are right and the rest of society wrong? Let me say plainly that I hold the men of letters to be right and the rest of society wrong.

Not, of course, that the men of letters are right at all points. But in their common feeling of uneasiness, in their vague suspicion or firm conviction that something radical is amiss with the kind of civilization that is characteristic of the nineteenth and twentieth centuries, in this I hold emphatically that they are right and that the rest of society—the politicians, the scientists, the ecclesiastics, the engineers, the industrialists, the professors—in so far as they complacently approve of the general trend of this civilization, are deceiving themselves to their own detriment. In the last resort, men of letters distrust or attack the Machine Age because they perceive, some only dimly but others very clearly indeed, that such a form of civilization makes steadily and inevitably for the elimination of the arts, crushes out and destroys those human values which the arts have always fostered and upheld, and substitutes for them other values definitely lower in the scale. In a word, the Machine Age, unlike every other form of civilization that the world has known, is stamping out the arts as fast as it can; and if its course is not checked, there will soon be no more literature, no more painting, no more sculpture, no more music, worthy the name. I can see no escape from this, to me, devastating conclusion.

If we are to judge by the *obiter dicta* of some leaders of our industrial civilization, they do not find the conclusion by any means so devastating as I do. They are polite, of course, these motor-car manufacturers and oil magnates and mining engineers. They regret that it should be necessary to eliminate anything which mankind has cherished in the past. They are even prepared to subscribe liberally to museums, libraries and art galleries in order that relics of these quaint, old-world forms of human activity, sculpture and literature and painting and the like, should be preserved for the amusement (or is it the derision?) of our enlightened, scientific and properly mechanized posterity. But they are quite sure that the loss is not serious. What were the arts anyhow but a rather childish and inefficient means of entertainment? Why, the Machine Age, by its characteristic methods of mass production and mass distribution, can supply much more efficient means of entertainment for the leisure hours of civilized adults. Look at the talkies (which Aldous Huxley prophesies will soon become the feelies); look at radio; look at our highly organized international sport. These are only feeble samples of what industrial civilization can do for the entertainment of the people.

Well, some of us are not moved to rapture by this prospect. We decline to believe that the arts are mere entertainment. The notion that they are, is one of the most damnable heresies invented and propagated by the Machine Age. We decline to believe that the Machine Age, by any of its characteristic devices, can give us human values greater than the values it is sacrificing by the destruction of the arts. And a few of us, of whom I am one, don't believe in the Machine Age at all. We regard it as a sham form of civilization.

Let me develop the indictment. It must needs be in pretty general terms, since space does not allow me to enter into much detail.

The contention which, in company with many other men of letters in the year 1932, I have to put forward concerning the Machine Age, is this: that the kind of civilization which European man has built up for himself in the last 150 years, and which he has tried, and is still trying, to impose upon the rest of the world, is a false civilization, a way of life that on the balance is more harmful than beneficial to mankind; or, to put it in another way, that in the latter half of the eighteenth century, European man, led, I regret to say, by the British people, turned up a blind alley in pursuit of a will-o'-the-wisp called Power over Nature, and has been racing at a constantly accelerating speed along this blind alley ever since.

The feature of our civilization which serves to distinguish it unmistakably from all other civilizations known to history, is the machine. That is common ground, as a lawyer would say. Both the supporters and the opponents of our civilization agree to call it the Machine Age. The change from older ways of life began with the invention of the steam engine. It has been carried on at a steadily increasing rate by means of later scientific discoveries and their application in such mechanical products as the electric dynamo, the turbine and the internal-combustion engine. All these things have the common quality of being extremely powerful instruments for the manipulation of natural forces. And it is our possession of such extremely powerful instruments, and our constant use of them in everyday life, which distinguishes us from the Ancient Egyptians, the Ancient Greeks, the Ancient Chinese, the Romans, the Italians of the Renaissance, the Elizabethans of England, the French under Louis XIV, and our own ancestors in Great Britain in the first half of the eighteenth century—I choose certain typical periods of high civilization. In all these periods men possessed and used many instruments of power—fire, the wheel, agricultural implements, metal tools of various shapes, the mariner's compass, printing type; these are a few examples. And it may be said that our instruments are only more complicated forms of theirs, that there is no difference in kind between, say, the internal-combustion engine that enables a South African to fly in a few hours from Cape Town to Johannesburg, and the wheels of the ox-wagon that enabled his great-grandfather to make the same journey on the ground, though more slowly and laboriously: both are tools, both instruments of power. To which I have two answers. First, that the difference in degree of power amounts, let the logicians say what they please, to a difference in kind; to pretend otherwise is to be deceived by words. And, second, that the invention of new instruments of power proceeded very slowly indeed in every civilization other than our own. Each advance came after a long gap, during which society remained relatively stable, relatively stationary. That meant that human beings enjoyed a reasonable time in order to adjust themselves to the new conditions introduced by invention A before they were called upon to adjust themselves to the new conditions introduced by invention B. They were never called upon to adjust themselves to fire, the wheel, the iron plough, the mariner's compass and so forth, all within a hundred years or thereabouts. Whereas, since 1750, and still more since 1850, the invention of new instruments of power has been pursued at an almost incredible speed, and, what is worse, at an accelerating speed. Society has never been stable for a moment. Before we have had a century of railways—and what is a century in the life of man?—a mere flash—we are called upon to scrap them in favour of motor transport and the aeroplane.

Everyone who thinks about the matter will agree that the conditions under which we live today, as a direct result of the machine, are vastly more different from the conditions under which our ancestors lived only two centuries ago than were their conditions of life from those of the Ancient Egyptians 5,000 years earlier. A significant fact, worth a little emphasis. By means of the machine and the power it has put into his hands, man has been able in less than 200 years to make vastly greater changes in his environment than he was able to do in more than 5,000 years before. He has altered it out of all recognition; he has made it almost unbelievably ugly in many places, but let that pass; he has made it, as everyone can perceive, almost unbelievably complicated. In 1750 it was possible for a man or a group of men to live in comparative seclusion from the rest of the world: what John Smith did or said or thought, unless he happened to be a very remarkable person, affected only himself and his family and a few of his neighbours. In 1932 it is hardly an exaggeration to say that a hasty word dropped by some insignificant John Smith in a tiny *dorp* in the Northern Transvaal may affect the production of oil in Oklahoma or precipitate a revolution in Brazil. By means of the machine we have reduced the whole word to the dimensions of a village. Unfortunately, this has not made life simpler for us; not by any means. It has made it immensely more complex and difficult. I for one believe that we have made our political and social environment so complex and difficult that we can no longer control it; it has got beyond our powers of management. For observe what has happened. We have altered the environment of man out of all recognition in less than 200 years, and some of us are proud of the feat; but there is no evidence to show that we have increased man's mental and moral capacities to any appreciable extent in more than 6,000 years. We are asking man, with the mental and moral capacities of an Ancient Egyptian, to master an environment ten thousand times more difficult and dangerous to control than any Ancient Egyptian ever had to deal with. It is like giving a child of two years old a loaded Mills bomb to play with in his nursery. Some of us are mortally scared that the child will pull the pin out of the bomb very shortly. That will be the end of the child *and* his nursery; in other words, the end of European civilization as we know it.

Until very recently everybody seemed to be satisfied that this difference between the Machine Age and the civilization of 1750 was a difference for the better, that the machine had been more boon than bane to suffering humanity, that, whatever might be true of the "backward" races—yellow, brown and black—the white races, gloriously led by the industrialists and engineers of England, Germany and America, had advanced and were still advancing along the primrose path of progress. And, of course, this view is still widely held. It has to be held by industrialists and engineers, and their salesmen; otherwise, like Othello, their occupation would be gone.

Now, to deny the benefits which science and the application of science have conferred upon humanity would be absurd. I don't propose to indulge in *that* absurdity, at least. Nor do I propose to compile a list of these benefits—such a list as would include high-speed and luxurious travelling, frigidaires, canned salmon from British Columbia, the broadcasting of symphony concerts, dictaphones, the dentist's drill and the surgeon's aseptic scalpel, and tractor reaping machines for the wheatfields of Soviet Russia. The benefits of mechanical civilization are obvious—when you consider them in isolation. And this—the consideration of things in isolation—is one of the habits we have acquired within the last two centuries, largely through our preoccupation with science and our growing indifference to religion, philosophy and the arts. Isolation, abstraction, specialization—these are the methods of science, eminently successful methods, as far as they go. The results which the scientist has obtained by them have been so startling that nowadays we all tend to imitate him in our consideration of our everyday affairs. That is how we have altered our environment so quickly and so radically: by dealing with it piecemeal. Each problem has been tackled in isolation, not in relation to civilization as a whole. But the mischief is that although you may invent piecemeal, you cannot live piecemeal among your inventions. The living thing is concrete, not abstract; you cannot split it up and isolate its problems and deal with them in the manner of the specializing scientist; at least, you cannot do so without lamentable and unforeseen consequences. Every event in life is inextricably interlocked with every other event, and more so than ever now, in the complex, highly mechanized environment that we have made for ourselves. How ironical it all is! The scientist, by isolating his problems, has created for us a kind of civilization which we cannot control by the same scientific devices. That is why I entirely disagree with Professor Phillips when he suggests that we ought to hand over more and more power to men of scientific training. They are the last people to give power to. A government of scientists, each trained to isolate his problems and solve them in isolation, would be a calamity only a little less disastrous than a government composed exclusively of businessmen. It is because we have listened with such docility to the claims of scientists and businessmen that we believe in the enormous benefits of the Machine Age. Each new product of the Machine Age may be good of its kind—good, that is to say, for its immediate and particular purpose. That is all the manufacturer of that product is concerned about. But there are general and mediate purposes as well as particular and immediate ones; and it does not follow that a product of the Machine Age, however good of its kind, is good in the whole economy of society. The scientist who invents, and the industrialist who puts upon the market, a new radio set giving better reception than any earlier one, assume that they have performed a valuable service to the community. But this assumption may be questioned. The radio as such may be more of a curse than a blessing to humanity. Some of us think so. To decide such a question we must needs consider, not whether such and such a receiving set is good of its kind, but what the total effects of listening-in to radio transmission are likely to be, in relation to the scale of values which we set before us as the highest possible in human life. We shall admit as manifest benefits the chance which radio gives us now and then of hearing good music, and of listening to some expert lecturing on his own subject—though, heaven knows there is little enough virtue in lectures; we shall regard as indifferent, neither good nor bad, the chance of hearing the news of the world a few hours before it appears in print in the newspaper; and we shall set down as very harmful indeed the general lethargy and passivity of mind which listening-in fosters, and also that habit of futile searching for new stations for the sake of getting new stations, a habit that appears merely frivolous until you realize that it is yet another expression of the typical modern belief that power over Nature is valuable in and for itself.

The main grounds on which the Machine Age may be condemned are these. In the first place, in proportion as it has bestowed on man increased power over Nature, it has withdrawn him from the influences of Nature. One does not need to be a Wordsworthian pantheist to believe that that is deleterious. One has only to recall in its barest outline the evolution of human beings through prehistoric and historic time. Until about the end of the eighteenth century the great bulk of mankind were subject, for weal and woe, to the direct influence of natural forces. They won their bread in the sweat of their brow and by the labour of their hands from Mother Earth. Sometimes Mother Earth was bounteous to them, sometimes niggardly, sometimes cruel. Man and

Nature were partners in the enterprise of life, sometimes friendly towards each other, sometimes at enmity; but never separated, never long dissevered. And that, for all its disadvantages, for all the disasters incident to it—the disasters of flood and field, famine, drought, pestilence, storm and frost—that is the kind of life to which man has adapted himself in the long ages of evolution. To adapt himself to a wholly different kind of life, a machine-made, power-wielding life that centres in the cities, is either impossible in any reasonable period of evolutionary time, or possible only by sacrificing most of the best gifts and capacities laboriously acquired in the age-long past.

In the second place, the Machine Age, by its concentration on the production of things, and still more things, is establishing a new scale of values in which things are the measure of the good. The good life is being measured in terms of enamelled bathtubs. This charge against the Machine Age has been put so often and so cogently by hostile critics that I don't propose to spend more time on it. No one can ignore it. I believe no one, not even Mr. Henry Ford, can reasonably deny it.

In the third place, the things which the Machine Age hands out to us, forces upon us, are increasingly all of a pattern, standardized, stereotyped, without variety and without individuality. This is not an accident but an inevitable consequence of basing our civilization upon the machine. For the good machine always does the same thing in the same way; that is one of its greatest virtues. And machine-made products, whether Ford cars or children sitting the Matriculation Examination, are notoriously all cut to the same shape. That is very convenient when you have to deal with them in bulk, or when you want spare parts. But nothing could be more disastrous than the resulting standardization of intelligence which we may observe taking place on all sides. In spite of all the well-meant but misdirected efforts of our scientists and engineers, the unexpected is still, and seemingly always will be, a factor to be reckoned with in life. No machine can deal with the unexpected. That is the function of intelligence.

> Our stability is but balance, and wisdom lies
> In masterful administration of the unforeseen.

But the more you standardize and mechanize intelligence, the less capable does it turn out to be for its own peculiar task. I have heard it suggested that the only hope for our civilization is to make it so completely mechanical that no one will have any intelligence left for the invention of a new machine. Well, perhaps that *will* be the solution of our troubles.

In the fourth place, the Machine Age develops in its human products a lethargy of mind, amounting at times almost to coma, on the one hand, and, on the other, and as if in compensation, a feverish activity that has no particular direction, but is just activity—like a dog chasing its own tail. It is the boast of our industrialists that by means of the machine they are steadily relieving human beings from the more degrading forms of toil, and by shortening the hours of labour, setting them free for leisure occupations. And right here, we are sometimes told, is the opportunity of the arts. When men and women need work only a few hours a day, what a glorious chance for the artist! He can have them to play with for the rest of the day. Alas! experience shows that mechanized work renders nine-tenths of the world fit only for mechanized play. We have taken to *organizing* our leisure. Was there ever a more appalling phrase coined than "organized leisure"? An American poet friend of mine has put the matter very effectively in a sentence or two. "It is common knowledge," he says, "that, wherever it can be said to exist at all, the kind of leisure provided by industrialism is a dubious benefit. It helps nobody but merchants and manufacturers, who have taught us to use it in industriously consuming the products they make in great excess over the demand. Moreover, it is spoiled, as leisure, by the kind of work that industrialism compels. The furious pace of our working hours is carried over into our leisure hours, which are feverish and energetic. . . We do not have the free mind and easy temper that should characterize true leisure. . . The arts will not easily survive a condition under which we work and play at cross purposes."[1]

And finally, and comprehensively, the Machine Age is spiritually damaging to its human products because it is coming more

---

1 Donald Davidson, "A Mirror for Artists," in *I'll Take my Stand*, by Twelve Southerners. New York, 1930

and more to rest on the belief that power is itself a good, an end in itself, instead of just a means that can be used for good or evil ends at choice. This time, let me quote one, Mr. Bertrand Russell, who is both a scientist and a man of letters, and who is therefore better able than I to see both sides of the question. "The scientific society in its pure form," he says, "is incompatible with the pursuit of truth, with love, with art, with spontaneous delight, with every ideal that men have hitherto cherished, with the sole exception of ascetic renunciation. It is not knowledge that is the source of these dangers. Knowledge is good and ignorance is evil. . . Nor is it power in and for itself that is the source of danger. What is dangerous is power wielded for the sake of power, not power wielded for the sake of genuine good. The leaders of the modern world are drunk with power; the fact that they can do something that no one previously thought it possible to do is to them a sufficient reason for doing it. . . In the conscious desires of the man who seeks power for its own sake there is something dusty; when he has it he wants only more power, and does not find rest in contemplation of what he has. The lover, the poet and the mystic find a fuller satisfaction than the seeker after power can ever know, since they can rest in the object of their love, whereas the seeker after power must be perpetually engaged in some fresh manipulation if he is not to suffer from a sense of emptiness. . . When I come to die I shall not feel that I have lived in vain. I have seen the earth turn red at evening, the dew sparkling in the morning, and the snow shining under a frosty sun; I have smelt rain after drought, and have heard the stormy Atlantic beat upon the granite shores of Cornwall. Science may bestow these and other joys upon more people than could otherwise enjoy them. If so, its power will be wisely used. But when it takes out of life the moments to which life owes its value, science will not deserve admiration, however cleverly and however elaborately it may lead men along the road to despair. The sphere of values lies outside science, except in so far as science consists in the pursuit of knowledge. Science as the pursuit of power must not obtrude upon the sphere of values, and scientific technique, if it is to enrich human life, must not outweigh the ends which it should serve."[1]

It is my contention that the civilization of the Machine Age *has* obtruded upon the sphere of values, and that scientific technique, by which must be understood the application of pure science to the production of instruments of power, has *not* enriched, but has impoverished human life.

Well, and what then? What are we to do about it? Are we to set back the clock to that wonderful year of 1750 when, by my supposition, civilization took a wrong turning? Were it possible, yes. But manifestly it isn't possible. So far as the greater part of Europe and most of the United States are concerned, matters have gone much too far. The machine is there, and we must make the best we can of it. What is going to happen in these regions of the world in the next 100 years or so, Heaven knows, not I. I won't pretend to be other than pessimistic in this regard. It is one of my firmest beliefs that the Machine Age, if it goes on as it is going at present, will destroy itself, perhaps catastrophically, perhaps simply by starving itself to death in the midst of plenty. As for those other regions of the world which are either not industrialized at all or industrialized only very imperfectly, there would certainly appear to be greater hope. But only on one condition: that the people of those regions look steadily at the Machine Age, recognize it for what it is—a sham and self-destructive form of civilization—and resolve, for their part, not to imitate it.

---

1   *The Scientific Outlook*, 1931.

The Holistic Attitude in Education

By
T. J. HAARHOFF
B.Litt., Litt.D.
Professor of Classics

The Holistic Attitude in Education

A man once asked me why General Smuts, in writing about Hōlism, as he called it, had been so careless as to omit the w. A classical scholar may be pardoned for suggesting that if you refrained from doubling the quantity of the first vowel, you would have no need to look for a w. For Holism, as you know, comes from the Greek τὸ ὅλον (the whole); and, as General Smuts used it in the sense of parts of Nature striving towards wholes, or "the fundamental factor operative towards the creation of wholes in the Universe," so I propose to use it of the unifying factor in various portions of education that are incomplete and sterile until they are combined into a significant unity. I speak of an attitude of mind, not of an attempt to cover all knowledge, which could lead only to superficiality; of the quality in a man, be his learning never so humble, that prompts him to keep the windows of his spirit open and to avoid the darkness either of ignorant isolation or of priggish pedantry. And this attitude is possible in the boy who learns a trade in a technical college as well as in the university professor.

Now this attitude of mind is more easily described than defined. It implies that we value in education not merely the acquisition of a set of facts and the professional skill that enables us to earn a living (I have known august educational bodies who have valued only these), but also the understanding of relationships, the forging of living links between an abstract subject and human interests, the realization of perspective, the desire to see how a theme fits into a whole, of which it forms a part. Thus, Holism, Greek by etymology, is Greek also in significance, for it was Plato who first recognized the synoptic point of view in education. "The detailed sciences," says Socrates, speaking of the Guardians, "in which they were educated as children, must be brought into the compass of a single survey to show the connection that exists between them and the nature of real existence." "Certainly," replies Glaucon, "this is the only kind of instruction which will be found to be abiding when once it has effected an entrance." To the Greeks the educated man was one who knew the connections between things, not just the things themselves.

And here let me remark on the relation between Holism and the great tradition of Humanism; not Humanism in its narrow sense of Renaissance scholarship, nor in the sense in which some theologians have used it, but in its wider implication; not a system that could be defined and formulated, but a spirit, intelligible to the wise, that reaches from Plato to Cicero and Vergil and Quintilian; from Erasmus to Goethe and Rudolf Steiner, to J. S. Haldane and Gilbert Murray. We have heard much about the development of science in modern times; but when Sir J. Arthur Thomson writes: "The great question today is: Is there one primordial substance from which all the rest is derived?" he raises the very problem that agitated the first Greek scientists in Ionia, in the sixth century before the birth of Christ. In reaction to excessive speculation of this kind, Socrates suggested that the proper study of mankind is man; and similarly today we need to correct the balance, and consider our problems from the humanistic standpoint.

For science, it would seem, spurning the low degrees by which she did ascend, became at last lop-sided. She became materialistic and dogmatic. Seldom was scientific formulation in the classical world so cock-sure and, in a sense, so limited, as that of those "classical" scientists who propounded the mechanistic theory in the nineteenth century. Not even Lucretius resembles these; passionately embracing the dogmatic materialism of Epicurus, as a means of escape from the pain of existence, he is yet haunted by the indefinable mystery of Nature. Moreover, modern science, through its by-products, the machines, has fostered a lop-sided view of life. She has induced many people to think of technical development as a synonym for civilization. She has caused a loss of historical perspective and obscured the moral and cultural basis of life. How easily she may become self-destructive is illustrated by the man who recently invented noiseless firearms. He kept the secret, because he felt it to be too dangerous; some other person may be less scrupulous; and when all those methods of destruction that were neatly docketed and filed at the end of the Great War are let loose, heaven knows what will be left of our Western civilization.

But the conversion of modern science, or an important part of it, to the mystery that lies behind the Universe, holds hope for the future—hope not only for education, but also for poetry and religion. Plato said that wonder was the beginning of philosophy; and now, after two thousand years, science sheds her proud claim to ultimate certainties and returns to the creed of Humanism—the creed of the finest and most cultured minds of all time. There is an ancient quarrel that Plato spoke of, between the poets and the philosophers or men of science, and it is not too much to hope that, in this new scientific spirit, parts too long unnaturally separated may once more find a way of forming a fruitful whole.

What, then, do I mean by Humanism? I mean the spirit that looks for significant connections; that seeks a harmony between man and man; between man and nature; that sought, in Cicero and Vergil, a unity, as distinct from uniformity, between Rome and Italy, between Hellenic and Italian culture, between Greek science and the ancestral rustic religion of the Romans; that seeks in a man like Professor J. S. Haldane for a re-interpretation of science in the light of our whole human experience; in Gilbert Murray for intellectual and moral co-operation between nations. It is a spirit instinct with sympathy and filled with pity for the blindness of human striving; appreciative both of the humour and of the pathos of life; a spirit strong enough to be unpopular in its steadfast pursuit of the best; almost, it would seem, necessarily unpopular, because it sees the position as a whole, and is therefore liable to be accused of disloyalty to its particular party; for even in the pride of national victory, it refuses to be blinded by chauvinism. It is thus opposed to a spirit seen in Europe and in our own country today, that seeks to establish a cause by rousing the passion of hatred and to win a victory by excluding everything that may show the other side in a favourable light; for it believes, in spite of everything, that truth will outlast party and that the lie in the soul is the ultimate degradation.

Thus, Humanism, in the sense described, is the parent of Holism: the descent is lineal and direct. That the holistic tendency is becoming one of the characteristics of the present time has been asserted by many thinkers. Thus, Eduard Spranger, who, with Werner Jaeger, to whom he dedicates his book, belongs to the modern Humanists, speaks of the "Trieb zur Ganzheit." Let us consider some examples of it in modern times.

The air has been thick with Outlines of History, Outlines of Science, Outlines of Christianity, Outlines of Everything. There is even an Outline of Knowledge. Valuable as all these Outlines are to the man who uses them properly, even though some of the authors have written so much more history than they have read, they constitute a terrible peril for the Babbitts of this world, who at once assume that knowledge, and even education, may be had in tabloid form. But summaries of this sort are symptomatic of the desire of our time to grasp the experience of the past entire, and to relate all the parts. Our time has seen the rise of the League of Nations and the first rudimentary steps towards real international cooperation; it has witnessed the first stirrings of the churches towards unity and towards the fulfilment of the hallowed prayer "ut omnes unum sint." In scholarship the different countries are much more aware of each other than they were in the past. One of the greatest scholars in ancient history to-day is a Russian, now in America, whose works are read by all serious students. An outstanding authority on Greek religion is a Swede, whose works are translated into English as soon as they are published. A leading classical journal publishes articles in all the main European languages. Even at this University we have had letters from countries like Italy and South America in regard to Vergilian studies prosecuted here. In economics we see mankind experiencing (learning would be too optimistic a word), painfully and recalcitrantly, that the part cannot be sound unless the interests of the whole are consulted. The co-operation that men reject on a higher plane is now being brought home to them on the lower plane of material welfare.

In psychology we have heard how the purely analytic methods of Wundt have been superseded by a more synoptic view, notably by that of the Gestalt-psychologists; and it is interesting to reflect that when Wundt was the acknowledged prophet (in the latter half of the nineteenth century) the lecture halls of the Berlin University were echoing to the thunders of Kirchoff as he rent the unity of the Homeric Poems; whereas little more than a generation later, I heard in those same halls the return to the Unitarian view of Homer, and Friedländer denouncing "die zerscheidende Kritik des Kirchoffs und Wilamowitz," while in the passage outside, the bust of Friederich August Wolf listened in immobile sorrow. Similarly, we may remember how the Odes of Horace fared. Walter Savage Landor wrote marginal anathemas in his copy and the words "better without" opposite many verses. Peerlkamp, with the ruthlessness of a pedant, boldly cut out whole stanzas. But a more synoptic study of Horace's mind has taught us to understand the Odes as a whole and to appreciate the underlying thought that connects seeming discrepancies. And you remember how the French editor of *As You Like It* came across the line "Sermons in stones, books in the running brooks," and with that brilliant logic for which the French are famous, changed it into "Sermons in *books, stones* in the running brooks."

So, too, in Greek sculpture the old concentration on the fifth century is giving way to a more catholic view, that restores to appreciation aspects of Hellenistic art and especially archaic art; some there are who even condescend to turn a kindly eye on the Ara Pacis and the peculiar contributions of Roman coins and sculptures. Again, in the domain of language, we have not only seen many attempts to produce an international code—the most promising and most recent of which is *Interlingua* or Latin without inflections—but we have witnessed a complete change in our view of language. Instead of regarding language as something static and exalting a chosen period with a supreme contempt for all other periods, we view the matter in the light of psychology and study a language as a whole, watching its different phases and tracing its growth with interest. No longer is the language that lacks inflections regarded as the guest that disgraced himself by coming to the feast without a wedding garment; and Afrikaans is recognized as a linguistic phenomenon that has occurred at least twice in the history of Western Europe.[1]

As for science, I am not competent to assess its development in detail. But perhaps you will permit me two quotations. Professor J. S. Haldane, the grand exemplar of Humanism in Science, writing

---

1 See my essay on Afrikaans in *Coming of Age* (Maskew Miller, Cape Town, 1930).

in the *Hibbert Journal* of April, 1923, rejected altogether the mechanistic explanation of life, chiefly on the ground that the upholders of that theory had failed to look at life as a whole, had based their conclusions on fragments or abstractions, had disregarded Holism. "The fundamental conceptions of physical science," he says, "represent only working hypotheses, corresponding under great limitations to partial aspects of experience. Extraordinarily useful as these working hypotheses are, in the absence of more detailed knowledge, they do not represent reality. This appears at once when we consider our experience as a whole. It is only when we neglect this consideration that we seem driven into a materialistic creed." Elsewhere, he maintains (and Plato and Vergil and all the great spirits of humanism would have agreed), that "the only real world is the spiritual world, the only real values, spiritual values."

From the side of physics there has recently come important confirmation. Max Planck, the eminent mathematical physicist, wrote in *Nature*, 18th April, 1931, "it is the concept of wholeness that must be introduced into the field of physics as well as into the field of biology, in order to enable us to understand and formulate the laws of Nature."

Forty years ago mechanistic theories were trying to formulate out of existence the mystery of the Universe; to-day the rigid foundations are seen to be wavering. "The science of the nineteenth century," says General Smuts, "was, like its philosophy, its morals and its civilization in general, distinguished by a certain hardness, primness and precise limitation and demarcation of ideas." The opponents of Science at that time were saying that Materialism was all very well, but it could not explain religion: to-day the scientists find that it won't even explain matter! And now they (or some of them) are talking in terms of creative wholes.

As regards philosophy, what more need I do than point to the father of these lectures, Professor Hoernlé, for does he not call himself a synoptic philosopher?

And yet, with all these tendencies towards wholeness, what is our plight in education? And how is Holism to help us? We know now (as Dr. Mackail pointed out ten years ago) that "education" does not mean "leading out what is in the child's mind," in spite of the robust assertion in our textbooks to that effect. It means supplying the right sort of food for the growth of the child and therefore corresponds exactly to our Afrikaans word "opvoeding." This food is to promote growth, it is to stimulate development. Why, then, is it so often made up into hard and unnutritious tabloids? Why does the classical teacher still read snippets of Latin and treat them like crossword puzzles? Why is Caesar regarded by schoolboys as a book of painful gymnastic, and not as a man? Why is the child in the primary school given no glimpse, as a rule, of the world of beauty that lies behind his toilsome spelling and inane recitation? Why is it that our university students select curricula in which Chemistry and Constitutional Law jostle each other in an explosive partnership? Why do we have our students coming back to us doctored but uneducated? Why are we producing, all over the world, that danger to education—learned barbarians?

I ask these questions in no superior spirit, but as one who is troubled by their reality, and who seeks a solution.

At the Commonwealth Conference held at Bedford College, London, in July, 1931, much attention was focussed on the idea of wholeness in education advocated by Rudolf Steiner, prophet of Anthroposophy and interpreter of Goethe. And in a book published last year, Dr. L. P. Jacks, the veteran editor of the *Hibbert Journal*, writes: "The modern man is at his best when he is dealing with analysis—his recent education has all tended in that direction. But he is something of a blockhead when it comes to synthesis. For breaking a thing up into parts and studying each part in separation, there has never been anybody to compare with the modern man. But when you ask him to put the parts together again, he is like one who has lost the use of its wits: 'Wholeness' seems to baffle him."[1]

Here, I believe, we are close to the root of the trouble. *We have overdone analysis and neglected Holism.*

Man is a destructive animal. He likes to pull things to pieces and when he applies the process to something organic, he finds that all the King's horses and all the King's men fail to restore it.

---

1 L. P. Jacks, *The Education of the Whole Man*, 1931

We should not be blind to the enormous scientific advances that have been secured by the analytic mind, from Aristotle onward; but we must beware of the effect it is having on our education.

I have said that Holism is an idea of the classical world, but it is a sad commentary on the extent to which the classics have become dehumanized in ordinary teaching, that the classical teachers have been among the worst sinners in regard to isolation and analysis. Starting with the notion that Latin is a dead language, they have made quite sure that it shall not come to life by placing it on the dissecting table and serving out the principal parts. Daily we find Latin butchered to make a teacher's holiday. Certain types of classical teachers consider it almost indecent if you suggest that the Classics have a meaning. Yet Latin literature is as living as any modern literature. "Is that old Italian speech dead and gone," asks Professor D'Arcy Thompson, "that murmurs in Lucretius a ceaseless solemn monotone of sea-shell sound; that in Vergil flows, like the Eridanus, calmly and majestically, through rich lowlands, fringed with tall poplars and rimmed with grassy banks; that quivers to wild strains of passion in Catullus: that wimples like a beck in Ovid; that coos in Tibullus like the turtle; that sparkles in Horace like a well-cut diamond?"[1] Roman civilization is an organic structure whose life may be traced and shown to be full of profound significance for our time; whose art, with that of Greece, contains a portion of human effort that is timeless, because in its perfection it rises above the vicissitudes that sweep most things away, and it is of importance to us because it lies at the root of our civilization.

If it is objected that there is no time to introduce all this into the curriculum, the reply is that a man who appreciates the significant links of the whole will find countless opportunities of suggesting to his pupils the potentialities of their subject. They will feel that he has an attitude of mind that is forward-looking, alive, whole-making; and that is worth more educationally than any number of facts carefully crammed.

---

1 *Science and the Classics* (Proceedings of the Classical Association, 1929).

I can remember classical teachers spending an hour over six lines; and at the end of the period their pupils departed with a large number of details, more or less unwillingly assimilated, and a profound loathing for Latin; whereas the man who is holistically inclined will perpetually stimulate their minds by revealing the true point of analysis and grammar—namely, the appreciation of literary beauty and significant values. He will contrive, for example, when his boys are reading Caesar, to put John Buchan's recent book before them. When he reads the *Aeneid* he will find that there is no time to read the whole in Latin; but rather than mangle a work of art and leave it in fragments, he will do what we do here and let his boys complete their reading by means of a good translation, so that the subject of the poem and something of its technique, if not its full literary meaning, may become evident. He will not dully grind out the grammar without relating it to his pupils' reading. He will treat Latin as a language, an instrument of human expression that can be used in conversation and above all in dramatic conversation. If you have seen children's eyes shine with pleasure while they act their Latin and make jokes in it, you will not want to revert to the dull old way. When the boy takes the sentence to pieces in order to "get it out" (a process often unavoidable), the master should insist on the sentence being read intelligently as a whole in the Latin order: only when you heal the wounds inflicted by the dissecting knife can organic life return. It is depressing and deplorable that the bad old advice about picking out the predicate and then the subject and then the object, without any attempt at subsequent synthesis, is still taught in all its ghastly destructiveness. We need Humanism and Holism, then, to supplement the work of the eye by the use of the ear, to bridge the gap between analytic reading and synthetic reading, between grammar and literature, between ancient literature and its influence on later letters.

I have spoken about my own subject, but what has been said applies to some extent also to the teaching of language in general; and lest the schoolmaster should regard all this as mere academic theory, let me say that it is based on personal experience and on the experiments of the Association for the Reform of Latin Teaching—a society that I commend to all our classical teachers.

If we regarded the child as a whole, we should realize that in his early years teaching should be especially directed to engage his emotions—not the emotion of fear only, as some still seem to think. We should make much more use of the dramatic method and press the ear into service as well as the eye. Instead of this eternal abstract dissection, we should teach the boy that language is an instrument for expressing things that matter to him, and we should take trouble to find the particular links that will make language significant to him. I knew a lad who was a born engineer, but who was bored by the standardized mathematics that his school put before him; when, however, he saw the connection between his mathematics and the construction work that he was keen on, the whole subject was transfigured with significance and interest. "Series iuncturaque pollet" (It is sequence and connection that count), said Horace. I believe that we often underestimate the potentialities of children. What we take for dullness is often lack of interest and in the monotonously simplified routine-lesson there is nothing to stimulate interest. I believe in setting the big things, on occasion, before quite young children—a play of Shakespeare, for example. They will fail to understand much of it, but contacts are made, echoes remain in the mind that bear fruit later; they get a glimpse of something worth striving for. Far too little good literature is read aloud to our elementary classes (such, for example, as may be had in "The King's Treasuries ") and far too much time is spent on purely analytical work and on snippets. There is no time to deal with other subjects; but think of the difference it would make if we read the books of the Bible as wholes, and not as artificially divided, long after their composition, into chapter and verse. (Our present arrangement of chapters dates from the thirteenth century, and our present system of verses from the sixteenth.) Few things have done more to destroy our understanding of the Bible than the dominance of the isolated verse. Think how our literary criticism would gain if, instead of concentrating on fragments and aspects, it tried to appreciate the direction or significance of a writer's work. Think how science would gain in interest if more of its history and growth and adventures were taught. During the recent visit of the British Association, Mr. E. R. Thomas showed us in his lecture on the atom, what humanized science could be. Think how history would gain in significance if water-tight compartments were abolished and if, for example, the Old Testament were linked to the History of the East, and the New Testament seen in its setting of Roman Imperialism. "No place or name was left a mere name," said a great scholar of his schoolmaster, "every one became an allusion to a story which we knew or to one which we might expect to learn. . . Alpheus was, of course, 'divine Alpheus . . . that renowned flood'; Hymettus was 'flow'ry hill Hymettus, with the sound of bees' industrious murmur'; Cyllene and Lycaeus were 'old Lycaeus and Cyllene hoar,' where 'nymphs and shepherd dance no more.' "[1] These are experiments in wholeness that make for living instruction. For analysis overdone kills. "Only wholes," says General Smuts, "are creative." It is in envisaging the whole, in seeing its connections and developments, its process of growth, that the mind itself becomes living, instinct with imagination. *Omne vivum e vivo* is an ancient principle; and if our teaching is to be living, it must proceed from a mind that is alive. Compared with that, training in method is of secondary importance. The facts that are communicated to a class may be either dead or alive. If they are treated as separate things-in-themselves, as a means of passing the examination, they are dead and damned. But if teachers realize Plato's dictum that knowledge is an activity of the mind, they will set ideas in motion, they will experiment and speculate; they will kindle in the student a sacred desire for knowledge and for scientific method. They will make illuminating contacts. Now contacts may be made in two ways. Remove your electric bulb and unscrew the fittings, and a great many things may be learned by examining the parts separately. That is analysis. When you place the bulb in the socket and it happens that your spring-contacts are out of position, you have connection, but no light. Here is the kind of synthesis that remains dead. But when you shift the spring-contacts so that they touch the leaden spots on the bulb, you have the life of the whole flowing through and the result is light. That is the kind of contact the

---

1 *Science and the Classics* (Proceedings of the Classical Association, 1929).

teacher has to look for; and, in that, no stereotyped professional training will help him.

Some of you may remember the address that Professor D'Arcy Thompson gave to our Classical Association in 1929. He told us that in the senior class under Pillans at the High School of Edinburgh, they were taught hardly anything except the Classics. But such was the stimulation of their lessons that the ancient world became alive for them and stirred their desire for knowledge; so that they ranged the fields in the afternoons investigating natural phenomena. "We had freedom to follow our bent," he said, "and leisure in which to teach ourselves." The result was that several of them became distinguished enough in science to be elected Fellows of the Royal Society. That is an example on the grand scale of knowledge as an activity of the soul. These are the teachers who are remembered by their pupils, not those who obtain the highest percentage of passes at the Matriculation by dint of efficient drilling.

All who have felt the spirit of Humanism, like Quintilian, Milton, Sir Thomas Elyot, have pleaded for breadth of knowledge. Cicero, too, following the tradition of Isocrates, stood for a training that included all parts of knowledge, and, furthermore, linked knowledge with morals. Today, we are being threatened with the appearance of the premature expert. We cannot hope to take in all the facts of knowledge; but we may cultivate the attitude of mind that I have called humanistic and holistic and remain sensitive to the contacts that light up our special subject. You know what the captious person said about the expert: an expert is a man who concentrates more and more on less and less, until he finally just concentrates. The satire is aimed at the danger of abstraction; and, indeed, abstraction and isolation are the great enemies. Intensify them enough and you have the monomaniac; that way madness lies, preceded by morbidity and neurosis. It is as though, in seeing things as a whole, we tap a spirit greater than ourselves, an *anima mundi*, whose influence is soothing and healing. The fever and the heat of partisanship drop away, and we are at rest in the heart of the universe.

We have far too many superficial generalizations, especially on racial and national subjects. What we need to learn, and not least the scientists themselves, is the patience and the impartiality that go to the making of a true generalization.

It may well be that the competition of our many specialisms will destroy the whole basis of culture. John Burnet tells how he attended a conference of archaeologists. The discussion was about the Palaeolithic Age. If a man talked about the Neolithic Age he was listened to with frigid politeness; but if an unfortunate gentleman mentioned the Bronze Age, he could not be heard for the heavy tread of archaeologists leaving the room. Already we find students of modern languages presenting themselves for advanced work without the linguistic and cultural background that they need. In Holland I found one of our students who was studying French, but was unable to take her degree because school and university training had not supplied her with the necessary prerequisite, namely, Latin. Far more co-ordination and co-operation are required, both between schools and university and between faculties inside the university. I am happy to say that courses in Comparative Literature are being arranged at this University, so that it will be possible for the student to trace the development of the epic from Homer and Vergil to Milton, or of the pastoral from Theocritus, through the Eclogues to Spenser and Hooft, or of seventeenth century drama in Europe back through the distorting medium of Seneca to Euripides in fifth-century Greece. Thus, the continuous study of a literary *genre* will become possible for the first time in our universities.

There are some who think that we ought to confine our studies to modern times, which is rather like a botanist studying a tree without knowing anything about its roots. It is the short view, as opposed to the long view; and the short view is responsible in human affairs for many bitter regrets. Most wars would never have happened if men had been able to see far enough; most acts of violence omitted, if all their consequences had been envisaged. And those studies that are decried as unpractical have a very important function in shaping the taste and the judgment. The Austrian socialist, Pernerstoffer, once defined education as "the sum of all we have forgotten."[1] What he meant was that all

---

1 J. Burnet, Romanes Lecture 1923.

the facts of our school reading may be forgotten, but in countless ways they have gone to form our attitude to life. It is not only such things as grammar and the multiplication table that can become automatic, but such elusive things as taste and judgment. The habits of mind formed in interested and willing exploration of great works, even when those works are forgotten, determine our reactions in matters of taste. As John Burnet reminds us in his Romanes Lecture of 1923, the actual facts a man knows are not the most important factor in his education. The full light of knowledge may illumine a definite portion of the field, but around that light lies a kind of penumbra of forgotten facts and potential knowledge. "A great mathematician and a child may both be said to know that two and two make four, and it would not be easy to show that there is any actual difference in the content of their knowledge at the time. The difference, which is really enormous, seems to lie wholly in the surroundings by which it is accompanied. In the same way, a schoolboy and a great scholar may give a verbally identical translation of a passage, but here again there is a wide divergence... It is like the difference in *timbre* between two notes of identical pitch sounded on different instruments. It is the presence or absence of overtones that makes the difference between the knowledge of the educated and the uneducated man, and it is plain that education in this sense is not a thing that can be handed over ready-made."

Let us never forget that the real test of education is what a man does with his leisure time (his *schole*, as the Greeks said—by an irony of history the word "school" is derived from it) as opposed to *anangkaion* (worktime); and if you have taught him nothing except the technique of his profession, you are likely to find him using his leisure in foolish or antisocial ways. Training for leisure means considering the child as a whole.

This consideration brings us to another side of the subject. For, ultimately, the application of the holistic-humanist attitude depends on something else. It depends on whether, in the ancient terminology, you are a *philosophos*, a lover of wisdom, or else a *philologos*, a lover of letters, and whether your interest is a disinterested interest. It is worthwhile reminding ourselves that even on the purely practical side our telephones and telegraphs, our X-rays and our wireless, spring from men who were disinterested seekers after truth. If the teacher lacks this quality, no amount of intellectual brilliance can make up for the deficiency. What does this quality imply? It implies, in its fullest sense, a faith that casts out fear and allows prejudices to fall into perspective; it helps us in our consideration of things like the Native Question. It implies something in the heart of the teacher that makes luminous the facts that he teaches and gives insight and quickens the imagination. He will have pity (like Vergil) for the things of life, because he sees them *sub specie aeternitatis* as well as *sub specie humanitatis*. He will contemplate the sublimity, which, as "Longinus" says, is the echo of a mighty soul; he will be interested in the *direction* of things even without achievement, more than in the successful accomplishment of petty detail. You remember Browning:

That low man seeks a little thing to do—
    Sees it and does it:
That high man, with a great thing to pursue,
    Dies ere he knows it.

The humanist will recall Plato's words, about the man who is ὡς ἀληθῶς πρᾶος, truly gentle, and reflect that it is the *impotens*, the violent man who has no control over his passions, who is in reality to be accounted weak. He will practise a tolerance like that of the Athenians at their best. Speaking of Aristophanes' criticism of the war-party in the *Archarnians*, Professor Gilbert Murray has recently said:

> "This is an astonishing scene. It would have been quite impossible in any country of Europe during the late war for a writer, however brilliant, to make a speech on behalf of the enemy in a theatre before an average popular audience. He could write a pamphlet; he could address a small meeting of those who agreed with him, but he could never make a defence of the enemy and an attack on the national policy in the midst of a performance in a national theatre. And if impossible in our time, it would hardly have been possible in any other period of history. This is one of

those points in which Athens definitely reached a higher level of culture than any other society known to us."

In a word, the humanist will stand for growth and expansiveness and abundance of life. So, he will communicate the divine spark: *Ex amante alio accenditur alius,* said S. Augustine, "one loving spirit sets another on fire."

It is when we add this spirit to the qualities of holistic Humanism that we shall be able to cope with the complex problems of race and nationality; and these we cannot shirk, for education must be education for citizenship. The problem is vast; but it may be suggested that if the English and Afrikaans cultures could be felt as wholes, unimpaired by prejudice or malice or unimaginativeness, a way might be found for co-operation in a greater South African whole; for the holistic attitude does not mean the suppression or superficial disregard of the parts, but fruitful diversity within a harmonious union. Thus it was (as I have pointed out elsewhere),[1] or nearly thus, that the Roman farmer, hardy, slow and courageous, became the ruler of Italy; despising and fearing at first the civilization that came to him across the sea, indignant at the change it wrought in his ancestral customs; but finding at length, when the individuality of his own culture was assured, a way of harmonious co-operation. The significant point about this historic operation of the holistic principle is that the final product—a Cicero, a Vergil, a Quintilian—was a finer gentleman and a better citizen, in general, than either the original Roman, strong but uncultured, or the original Greek, cultured but frequently unstable. The bi-lingual Roman of the time of Augustus had two distinct streams of culture flowing in him. "I for my part," says Cicero in the Pro Archia, "maintain this, too, that when to exceptional and brilliant natural gifts there has been added a certain scientific method, and the moulding force of learning, there is wont to result something indefinable that is both distinguished and unique." Cicero is thinking here of the alliance of the practical virtues of the Roman farmer with

---

1 Vergil and South Africa (Blackwell, 1931)

oversea Greek culture; and his appreciation of two cultures did not weaken, it enriched him and made him more tolerant.

In vain do the scientists "storm the bastions of Heaven," in vain does analysis strive to force from life her secret. But the creed of the humanist remains. In our time it has been reinforced and inspired by a great hope: the return of many prophets of science to what may be termed a humanist standpoint. Humanism needs Science with her cold, clear methods of research; Science needs Humanism with her care for man as a whole. If, in view of the changes that are taking place in scientific philosophy, Science and holistic Humanism could join hands, and Lucretius, *e.g.*, be accompanied by the history of the atom, the educational future might be rich in fruits. So, perhaps, we may withstand the assault on Humanism that this generation has seen; so, the ghosts of the sentries that guarded Hadrian's Roman Wall in the north of England (and among them were cohorts of our Dutch ancestors) may rejoice that the Great Tradition of Humanism has been saved even now, even as the Wall in some sense helped to save it.

But there are times when mankind, painfully learning and then rejecting wisdom, striving to work together and then blindly spoiling its own efforts, drives us almost to despair.

> See, in the rocks of the world
> Marches the host of mankind,
> A feeble and wavering line.
> Where are they tending? A God
> Marshalled them, gave them a goal.
> Ah, but the way is so long!
> Years have they been in the wild!
> Sore thirst plagues them, the rocks,
> Rising all round, overawe;
> Factions divide them, their host
> Threatens to break, to dissolve.
> Ah, keep, keep them combined!

(So wrote Matthew Arnold, the Humanist, Arnold, who admired Sophocles because he "saw things steadily and saw them whole.")

And then, apostrophizing the noble and the great who have been faithful to the Great Tradition:

> Then in the hour of need
> Of your fainting, dispirited race,
> Ye, like angels appear,
> Radiant, with ardour divine!
> Beacons of hope, ye appear!
> Languor is not in your heart,
> Weakness is not in your word,
> Weariness not on your brow. . .
> Eyes rekindling and prayers,
> Follow your steps as ye go.
> Ye fill up the gaps in our files,
> Strengthen the wavering line,
> Stablish, continue our march,
> On, to the bound of the waste,
> On, to the city of God.

With allies like these, we may learn to obey Goethe's exhortation: "Im Ganzen, Guten, Wahren resolut zu leben," to live steadfastly in the Whole, the Good, the True.

Our Changing Economic World

By
C. S. RICHARDS
M.Com.
Professor of Commerce

Our Changing Economic World

Several times since I selected the above title for my lecture I have wished that I had chosen a different one, for affairs in the economic world are changing so rapidly that it is extremely difficult to give any sense of perspective, though the position is not quite so bad as a recent correspondent to our University paper would have one believe when he said ironically that "to all who have studied economics as recently as even last week it is evident that what they have learnt is absolutely out of date."[1] In any case, its obviously changing character, often, indeed, more obvious than real, relieves one of the necessity of proving it; nor is our economic world apparently nearly as bad as the physical universe, which, according to a recent writer, "was once upon a time all tidy, with everything in its proper place, but ever since then has been growing more and more disorderly, until nothing but a drastic spring-cleaning can restore it to its pristine order."[2]

That flux and change are inherent in our economic world should be obvious to all, though the fact of change is not readily recognized by many, whose concern it is, with unfortunate results to Society; or, often, what is changing is frequently misunderstood. Variations in standards of living, changes in the mobility and supply of labour, alterations in the amount of capital available for investment, changes in the birth and death rates, exhaustion of supplies of raw materials and the substitution of others, changes in demand and in price levels, in the fruitfulness of the earth and the plenteousness of Nature, combined with new inventions and new ideas of economic organization make economic co-ordination much like doing "a jigsaw puzzle on a rolling ship."

The changes I have enumerated are often more obvious than real, more apparent than basic, and I want this evening to distinguish if possible between these two kinds of economic change, between what is superficial and what is fundamental, and

---

1 *Wu's Views*, University of the Witwatersrand, 12th August, 1932.
2 *The Scientific Outlook*, Russell, *p. 119.*

endeavour to leave you in the possession of certain principles in the light of which the present apparent chaos can be judged.

I shall, therefore, treat first of the philosophy and organization of the economic system as it existed before the War; then of the changes both in ideas, institutions and structure introduced during the War and post-War period; and finally (greatly daring, perhaps) I shall attempt a dip into the future, both immediate and more distant, to see what it appears to hold for us. I would only ask you to remember that the subject is too vast for anything but a cursory survey in the space of one brief lecture.

The Economic Problem and the Nineteenth Century Solution.

The economic problem as it faces us in this world is one of organization;[1] of utilizing man's capacity for *joint* action so that provision is made for his material welfare. Now just exactly as it is possible to build many different types of house, so it is *possible* to organize Society in many varied ways in order to make provision for its economic needs. While at the present moment in the world there are many types of organization, the one which is mainly characteristic of most civilized countries, and the one which in modern times has lasted longest, is that known as the Individualist Solution, or that of Capitalism, Competition and Freedom of Enterprise, commonly summed up in the general economic doctrine of *laisser-faire*.

This economic system, which exists in most countries of Western civilization, is relatively modern—a product or co-partner of the Industrial Revolution and starting only from the middle of the eighteenth century. Though considerably modified since, fundamentally it is still the same. To quote Hawtrey: "Our economic system remains predominantly and in principle individualist."

The era which opened in the middle of the eighteenth century, with its concentration on machinery and power, and which continued right to the War, can best be described as one of unconscious, unplanned but nevertheless deliberate "specialization and exchange." It has been described by the economist, Professor

---

1   *The Economic Problem,* Hawtrey, p. 2.

Commons, as the Era of Abundance, as its immediate predecessor was that of the Era of Scarcity, and its successor is to be, in his opinion, the Era of Stabilization. The development of this exchange economy, which finally spread all over the world and made it, to all intents and purposes, a single co-ordinated unit, gave rise to the two great economic schools of thought embodied in Liberalism (*i.e.*, the Individualist Solution—*laisser-faire*) and Socialism, the former having its birthplace in England and France, in the middle of the eighteenth century, the latter, a universal movement, making its appearance as a conscious reaction against the worst features of the epoch of economic freedom and demanding, in general, the "abolition of the private domination over the means of production, the central organization of production and the attainment of equality in distribution."

The characteristics of this Era of Freedom were manifold: An era whose economic institutions and organization were built up largely on the postulate of *laisser-faire*, whose driving force was private profit and whose stimuli were capitalism, private enterprise and private ownership; whose glorification was that of the individual, whose civilization was one of unashamed materialism and whose philosophy was that "the end justifies the means." It was an era of abundance but of selfishness; an era of great and rapid development, both materially and geographically; for it spread its philosophy and extended its tentacles far to the East, until the slow-going Oriental was infected by its ideas and emulated its achievements, so that the whole world is now imbued with an economic doctrine, namely, the dominating importance and sanctity of the idea of the export market, a policy feasible enough when only a few nations are industrialized but impossible when all practise it; an era likewise of exploitation of the "newer" parts of the world, of concentration, and the subordination of the individual through the growth in the size of industrial units; an era of achievement, but not of culture; an era of power and machinery; of saving and investment under the principle of joint stock and limited liability, but also of meanness and pelf; an age of contrasts, enormous wealth and great poverty; an epoch which witnessed the greatest increase in population ever seen in the history of the world, in which not only migration of population but also of capital opened up the four quarters of the globe, and through its railways, steamships, its telegraph and telephone, eliminated barriers, both of space and of time; an era too, which, as it became more complex, became more dependent for its survival upon a single factor which was treated empirically and fatalistically[1] namely, relative stability in the purchasing power of money. Though this era reached its zenith at the close of the nineteenth century, it was, ostensibly, at least, everywhere triumphant before the War.

But, coincident with its rise grew the chorus of antagonism and criticism, embodied politically in the development of Democracy, economically in the growth of Socialism, and legislatively in the development of Nationality, expressed in tariff barriers and a whole doctrine of State restrictions. This criticism concentrated on some of the adverse features of the age of development—the growing inequality of incomes; the growth in the size of business units and the tendency to concentration and monopoly; the appearance of democracy with the reality of economic oligarchy; the periodical fluctuations of business and industry with their consequent unemployment and distress to millions, fluctuations which, it is now well recognized, are a by-product of the institutional processes involved in this form of economic organization. It drew attention to the industrial insecurity of the worker both as regards tenure of work and provision for unemployment; to the three characteristics of all such industrial societies, namely, the numerical preponderance of wage-workers; the remarkable degree to which the wage earning section of the population tends to be distinct from the section which owns property (in England, according to Sir Josiah Stamp, one per cent, of the population in 1919 owned about two-thirds of the aggregate wealth of England[2]); and the sharpness of the division between the upper and lower grades of the economic hierarchy.

The battlements of the fortress of *laisser-faire* were, therefore, continually being breached throughout this epoch and

---

1 "The First Necessity of Thinking To-day on Social Questions." Sir Josiah Stamp in *The Movement for a Sounder Money*, p. 33, issued by the Stable Money Association. New York, 1929.

2 *Equality*, Tawney, p. 81.

such breaches were continually enlarged; the growth of Trade Unionism, the passing of Factory Acts, the limitation of working hours, the fixation of minimum wages, the increase of progressive taxation and consequent redistribution of incomes, the growth of Co-operation and the development of Social Insurance, were but the advance guard of an army whose objective was the elimination of grave industrial abuses and whose goal was greater social control over the economic machine—a control which has grown so greatly that in some cases it threatens the very functioning of the machine itself, a control now so great as to prompt Mr. Keynes to write his pamphlet on "The End of *Laisser-faire*."[1]

Nevertheless, prior to the War, the world *was* one economic unit with virtually a world currency, gold, and the abundance of one area made good the deficiency of another, and capital and labour were directed to the points of highest return. The bases of the "system" were seldom analyzed and even less recognized— its dependence on such things as mobility of labour, the export of capital, the relative stability of its international currency unit, and its rough international division of labour between two groups, one, the highly industrialized manufacturing countries with high standards of living, such as Great Britain, Germany, France and the United States, and the other, the raw material or primary producing countries, comprising the backward countries of Europe, the countries of the New World and the Dominions. The very rapidity of the Industrial Revolution and the enormous changes wrought in so short a space of time blinded people to its real features, to its complex character, to what was temporary and what permanent, to the haphazard nature of its development and to the fact that the "machine" was in grave danger of becoming "end" and not "means."

War and Post-War Changes in the Structure of World Economics.

On this delicate structure, this finely balanced piece of mechanism, compounded of ideas and institutions, already, however, showing signs of rust and developing internal creakings, the War

---

1 *Essays in Persuasion*, Keynes, p. 312.

fell with full force for over four years. It is not to be wondered at, therefore, that the effects of that cataclysm should be deep and far-reaching, extensive in their scope and, in certain directions, fundamental in their results. It is necessary to review very briefly the principal results of that conflict and the alterations they have produced both economically and politically, philosophically and geographically, before we can make any attempt to visualize the strengths or assess the weaknesses which they are exercising towards the world's future development.

Politically, through Europe, it has resulted, strangely enough, in the virtual disappearance of the despotism of kingship and the substitution of the despotism of dictatorship, either individual or bureaucratic. Italy, Spain, Poland, Czecho-Slovakia and Russia, to mention only a few, are each working out in different forms and with varying degrees of success or failure new philosophies of the State. The British Empire has also undergone an enormous change and if it be true that "the measure of a country's vitality is its power to create common institutions,"[1] then this constitutionally curious entity of a centralized State and an embryo federation of States is still capable of contributing its quota to world development. Politically, too, the East has stirred and India, China and Japan are undergoing a reorientation of ideas and have become imbued with the philosophy of democracy; though it is open to grave question as to whether the democratic ideal, which may be suited to Western ideas can be transplanted and flourish with equal success in the Orient, where outlook, age-old tradition, custom and religious belief are its complete antithesis.

It is in the economic sphere, however, that the changes produced by the War and post-War period have been greatest and are most clearly seen. Apart altogether from such features as War Debts and Reparations, now we hope happily settled by the Lausanne Agreement, and the great influx of women into industrial life, the post-War period has been marked by many notable changes both in ideas and institutions, some of which have radically altered the structure of world economy.

---

1 *Changes in the Structure of World Economics since the War*, Somary, p. 46

There has, in the first place, been the great growth in the spirit of economic nationalism, fostered by the conditions of the Treaty of Versailles, and the development of national self-sufficiency. The full and unfortunate effects of this doctrine are best seen in Europe—a mosaic now of twenty-six relatively small countries, practically all of which are in fee for capital requirements to the United States, all of them surrounded by ridiculous and impossible tariff barriers which impede trade and reduce exchange, all endeavouring to promote self-sufficiency, all with restrictions on mobility both of capital and labour, all disintegrated and jealous, disunited and mutually suspicious, all of whose problems appear, and are made, all the more difficult as the nationalism of each country extends to the economic field. As already pointed out, prior to the War, the whole trend of world economic development was towards unity—the world economically was, in fact, one, based on the principle of exchange and a universal monetary medium, gold. Labour and capital flowed freely all over the globe and the interchange of ideas no less than the interchange of goods made economic unity a more or less accomplished reality, and seemed to foreshadow the fruition of the poet's dream of the "Parliament of man, the federation of the world." All that the War changed, and though initially fought for an idea, the idea of freedom and liberty, in its place has been enthroned its international antithesis, Nationality.

Dr. Somary, writing of the present condition of Europe, states that the awakening of Nationalism is the main reason why Europe is at present completely disintegrated, adding "the fact that a man is not a citizen of a certain country has almost become a crime, and it is particularly in the pigmy countries that this idea is carried to an absurd extent."[1] Nationalism has given birth all over the world to a host of infant industries, most of which, it is now being realized, are either stillborn or most unpromising infants which can never grow into lusty manhood. In the economic sphere, anyway, Nationalism is retrogressive—it has outlived its day and generation.

---

1 *Changes in the Structure of World Economics since the War"* Somary, p. 101.

A further effect of the War has been that the economic life of the world has been subjected throughout the whole period to an unprecedented degree of political interference. Absurd tariff restrictions, import prohibitions, quotas, wage boards, all necessitating hordes of unproductive State officials and, in many cases, resulting in quite unnecessary interference, have largely impeded fluidity and elasticity in the system, such as existed before the War, have greatly impaired the Individualist technique of adjustment, and have substituted nothing in its place. This political interference, coupled with the rigidity which it has introduced into the world economic structure, acting on a business atmosphere, "which has inherited from the period of violent inflation which preceded the restoration of the gold standard, a nervous apprehension of the possibility of a currency becoming worthless,"[1] has destroyed the postulate of supply and demand, introduced maladjustments of its own and prevented the adaptation of the system to changing conditions—in a word, to quote Professor Gregory, "there have been tendencies at work in many countries preventing a rapid adjustment of the level of money incomes to changes in the general economic situation."[2]

But the outstanding feature has been the transformation of the United States of America from a colonial into a world power—from a debtor country, in which European countries had invested large capital, to a creditor country holding Europe largely in fee. The extraordinary mechanization of her industry, the growth in the scale of her manufactures and competition with European countries, the complete change in her traditional policy of unrestricted immigration from Europe (a further bar to mobility), the increase in her export and capital surplus, the accompanying but at the same time contradictory policy of increased tariffs (which policy is greatly to blame for her present stagnation, for a creditor country must import visibly more than she exports visibly, or continue to lend abroad—and America has shown a reluctance to do either), have fundamentally altered, not only her own internal economy, but also that of Europe. Moreover, coincident with her

---

1 *The Gold Standard and its Future*, Gregory, p. 31.
2 *The Gold Standard and its Future*, Gregory, p. 33.

growth as an industrial and manufacturing nation, has been her growth as a financial and monetary power—a growth so rapid that it has outdistanced the development of the necessary financial technique, for banking is not an art which can be comprehended on mass production lines—the psychology to operate the machine of mass production has little in common with the subtlety and delicacy required to operate and control factors largely psychological in their origin. The doctrine of self-sufficiency, self-containedness and Economic supremacy, which dominated American political and economic life in the post-War period till the present depression, is now stated with less certainty and dogmatism.

A fourth effect of some consideration is the rapid industrialization of the East. Before the War, the world's position was roughly its division by countries into two groups, creditor countries such as Great Britain, Germany and France, highly industrialized with relatively high standards of living, and principally engaged in manufacture, and the debtor countries, the South American Republics, the British Dominions, China, India, Japan, etc., principally supplying raw materials and primary products to the former. There was, therefore, a rough division of labour in the world on these lines. But since the dominating idea of Capitalism is profits and since forethought, except for its own day and generation and its own immediate benefit, is not an outstanding feature of capitalistic enterprise, not only were consumable manufactured goods exported, but also capital equipment in the form of machinery and technical skill—the ultimate was sacrificed to the immediate, the future to the present, permanency to expediency, so that even before the War the repercussion of these processes was being felt, from countries like Japan, in countries of Western civilization in the form of increasing competition. The pre-War movement of industrialization has therefore gained great impetus and has resulted in the industrial development of:

(*a*) The previously more backward countries of Europe;
(*b*) The Eastern countries like Japan, China, India.

The monopoly which Western countries previously enjoyed for their manufactured goods in the markets of the world is each year being more vigorously assailed. It would seem, therefore, that the principal effect of this fundamental alteration must be, at first, and for some time, anyway, the progressive redistribution of world income in favour of the more backward European countries and the East, and adverse to the older industrialized countries such as Great Britain, Germany and the United States, and therefore the wage standards and general standards of living of those latter countries will, *ceteris paribus*, see progressive relative diminution for some time[1]. If this result is to be avoided or retarded, then a rapid adjustment of their productive organization will be required in the countries of the Old World, but, unfortunately, Government interference and consequent rigidity of the economic structure, combined, perhaps, with business inertia, will greatly hinder this adaptability.

The fifth factor, more important at the moment from an ideological point of view, than from that of a new competitor in world's markets, is the great Russian industrial transformation and the Five Year Plan. On this experiment in organized State planning I have time to say only three things: First, it is quite impossible to give an opinion at the moment as to its ultimate success or failure, and one should avoid dogmatic conclusions as to its success deduced from overdrawn accounts of hurried visits paid by ardent but uncritical enthusiasts who see no more than they are intended to see; though obviously there is much we can learn from Russia. Secondly, profit, that bugbear of Marxian Socialists, is virtually the chief concern of the Russian State, is in high favour and is found to be vitally necessary to the first country that has tried to put radical Socialism into practice. Thirdly, the possibility of the Russian experiment succeeding is greatly conditioned by the fact that Russia is a country which, like the United States, is potentially, at least, more or less self-supporting—and, in addition, has an enormous population largely docile and quite uneducated, a fertile field for economic experiment. Whether capitalist States

---

1 *Business, The Universities and the Economic Outlook*. Inaugural Lecture by Professor C. S. Richards, University of the Witwatersrand Press, 1932, p. 19.

can continue to exist side by side with a Communist State is a matter for conjecture.

The Immediate Future.

If the foregoing analysis is at all a correct interpretation of events, out of the welter of the War and its aftermath, out of the conflict of the old and the new, out of the antagonism of ideas and institutions, there seem to emerge three factors or problems, embodying three ideas, which will engage the attention of all of us for some years to come and dominate the stage of international discussion for the next decade. The present depression, acting as a furnace separates metal from slag, has brought them into sharp relief and none of us can escape the heat of their influence and effect. These problems seem to me to be clearly discernible as follows:

1. Is Nationalism or Internationalism, in its economic aspect, to be the ruling ideal and to dominate the scene in the years that lie ahead?
2. Is the economic concept of Liberalism, *i.e.*, freedom, or of Socialism, control, to supply the motive and provide the basis of future economic organization? Will it be a combination of or a compromise between these two, or must we seek an entirely new postulate?
3. Whatever the answer to the second problem, is the next economic epoch to be one of conscious planning or of haphazard development? Is it to be an age of Stabilization and Certainty or of Instability and Uncertainty?

We stand, therefore, on the threshold of a new era. What is it likely to hold for us? What factors must we take note of and what finality are we likely to reach? I turn, therefore, to a short consideration of these three fundamental problems and the minor considerations which depend on them.

1. No question, to my mind, is more important than that of Nationalism or Internationalism as a factor in world economic affairs. I have already indicated some of the ways in which

it has adversely affected, either actually or potentially, world prosperity, how it has destroyed the pre-War economic technique and machinery, hindered the flow of labour and capital, increased national antagonisms, given birth to ridiculous industrial enterprises, split the world up into innumerable small trading areas, created bureaucratic organizations for carrying out its behests, enormously enlarged the civil services and parasitic services also, and extended the scope and greatly increased the cost of government. It is a movement retrogressive of world movements in science and art, in industrial technique and in improved transport facilities. Writing of Nationalism and patriotism in his book *Marriage and Morals*, Bertrand Russell says:—"Undoubtedly, patriotism, so-called, is the greatest danger to which civilization is at present exposed and anything that increases its virulence is more to be dreaded than plague, pestilence and famine" (pp. 172-3).

I have stressed this factor because economically there is no gainsaying its importance. That, however, is not to deny that there are other factors, more purely economic in their origin, which will, so far as one can tell, lead to an alteration in international trade in the course of the next half-century, markedly different from that obtaining in the nineteenth century, an alteration definitely in the direction of a *permanent* decline.

"The economic development of the world during the nineteenth century is usually looked on as a complete justification of the doctrines of the Manchester school of Free Traders. While the tariff as an agency of economic acceleration admittedly played little part during the nineteenth century, it is seldom realized that the free trade arguments and consequent international development rested on five factors of a transient and not a permanent character, namely, the growth of technique, the use of steam power, then of oil; the unequal distribution of financial resources which involved the necessity of international capital movements and then of interest payments; a progressive improvement in freedom of communication, *i.e.*, consolidation of areas permitting of the free passage of goods; lastly and more important of all, the world was being peopled, and the constant growth of population, together with a rising standard of life, provided a seemingly inexhaustible market for raw materials in the manufacturing areas and for manufactured goods in the 'overseas' areas. How far have the above conditions *permanently* disappeared?

"Apart from the increase in the number of sovereign States and the fact that national frontiers have increasingly tended to become economic frontiers, other economic changes have intervened, militating against the growth either directly or indirectly in the volume of international trade. Firstly, social changes not necessarily permanent in character have in certain cases reduced the ability to export, *e.g.*, the break-up of the great estates in south-eastern Europe has reduced their wheat producing capacity; unsettled conditions in China have had similar effects. Secondly, there has been a marked shift in recent years in the real ratio of interchange between raw materials and manufactured articles, resulting in a reduction in the physical volume of the latter, which has to be given for a given quantity of the former. This has led to an increase in unemployment in exporting industries in the manufacturing countries and an increase in unemployment among primary producers in the agricultural countries and is therefore a most important factor making towards the industrialization of the latter countries. Thirdly, nationalism has everywhere fostered the growth of the feeling against the dominance of the agrarian and raw material producing States by the industrial. It should be emphasized that concentration upon mining and agriculture by no means necessarily implies inferior economic strength, but in so far as it voices the social desirability of diversification of the economic life of a country the demand for industrialization is comprehensible on rational grounds and is likely to be an element of increasing importance in future.

"Moreover, profound technical changes are at work which make it likely that a greater degree of self-sufficiency and therefore a relative decline in the volume of international trade will characterize the immediate future. The increasing importance of 'services' and other sheltered occupations which cannot be imported, a slackening in the growth of population and therefore in the demand for crude foodstuffs and raw materials; technological changes in agriculture on a large scale, resulting in a greater productivity but also increasing agricultural unemployment, will all tend to stimulate local manufacture and therefore reduce the relative volume of international trade.

"The above statements do not weaken the arguments for international trade based upon the possession by particular areas of specialized kinds of skill, experience or product—they are statements of what is likely to happen for some time at least and not what should happen, and the element of growth, if there is to be such, will be provided more by luxuries, less by the necessaries of existence, for the problem today is no longer the high cost of carriage but the increasing degree to which science is making the whole world independent of local circumstances in the production of necessaries coupled with an increasing determination on the part of the agricultural peoples to emancipate themselves from the dominance, as it is considered, of the advanced industrialized States."[1]

The above would appear likely to be the position for some time to come. Ultimately, however, the economic disadvantages of these results will be realized, for economic necessity is a greater compelling force than any nationalism. Depression and disaster are already educating the world into a proper appreciation of political and economic values—and the development of larger economic areas is already receiving an increasing amount of attention. Though obstacles are vast and difficult, the idea of a United States of Europe, the dream and almost the accomplished fact initially of Napoleon, may not be so Utopian as it sounds, for the "fate of Europe in the future is the chief problem which faces modern civilization, and if Europe cannot find a formula for such a union she will be able neither to uphold her economic position in the future nor maintain her population at its present level."[2]

This concept of larger economic areas born of economic necessity will, I venture to suggest, possibly spread. A closer economic unity of the British Empire would appear to be already an accomplished fact. Moreover, a closer economic unity between the two Americas, and, though more Utopian at the moment, an

---

[1] "Permanent Decline in International Trade," Professor T. E. Gregory. *Natal Advertiser*, Durban, 5th and 6th February, 1932. Article syndicated by London General Press.

[2] *Changes in the Structure of World Economics since the War*, Somary, pp. 94 and 103.

economic working agreement between Asiatic countries, may neither be impossibilities in the not too distant future. This would virtually reduce the large trading areas to four in number and would greatly reduce the causes of international friction and difficulty. Until it is fully realized all over the world what the insistence on nationality is costing in material welfare, we can hope for no improvement. But I believe that out of this present world depression will grow forces working towards that end; working ultimately, perhaps, though in the very distant future, towards a World State. The sooner it is realized that the worship which at present attaches to a favourable trade balance (and which has led to the ridiculous attempts of most countries to obtain such a balance and to the conception of the world split up into a number of isolated units all attempting to show a surplus[1]), has sanction neither in economic doctrine nor yet, for that matter, in common sense, the sooner shall we reach sanity. But politics and economics are, unfortunately, at the moment, uneasy bed mates, and so far most of the economic bed as well as most of the bed-clothes have gone to the politician—he usually pulls the hardest and has most pertinacity.

2. Turning to our second problem, whether Liberalism in its broadest sense, *i.e.*, economic freedom, or Socialism in some form, is to provide the basis and postulate of our future economic organization, it is still an unsettled matter, though many factors would make it appear that the apparent eclipse of Liberalism has been but temporary and that once again the tide is turning in its favour.

The future economic organization of society is frequently pictured as a conflict between Individualism and Socialism, between freedom of enterprise and social control of business, between means as means and means as ends, between materialism and spirituality, between machinery and man, wealth and welfare, getting a living and knowing how to live. The ultra-Socialist points to the benefits of national enterprise—the individualist

---

1 *The World Political Crisis and its Economic Consequences*, Quigley, p. 7. Paper read to the Purchasing Section of Management Research Group No. 1, 28th April, 1932.

to the wealth which has accrued from freedom, and a picture is drawn as though it were a study in contrasts.

I do not share this attitude, nor do I think the picture at all in accord either with history or with fact—and when I hear those least qualified to judge exploiting our present discontents and pencilling in overdrawn pictures of the horrors of the machine age, I feel their criticism to be equally as mistaken as the enthusiastic encomiums of those who still live in and think of an era of economic freedom which to all but static minds has gone forever. Neither of these extremes is accurate. Three generations of critics have attacked Liberalism for making economic progress its aim; and many do it today, but without material prosperity there can be little real culture except for the favoured few. Material prosperity is nevertheless means and not end, and criticism directed against the scheme of things as end, as it is to many people, is justified.

We have long moved far from the position of unrestricted economic freedom—we have a long way to go before we reach, if we ever do, the Socialist's Utopia. Individualism means different things to different people—and Socialism is capable of as many interpretations as there are Socialists: "As a criticism it is unanimous, as a method it is divided, as a reconstructive process it is hopelessly at sea," wrote Orth[1] many years ago, and his criticism is equally valid today. The truth is that the possible combinations of organization between absolute freedom and complete control are numberless. There is a sphere for both Individualism and for State Enterprise, and a large shadow land between where various types and varying forms of joint organization and control are economically the most efficient. The manufacture of cotton fabrics is clearly the sphere of private enterprise where risks both of demand and supply are great, where substitutes are always possible, and where elasticity and flexibility are essential to an efficient organization. At the other end of the scale, the provision of public utility services, such as gas, water, electricity, etc., where monopoly is inherent and demand fairly stable, is obviously the sphere of public enterprise. In between are various gradations of private ownership and public control or public ownership and private

---

1   *Socialism and Democracy in Europe*, Orth, p. 12.

working, such as are seen in the British railways, the French railways, the South African Electricity Supply Commission or the South African Reserve Bank. The controversy between the two ideas is therefore quite mistaken, and it is as difficult to adopt the attitude of the ultra-Socialist as to agree with those of an older generation and a former economic regime who gaze longingly into the past and think, with Soames Forsyte, that the pearl of economic wisdom resides only in those who still regard as sacred, freedom of enterprise, private property, the right of inheritance and the five per cents.

Private enterprise in certain directions there must be, and likewise competition, if we are to maintain freedom of demand and choice, the mainspring of economic progress: but Society will never revert to the days of unrestricted freedom—that era which gave us our great development but likewise laid the foundations of many of our present-day social problems: our great inequalities in income, our conception of men as "hands," our slums, our horrid tenement houses—and our Victorian architecture and the Albert Memorial. Social control has come to stay, but we have yet to work out suitable formulas for its operation in different directions. Unfortunately, the War forced the pace of the growth of social control long before the bases had been established, and the politician, with typical pertinacity and cheerful inattention, still mounts guard outside much of the field he has browsed over for so long, and is reluctant to relinquish the smallest area, despite obvious evidences that his husbandry is anything but successful.

There will, I feel convinced, have to be many relinquishments or alterations of social control in certain directions where it exists at present: in the methods of Wage Boards, to cite one case only. But likewise the frontiers of social control will have to be extended in other directions, particularly in doing those things which at present are not done at all: in the collection and dissemination on a great scale of data relating to business, especially banking and currency, where private property and secrecy is definitely socially harmful, and possibly, too, in the direction of capital investment. Labour, quite rightly, I think, is more and more refusing to be regarded as a chattel and a market commodity, nor is it to be blamed for drawing attention to the fact that the immediate influence of machine introduction is usually "labourer saving" and not "labour saving," and that pious references to "long run" tendencies, when more labour will undoubtedly be employed, is quite useless to those who, through no fault of their own, are sometimes temporarily, but sometimes permanently, thrown on to the industrial scrap-heap. In the long run we are all dead, and the present insecurity of the industrial worker is, in this age of productive power, barbaric in its crudity and cruelty. Safeguards against industrial malingering would obviously have to be provided, but it is not irrelevant to suggest that increased productive power should sometimes connote reduced working hours and more satisfactorily employed leisure time.

The solution of the problem of poverty, and its companion, unemployment, as long as it is with us, must therefore engage more and more the public attention and be more and more subject to social control, though it is indubitable that much unemployment at present is caused by political interference, and one might suggest that next time an Unemployment Commission is appointed (as has recently been done in South Africa), it might not do any harm, since unemployment is a difficult economic problem, to include an economist or two!

Though we are still largely dominated by the ideas prevalent in a society not then certain of its food supply and still under the influence of Lamarck and later of Darwin, I feel certain also that the demand for greater economic equality will rightly or wrongly receive increasing attention and wider recognition. It is as well to realize what is meant by economic equality. "Humanism," says Tawney, in his brilliant essay "Equality," the Halley Stewart Lecture for 1929, "is the antithesis, not of theism or of Christianity, but of materialism.

". . . The humanist spirit, like the religious spirit, is not indeed indifferent to those things which, on their own plane, are obviously important; but it resists their encroachment upon spheres which do not belong to them. It insists that they are not the objects of life, but its instruments, which are to be maintained when they are serviceable and changed when they are not. Its aim is to liberate and cultivate the powers which make for energy and refinement, and it is critical therefore of all forms of organization which sacrifice spontaneity to mechanism, or which seek, whether in the name of economic efficiency or of social equality, to reduce the variety of individual character and genius to a drab and monotonous uniformity. But it desires to cultivate these powers in all men, not only in the few. Resting, as it does, on the faith that the differences between men are less important and fundamental than their common humanity, it is the enemy of arbitrary and capricious divisions between different members of the human family, which are based not upon what men, given suitable conditions, are capable of becoming, but on external distributions between them, such as those created by birth or wealth.

"Sharp contrasts of opportunity and circumstance, which deprive some classes of the means of development deemed essential for others, are sometimes defended on the ground that the result of abolishing them must be to produce, in the conventional phrase, a dead-level of mediocrity. Mediocrity, whether found in the valleys of society or, as not infrequently happens, among the peaks and eminences, is always to be deprecated, though it is hardly curable, perhaps, as sometimes seems to be supposed, by so simple a process as the application to conspicuous portions of the social system of sporadic dabs of varnish and gilt. But not all the ghosts which clothe themselves in metaphors are equally substantial, and whether a level is regrettable or not depends, after all, upon what is levelled.

"Those who dread a dead-level of income or wealth, which is not at the moment, perhaps, a very pressing danger, do not dread, it seems, a dead-level of law and order and of security for life and property."[1]

Many who hold such views and worship at the shrine of Mammon are clearly included in the scope of Sydney Smith's reply to a man's boast that he was "self-made": "You take a great responsibility off the shoulders of the Almighty." And when it is clear from innumerable investigations (notably the researches of Professor Ginsberg, Mr. Wedgwood, Professor Clay and Professor Cannan), that "inheritance is by far the most potent cause of

---

1   *Equality* Tawney, pp. 110-112

inequality in the actual distribution of property,"[1] a new meaning is given to the advice "to be wise in the choice of one's parents." The principles of inheritance and bequest are fighting a losing battle, and while inequalities there will always be, while some must continue to direct and others to be directed, and while there will continue to be differential rewards, not power and inequality, but irresponsible power and capricious inequality, will gradually disappear.

The sphere of private enterprise need not necessarily, therefore, suffer great contraction in the future, provided the social effects of private business contracts are realized. But social control allied with private enterprise will hammer out and perfect new forms, new combinations and new conceptions of economic organization and the business unit; in some cases, joint control by capital and labour or combinations of private and State enterprise; the experimental habit of mind is a difficult one for most people to maintain—yet nothing is more necessary in the field of social organization.

The co-operation of the two forms of economic system, State-controlled and free, benefits the former much more than the latter. State control can only learn the principles of economic calculation and can only avoid monopolistic lassitude by co-operating with private enterprise. While the State, therefore, is assured of a large part in the ordering of economic life, I see no other way for a more solid economic life for the world than by the conservation of private initiative, the maintenance of free exchange as well as of private property as the central legal institution, the creation of larger economic areas and the penetration of State enterprise by the spirit of rational calculation. Immense difficulties, as we have seen, stand in the way, but if the world can be brought to a measure of general agreement as regards the ends, the means will ultimately follow.

3. I turn finally to the third problem for a brief consideration of the principal points involved in the concept of Stabilization, or of conscious and organized planning. It is only natural that the flux and change inherent in competitive organization should

---

1   *Equality* Tawney, p. 162

breed its logical antithesis, stabilization, not only among Socialistic thought but also in Oligarchic trusts themselves. Much of what I have already said will provide a clue to the general standpoint from which this idea is to be viewed. Like all other ideas, it has in it elements both of good and evil; of usefulness and absurdity.

As usually expressed, the prerequisites for stabilizing the economic system must be:

(i) A stationary population, as immobile as possible.
(ii) Stationary demand, and
(iii) Abstinence from the adoption of new inventions.

When put in this way, absolute stabilization is immediately seen to be what it actually is, a visionary and impossible dream. It means not stabilization but stagnation, for flux and change are of the very essence of life itself. Moreover, it is never very clear from discussions on the subject as to whether it is stabilization of production, or stabilization of prices in general, or stabilization of particular prices which is desired. The first and the third would appear to be both undesirable and unattainable, while the second may be both desirable and attainable though even here exist technical difficulties which I shall mention later. Wealth and culture go hand in hand and therefore invention, which causes the greatest disturbances in economic life, is necessary to promote economic progress and culture. No class would suffer more from such a retrogressive movement than the workers, though that is not to deny that inventions which lead to greater productivity should also logically lead ultimately to a shorter working day.

But to point out the absurdity of the extreme position regarding stabilization is not to affirm that great progress is not still possible in obtaining a better adaptation of means to ends, a better co-ordination between efforts and rewards, a better co-operation between demand and supply. The recent destruction of a large portion of the Brazilian coffee crop so as to maintain the price of the remainder, the fact of millions at this moment willing but unable to find work, bounteous harvests and granaries overflowing with grain, on the one hand, and starving millions on the other, are but instances of an economic disease and epidemic which periodically affects society. In the past the economic problem was that of providing sufficient food, adequate housing and necessary clothing. Now it is a question of organization, of co-ordinating adequate resources and of conscious planning versus haphazard development. But this conscious planning cannot, I hazard the opinion, be found through the medium of large State Central Organizations controlling and directing our whole lives, deciding what shall be produced and when, how much each of us shall have and what, and shepherding us with a combination of maternal care and paternal solicitude from the cradle to the grave. As Professor Gregory has pointed out, "owing to the much greater pressure which organized business and labour interests can bring to bear on Government, there has been a general advocacy of 'stability,' which has in practice meant that particular groups could stabilize their own position, without any, or enough, attention having been paid to the result of such stabilizing action on other parts of the economic field or to the long-period results of such action. Raw material producers have been allowed, with the aid of governmental or quasi-governmental assistance, to 'stabilize' the prices of particular raw materials without regard to the fact that consumption might thereby be discouraged and production encouraged. In industry and distribution there has been a growth of large-scale organizations which have not always been willing to adjust prices to the trend of the market, thus adding in the end to the losses which had to be suffered on stocks when liquidation finally became necessary. In the sphere of labour there has been in certain countries a development of unemployment insurance schemes or similar relief measures which have prevented wage rates from falling, whilst in others public opinion, reinforced by Government propaganda, has had very much the same effect."[1]

There is grave danger of the principal function of "price" being completely overlooked, namely, its function in adjusting demand to supply and in indicating to producers whether more or less of any particular commodity or service is required. All schemes for the "stabilization" of the prices of particular commodities

---

1 *The Gold Standard and its Future,* Gregory, pp. 32-3.

or services are open to this grave objection—the results of such action are only too patent in this country in many directions.

That is not to deny, however, that there is ample room for a better adjustment of supply and demand, of production to consumption, but such improvements can, I believe, only be found within the form of organization which we already possess (since it is in the production of those commodities which are specially suitable for private enterprise that variations are greatest and adjustment most difficult), by the spread of knowledge, improvements in technique, and a better understanding among business men of the relation of their own units to those of the rest of the individual world. What we have lacked in the past (and what we still lack to a great extent), particularly in regard to "business fluctuations," is information on all phases of our complex and complicated life, a knowledge, for example, not only of past but also of projected production, statistics of production of raw materials and manufactured goods and, perhaps more important than all, adequate banking and currency statistics. These we now possess in much greater measure than formerly, together with a whole host of agencies whose work it is to study and, if possible, discern the causes of and eliminate the business cycle. Many large business units in England, Germany, the United States and elsewhere, and the most important banks throughout the world, and practically all the Central Banks, issue "Monthly Letters" or "Bulletins" giving the latest information, though it is significant that the Bank of England issued its first Statistical Summary in January this year. The information supplied by the League of Nations and such accurate statistical surveys as that of the London and Cambridge Economic Service are providing the material and developing a technique which should lead to greatly improved adaptation. But what is also wanted is an appreciation by businessmen of the value of such information, of the value of research in business and the development of the technique to use it. There is still a sneaking feeling among many who pride themselves on being "practical" men that such information is academic, theoretical and highbrow, with little reference to the world of reality. The sooner there is a change of attitude the better, both for their pockets and for society; but Anglo-Saxons are notoriously conservative and the growth of such an enlightened attitude must necessarily be slow, though it is the rule rather than the exception in America, where the recent *Report on Long Range Planning for the Regularization of Industry* (the report of a Sub-Committee of the Committee on Unemployment and Industrial Stabilization of the National Progressive Conference) is symptomatic of the general trend. Conscious planning and deliberate organization of this description, especially if it includes deliberations between governments, holds out great hopes, even if it is an admission of limitations; and national dovetailing of private and public demand is another way in which excessive fluctuations can perhaps be reduced.

It is possible, too, that the League of Nations or some similar form of organization may ultimately play a large part. A great task awaits the world, even with regard to its population problem, not so much in its qualitative as in its quantitative aspects, though the former in these days of democracy and mistaken religious ethics is also urgent. Unless some body, such as the League, undertakes the conscious and deliberate spread of population to areas and centres where it can subsist, it is quite certain that pressure of population alone, caused through its unequal distribution, must be a cause of international friction, if not of war. Without attempting to pass any opinion on the merits or demerits of the case, I fail to see, for example, how for any length of time a continent like Australia, capable of holding a greatly increased population, can be retained for the exclusive use of six million Europeans, when other lands, not too distant from it, are overflowing with teeming life, plentiful as ocean sand. It is just here that the creation of larger economic areas would increase mobility and contribute to a solution of some of our pressing problems for years to come.

Turning to the monetary system of the future, stabilization of the general level of prices is by no means a remote possibility, but is in fact an urgent necessity. A scheme of economic organization like our own based on exchange *must* have a relatively stable unit of exchange, relatively stable, that is, in purchasing power. It is as well, however, to realize that there are many price levels, each fluctuating to a large extent independently of the other, though related in some way. The three price levels of principal importance are:

1. The International Price Level, *i.e.*, the price level of those goods, *e.g.*, wheat, wool, cotton, etc., which are in international demand and whose values at any time are fixed by world factors of supply and demand.
2. The Wholesale Price Level—an internal level.
3. The "Cost of Living" Price Level.

Reference to the value or purchasing power of money is always in relation to the latter price level. Now reasonable stability of this level is absolutely essential, for changes in the value of money, especially rapid and large changes (50 per cent. in the past three years), destroy the basis of the whole economic system, arbitrarily alter every contract, "transfer wealth from one to another, bestow affluence here and embarrassment there and re-distribute Fortune's favour so as to frustrate design and disappoint expectation."[1] The enormous changes in all price levels during recent years are at the root of much of our present trouble, and have drawn forcible attention to the fact that civilized society simply cannot continue to exist in the face of such enormous fluctuations, particularly the heavy fall which we have experienced recently, for in a society whose stimulus is "profit," falling prices reduce that margin or eliminate it altogether and lead to a curtailment of business all round and consequent unemployment—the position throughout the world at present.

This is neither the place, nor have I the time, to enter into a discussion of monetary stabilization, to examine its general desirability, its theoretical and practical possibility, the difficulties to be overcome, the various plans proposed and the methods whereby stability may be achieved. These constitute too big a field for discussion here: they can be studied in appropriate literature. Stabilization, however, does involve management in some form or other, and the degree of management which is postulated by advocates of a managed (and often a paper) currency is not at the moment at all *universally* possible, involving as it does contentions as to aims, ideals and particular interests. For that reason, despite its many faults, both latent and patent, we shall once again,

---

1 *A Tract on Monetary Reform*, Keynes, p. 2.

when this period of distress is over, have to rely largely on the internationally acceptable medium, gold, most probably at levels different from its present level. Though Professor Kemmerer has recently suggested that "the commodity price level will probably rise to something like what it was during the eight-and-a-half-year period of comparatively stable wholesale prices which ended with the stock-market crash of late 1929,"[1] it is quite certain that without a rise in commodity price levels there can be little hope of real recovery from the present depression.

Co-operation between Central Banks may in future help to mitigate the worst features of the international gold standard and bring some semblance of sanity into a disordered monetary system. But a banking system has to be operated by bankers, and, to quote Keynes, "one is often warned that a scientific treatment of currency questions is impossible because the banking world is intellectually incapable of understanding its own problems. If this is true, the order of society which they stand for will decay."[2] Though this was written almost a decade ago, recent experience in this country suggests that it may still contain an element of truth. Banking is still looked upon by many as an occult science, similar in character to religion and metaphysics; and in truth there is much to support that view, particularly as the attitude of bankers themselves lends colour to it. supported by the general air of secrecy which is supposed to surround all banking transactions, the inadequate and unintelligible banking statistics which are usually issued, and the general attitude towards research workers.

Though it would not be true to say that there has been in recent years new sound monetary instruction available which the practical bankers have deliberately ignored, it is nevertheless true that they have not assisted very vitally, if at all, the movement to obtain from banks "exact quantitative information concerning contemporary economic transactions" in order to "eliminate impressionism," as Dr. Miller, of the Federal Reserve Bank, has put it. In this respect, America is far ahead of all other countries,

---

1 "Gold and the Gold Standard," Kemmerer, p. 100. *Proceedings of the American Philosophical Society*, Vol. LXXI, No. 3, 1932.

2 *A Tract on Monetary Reform*, Keynes, Preface, p. vi.

especially Great Britain, where the economic inquirer has been looked on—by the Bank of England and the Big Five alike—as though he were the policeman in the pantomime who warns the fellow under arrest that "everything he says will be taken down, altered and used in evidence against him."[1]

Fuller and more adequate banking statistics, together with a freer access to them, and greater readiness on the part of the banks to adopt the most satisfactory results of such investigations, will greatly assist in the development of a better banking technique for the elimination of unnecessarily wide fluctuations in the value of money. Banking statistics, incidentally, with regard to this country, are extremely meagre and an increase and improvement is urgently necessary. Increasingly in future, too, much of the statistical data of private business, at present available only to accountants, and, by them, for various reasons, completely unutilized, will have to be made accessible.[2]

Before concluding this section on Planning, I venture to repeat some of the suggestions which I made in May last year for a better co-ordination of economic effort.

1. A Permanent International Monetary Council, acting in conjunction with the newly established Bank of International Settlements, the Central Banks of the chief Powers, and also the financial section of the League of Nations, whose chief function would be to study means and ways of obtaining and preserving the highest possible degree of stability of the world general level of prices. Such co-operation is already virtually in existence to some extent between Great Britain, United States and France, through the informal conferences of the Central Bank governors. The above plan would, therefore, be a conscious and deliberate adaptation of existing but indefinite machinery.

2. A General Economic Council for the world, composed of carefully selected and trained representatives from the principal Powers, whose main function would be to work out suitable

---

1 *A Treatise on Money*, Vol. II, Keynes, p. 407.
2 For a good account of this, see *Current Problems in Finance and Government*, by Sir Josiah Stamp, the paper entitled "Economics as an Exact Science—An Appeal to Accountancy."

formulas for the settlement of important world economic problems, *e.g.*, the present urgent problem of international tariffs and the population and racial relation problems.

3. A recognition of the necessity for definite economic training for statesmanship. As an ideal, the democratic form of government may have many advantages, but it has many disadvantages. It was evolved when the emphasis, as regards functions of government, was on constitutional rather than on economic problems, which engage practically the whole time of Parliaments to-day. Though conditions have altered, the organization and machinery for handling them is virtually the same. Competence to sway the fickle public and allegiance to a particular political party can scarcely be regarded as the best qualifications to assist in the solution of present day Parliamentary economic problems. Parliamentarians need training just as much as, if not more than, other "professional" people.

4. Each country should have a General Economic Advisory Council to advise the government on policy. Great Britain has had one for the past three or four years, and the suggestion recently made of one for this country is worthy of the most careful consideration.[1]

5. The dissemination of sound economic knowledge should, in democratic societies, where adult suffrage is applicable to women as well as to men, be regarded as a first necessity.

The Distant Future.

Truly these are the days of pessimism—the optimist is in eclipse, and the prevalent disease is not physical but mental: economic melancholia. Businessmen seem to take delight in commiserating with each other and in agreeing how bad business is, consoling themselves apparently with the thought that it can still get worse. Many are imbued with the idea that we must get back to 1914 values, which by some strange mental twist are regarded as "normal." It would be equally as valid to suggest getting back

---

[1] *Journal of the Economic Society of South Africa*, Vol. IV, Part 2, No. 8, pp. 75-6.

to the sailing ship as the normal form of ocean transport. It is this rigid attitude among bankers which has been mainly responsible for the post-War policy of deflation which has fortunately broken down because the world has been quite unable to carry out its full implications. While there is undoubtedly ground for deep concern, I believe that pessimism has exaggerated the facts of the case and represented the future as much worse than it is likely to be. Though there are about two million unemployed in Great Britain, there are approximately ten times as many usefully employed; though eight million are reputed to be out of work in America, many times more than that number are pursuing their daily avocations. The deep shadows of the economic picture are overemphasized and the highlights underestimated and an entirely wrong perspective is given. With those who predict the end of civilization, and the approach of the second Dark Ages, I can by no means agree. If balance, tolerance and perspective be the qualities of an educated man, it is just such an attitude we should cultivate towards our present difficulties—and since I myself may be accused of over-stressing in this lecture the darker sides of the picture, I want to conclude on a more optimistic though perhaps also somewhat exaggerated note.

Mr. Keynes, in a recent brilliant essay entitled "Economic Possibilities for our Grandchildren,"[1] has sketched an imaginative picture of economic life a century hence. Drawing attention to the enormous rate at which capital accumulates at compound interest (£1 invested at 3¼ per cent. compound in 1580 would now amount to £100,000), he points out that if capital increases at the rate of 2 per cent. per annum it will be, in 100 years' time, seven and a half times as great as it is now, which, translated into terms of material things, houses, transport, machines and capital instruments generally, means an enormous increase in our productive capacity. This, together with the great technical improvements which are every day being made and which at present show themselves in technological unemployment, *i.e.*, unemployment due to our discovery of means of economizing the use of labour outrunning the pace at which we can find new uses for labour, leads him to

---

1   *Essays in Persuasion*, Keynes, p. 358.

draw the conclusion that, assuming no important wars and no important increase in population, the *economic problem* may be solved, or be at least within sight of solution, within a hundred years, and that mankind will therefore be deprived of its traditional purpose, namely, the struggle for subsistence. This will bring in its train difficult problems of adjustment, and of the right use of leisure time. There will be great changes in the code of morals and we shall be able to assess at their true valuation some of the most distasteful of human qualities—such as the love of money as a possession—which are at present exalted into the position of the highest virtues, and shall be set free to return to some of the most sure and certain principles of religion and traditional virtue, and once more value ends above means and prefer the good to the useful. "The *pace* at which we can reach our destination of economic bliss will be governed by four things—our power to control population, our determination to avoid wars and civil dissensions, our willingness to entrust to science the direction of those matters which are properly the control of science, and the rate of accumulation as fixed by the margin between our production and our consumption."

But the time for all this is not yet—the vision is too distant, though it may help us to see things in their true proportions and nerve us to distinguish even now between the means and ends of life. "For what is to be gained by merely heaping up that material wealth with which, in comparison with our spiritual development, civilization is already too heavy? Wealth and ever more wealth. Is this to be our everlasting cry? For ever grasping at the means and forgetting the ends of human life and welfare? The need of the world at the moment is not so much more wealth, but more wisdom in the art of using wealth toward rational aims. This is the slowly attained ideal of the worthiest economic thought of our time. It makes economics not the slave of industry, rather would it make industry the servitor of mankind."[1]

---

[1] *American Economic Review,* March, 1925: "The Economists and the Public," pp. 25-6, by Professor Fetter.

Africa in the Re-Making

By
S. HERBERT FRANKEL
M.A., Ph.D.
Professor of Economics and Economic History

Africa in the Re-Making

We South Africans are not in Africa alone. Our European civilization is in the main the product of successive waves of the dominant world culture of the West.

At least it is foolish for us to attempt to ignore changes in the worldviews on matters that affect our society; at most it may prove extremely dangerous to the future of the South African State.

One sphere in which worldviews have been changing rapidly is in the relationship between Western civilization, the more static cultures of the East and the so-called primitive peoples, such as the Bantu and other Negro tribes of Africa.

It is the fundamental character of this change and its great importance to the citizens of Africa which is my excuse for attempting to deal with the subject of this address, aware as I am of the vast field into which I am entering, armed only with the all-too-inadequate tools of the economist and the economic historian.

Moreover, the method of approach of the economist tends to be unpopular. He is interested primarily in discovering the sequences between social factors, and the discovery of the real sequences is often inconvenient to vested interests and irreconcilable with long-cherished traditional beliefs. But fundamental sequences persist and eventually the scientist succeeds in establishing this truth even in social relationships.

A most fundamental cause of all economic difficulties, apart from the fact of scarcity, is the fact of change in human wants and desires.

Such changes are not, as many think, in themselves merely capricious. They are inherent in the simple fact that it is not possible to guarantee that man at no time in the future shall think otherwise, and therefore act otherwise, than he does today; that at no time he shall change his conception of his environment or his powers over it. We know that these changes may be so slow as to be almost imperceptible or so rapid as to spell tragedy to those subjected to them. But we know also that they can never be eliminated entirely.

Moreover, it is not possible to guarantee that change will always be beneficial to all. On the contrary, it is inherent in the nature of change itself that it is almost invariably detrimental to some, even if it be beneficial to very much greater numbers of others.

Let us take an imaginary example. Assume a pastoral society such as the early Bantu, possessing much land and cattle. Assume next a discovery by one of the group in advance of the other members that the contact with this cattle is the cause of a disastrous disease that has long affected the group. Assume, lastly, that it is decided to kill the cattle and in future to live only upon arable products. The change, quite apart from the ownership of the cattle, is bound to affect many very adversely. Those who have a specialized knowledge of cattle will now have to stand in a personally less desirable relationship to the group. More fundamentally, the group may not be able for a long time to produce as much under the new circumstances as under the old. Their range of activities may be much curtailed, some specialized occupations may become impossible, almost all may have less satisfactions of one kind or another than before, some may even die of starvation. Yet the change may be a most beneficial one for the future of that society, notwithstanding its disastrous effects in the present.

For some three hundred years large areas of the West have been subjected to a rate of change in social relationships much more rapid than that which has taken place in the East.

There is, perhaps, no better way of expressing the nature of the change than by regarding it as an unprecedentedly rapid conquest of distance—a conquest of distance both in the sense of narrowing it by better means of transport and communication, and of widening it by enlarging the horizon, the range of co-operation, and the range of interdependence of social groups and human cultures.

The essential difference between the feudal village society of the Middle Ages and the modern Western State is that in the earlier one the majority of men are, as in India to-day, earthbound and space-bound—bound by the traditions of the past and the exigencies of the present—with little opportunity of moulding the future. They are bound by group loyalties, group seclusions, group fears and group ignorances of other societies and of the outer world. They form small, unconnected, peasant or village economies in which there is little production in excess of the local needs of the producers. Their relatively undifferentiated and unspecialized methods of toil yield the possibility of satisfying only a small range of wants.

Save in the regions given over to nomadism, the human world of a few centuries ago was a world of small localized cultivators, resting "on the indefatigable toil of the man with the plough and spade working in the vicinity."[1] It was a world cut up into innumerable autonomous self-supporting economic units. Men might, as in India or China to-day, starve or be exterminated ruthlessly in one, or feast in superabundance in another, without affecting the well-being even of neighbouring communities, for these groups were neither competitive nor complementary. They affected each other as little as the Basutos in their mountain fastnesses affected the little groups of Voortrekkers subsisting, isolated from the outside world, on the lands they had conquered in the Free State and across the Vaal.

The modern world rests on a different foundation. It depends on the correctly attuned and integrated toil of men in the four corners of the earth.

The secret of the dynamic forces of modern Western society lies in the increased diversification of functions—the division of labour—by means of which the modern State draws into its orbit larger and larger communities for the minutely divided, but at the same time integrated and co-operative work of society. In it fewer than ever before are now the tasks which are both begun and completed by the same individual, or those which are both begun and completed in the same village, in the same town, or even in the same continent. Never before has the space and time span of the work process upon which civilization rests been as lengthy or as dependent on the interacting individual responsibilities of such a variety of men.

It is wrong to picture the dynamic forces of the West as a mere mechanical sub-division of tasks and application of scientific

---

1   Cf. H. G. Wells: *The Work, Wealth and Happiness of Mankind.*

devices. This far-flung world traffic has been made possible only by the evolution of a vast complex system of law, education, and political organization. It depends on the growth of private and social foresight, of civic pride, of state—even of world—loyalties and obligations. It depends on the growth of individual responsibility and personality in the workers of modern society. The substitution of this high degree of individual responsibility for feudal absolutism, slavery, serfdom, gang coercion and ruthless exploitation, is the *sine qua non* of modern development.

The modern developments of Western civilization are impossible on the basis of slavery and serfdom. They depend to an increasing degree on the appeal to the personality and the objective interest in their work of millions of employees, officials and organizers, but not on the coercion of dictators or the commands of autocracies. It makes no difference whether this appeal is solely to mere material reward, or in whole or in part to other motives, such as patriotism or professional pride. The essential point is that the success of modern economic development in the widest sense is inversely related to force and command as incentives to action.

Perhaps one can sum up the whole matter by saying that the West has discovered that in human relationships the longest way round is often the shortest way across and is applying the discovery to an increasing extent. Brute force is the shortest way round. The longer way is characterized by the continuous subdivision of responsibility until men work together at the common tasks of civilization by free objective association with each other.

The future development of Africa, in my opinion, will depend, more than on any other factor, on the method of organization of the efforts of African society. It will depend on the extent to which those efforts are based on mass coercion or on the development of individuality, personality and human dignity.

The problem of Western colonial statesmanship in Africa, as in the East,[1] is today the problem of breaking down the existing static social structure of indigenous peoples and of fostering in its

---

[1] Cf. Dr. A. D. A. de Kat Angelino: *Colonial Policy*, Vol. I. The Hague: Martinus Nijhoff, 1931.

place the growth of societies which will be able to take their place in the new dynamic system of world traffic and world co-operation.

The essential difficulty of that problem is no other than that which Europe itself often failed to appreciate and to deal with adequately throughout the period of transformation during the last few centuries, and particularly in the last 150 years. It is a problem of developing methods of education for social control of, and social defence against, the ruthlessness of the forces of change.

We know the hardships which accompanied the destruction of the old European economic order and the hopelessness of those who were unfitted by the rapidity of the change to find their foothold in the new. We know the strength of the forces of greed and exploitation to which they were subjected, the lack of political and social machinery to prevent their degradation, and the frequent use of their efforts for merely personal gain to the detriment of the real welfare of the society of which they were a part.

The problem of the re-making of Africa is no different in essence from the problems which were involved in the past, and which are still involved in a different degree in the present, in the re-making of Europe.

It is the problem of devising means on the one hand of inaugurating change and on the other of defending those who will be subjected to it against its most serious evils. It is a problem of political and economic organization, and only secondarily one of race or nationality. Lastly, as Dr. de Kat Angelino has rightly stressed,[1] it is a task of leadership that eventually would have been thrown on Eastern or African societies, even if they had not been subjected to conquest by foreign empires.

To the Chartered Companies and the concessionaries of the nations of the West who frantically pegged out Africa from 1882 onwards, the idea would have seemed preposterous in the extreme that the future development of this vast continent would depend less on their thundering commands, their armaments and their diplomatic niceties, than on the successful re-awakening of the long-stagnant society of its indigenous peoples.

---

1 *Loc. cit.*

To most of them it appeared in the first outburst of imperialism that one could colonize Africa in the old sense of the word, *i.e.*, that the Germans could make a German Australia out of Tanganyika, and the French a French Australia out of Senegal.[1] It was simply a question of clearing the continent of everything that stood in the way, whether it be of forests or swamps or Native peoples. The presence of the latter might, in fact, simplify the process, as the Natives could be used to do the clearing and exploiting of natural resources in the same way as elephants can usefully be employed to assist in the work of clearing the Indian jungle.

In so far as any of these Europeans thought of the future of Africa at all, and were interested in more than the shares and dividends of their companies in Berlin, Paris, Brussels and London, they thought of it as a land which would be developed by millions of men and money from Europe, in the same way as America had been developed by a like process. They, like their fellow imperialists who opened up the diamond and gold mines of South Africa, saw an unending stream of immigrants follow in the wake of the hasty trail they were blazing; hordes of immigrants that would utilize and swamp, perhaps eventually even exterminate, the Native peoples.

Of course, in the crudest of the stages of exploitation, whether it be exploitation in the form of soil robbery, which completely destroys the fertility of the land, or whether it be the ruthless destruction of human beings, there is no thought for the future at all. This kind of exploitation is, as is well known, illustrated by the policy of King Leopold of Belgium in the Congo Free State, which he declared was formed for the purpose of promoting the civilization and commerce of Africa, and for other humane and benevolent purposes."

In accordance with this aim, he destroyed the peoples of the Congo in the same way as modern whaling fleets are exterminating the whale.

Open extermination of this kind eventually meets with humanitarian opposition, and it is usual to ascribe the cessation

---

[1] Cf. Stephen H. Roberts: *The History of French Colonial Policy*, Vol. II. London: P. S. King & Son, 1929.

of this policy in the Congo to the world outcry which it finally aroused.

The policy, however, has to be discontinued, in any case, for another reason, namely, the eventual shortage of labour with which the resources of the land can be carried away.

In the next stage of Congo policy there was still the assumption that one could simply appropriate the wealth of Africa by brute force. The Congo authorities now embarked on an open and official policy of reducing the whole indigenous population to semi-slavery. This change was brought about also by the realization that large areas of Africa, such as the Congo, were not colonizable except on the basis of the labour of black men.

Roberts[1] has summed up this phase of Congo policy as follows:

"In detail, the Belgian theory meant the initial destruction of all that was vital in Native life and then the reduction of the amorphous mass that remained to the status of a vast black proletariat."

By every means possible, the Belgian authorities for years smashed the social organization of the indigenous population until "they could resort to direct administration without the intermediary of any native officials either old or new . . . This policy sums up the history of the French Congo and of certain other French colonies in Africa as well. . . The Natives were refused rights; regional guards dragooned them into slavery; all unoccupied land was viewed as belonging to the State, and the interests of the concessionary with whom the Government worked in a narrow collaboration alone counted."

This policy largely remained in force until about 1917, when the Belgians were brought up at last against the uselessness of enslavement as a method of production in the modern world economy. As long as their main consideration had been the mere draining of rubber from the Congo rivers, slavery was still possible.

"When, however," says Roberts,[1] "after about 1917 the draining stage was over and production needed to be fostered artificially, the newer considerations (such as the British policy of

---

1 *History of French Colonial Policy*, Vol. II, p. 668.

indirect rule and the development of Native peoples on their own lines) obtained a hearing."

In other words, when colonization in the Congo became an industrial proposition, more was needed than the military commands of the governing State on the one hand (even although it enforced its decrees by black officials), and the disorganized, illiterate, uneducated rabble proletariat on the other.

Finally, the Belgian Minister of Colonies announced in 1920:

"We absolutely break with the policy of assimilation. We claim that the Native society should freely develop after its own manner, its own nature, its own milieu. We must respect and *develop* Native institutions and not as heretofore break them."[1]

There is nothing really surprising in this Belgian conversion. Other colonizing nations and, in particular, the Dutch in the East Indies, had long discovered the same basic facts. Today, after going through all the stages of colonization which are possible on the assumption that the real development of indigenous populations can be ignored or can be dictated, the Dutch have become the pioneer reformers in dealing with the problems which arise in the impact between more developed and less developed cultures. The basis of their policy is that of the maximum possible Native self-government consistent with native social development. They aim at the maximum Native economic development. The latter is fostered by every means possible, *e.g.*, by co-operative agricultural banks, by model agricultural colonies, by agricultural demonstrators, by encouraging Native proprietorship, and by endeavouring to facilitate the growth of a cultured Native middle and professional class, and by special educational measures.

The Germans, as is well known, ruthlessly adopted the policy of the iron hand, in the belief that Native interests must be bludgeoned into subordination to the economic interests of Germany. But they found that this policy was not compatible with their many attempts to increase the production of the colonies by scientific measures. Already by 1907 their policy was being

---

1   Roberts, *loc. cit.*, p. 670.

challenged by prominent colonial experts,[1] and they were beginning to move towards the same system of Native welfare, both as regards Native officials and Native plantations, that the British were working out in Nigeria and East Africa.

Nowhere can the dead hand of a bureaucratic, over-centralized control and dictatorship of indigenous peoples be seen more clearly than in the French colonies, particularly those in Africa, notwithstanding the considerable degree of sympathy which is developed in many directions between the French and indigenous populations. The destruction in most of the French territories of Native institutions, and their government by French European officials down to the very lowest ranks, as if they were a province of France, has made the French colonies the least developed economically in Africa.

In every direction in Western colonial policy one finds, both on humanitarian and on economic grounds, attempts to reverse the policy of exploitation of the past. Everywhere there is at least a definite tendency to move towards the modern British colonial policy of allowing these colonies to develop as independent social groups allied to the mother country by ties which are as loose as circumstances permit.

It has at last been realized fully that the wealth of Africa does not lie ready to hand in the way in which the imperialistic optimists of the nineteenth century apparently thought. It will have to be developed, unearthed and constructed by the labour of many generations and with the help of every scientific device that Western civilization has been able to evolve in the fight with Nature. Obviously, the application of science in this way requires the highest degree of skilled effort in the populations that make use of it.

---

1   For example, by the Colonial Minister, Bernard Dernburg, and by Schultz, who gave practical expression to his system in New Guiana, and insisted that "our colonies are colonies of plantations by and for the natives and their future depends entirely on the cultural development of the natives" (quoted by Roberts, *loc. cit.*, Vol. II, p. 666).

We know today that the dream of a flow of millions of immigrants from Europe to Africa, to develop its resources, is an idle one. It is, in my opinion, an idle one even in those areas where the climate permits of the white man's becoming an actual labourer. The trend of the population of Western Europe is in the reverse direction to that which inspired the optimism of the nineteenth century.[1]

Moreover, I believe that in the future the populations of the West will be more chary of the manner in which they will sacrifice capital for the development of other continents than they were under that particular organization of Western society in the nineteenth century, which so very much favoured the appropriation of capital by certain sections for use wherever it seemed to yield the greatest amount of immediate private profit.

The resources for the development of Africa will depend increasingly on the social and economic progress of Africans themselves. Much of the capital naturally will have to be created by Africans who have been taught how to create it, how to conserve and how to apply it in the best directions.

It is absurd to assume, as some who speak about the development of the Native peoples on their own lines do, that this knowledge and these enormous changes can be left to the initiative of the Native peoples themselves. European civilization is essential to the development of Africa. As the Hilton Young Commission has pointed out:

"Its religion, its stores of literature, political experience and scientific knowledge, its wealth of material resources, hold out, if European civilization gives of its best, the one great hope of progress in Africa. Western science is alone capable of combating the diseases by which the continent is ravaged. Through Western science alone can its great agricultural possibilities be realized. Only from non-Natives can the Native peoples obtain the education which will enable them to advance to higher levels of civilization and to turn to advantage the natural resources of their land."

Those who assert that European nations have a great task before them in Africa are not making merely hypocritical statements. As De Kat Angelino, in his remarkable book on Dutch

---

1 Cf. League of Nations: *World Economic Survey*, 1931-1932, p. 12.

colonial policy, has rightly stressed, the policy of abstention by European Powers in the development of native territories, due to ignorance, misplaced sentimentality, or sheer inertia (as appears to exist in certain of the British Protectorates adjoining the Union), is as much to be condemned as the policy of enslavement and extermination. The real problem of colonization is therefore the problem of knowing at what rate to bring about modifications or to destroy, and how to replace what has been destroyed.

Now the basic difference between the attitude towards this vital question which characterized past and which characterizes modern tendencies in colonial policy can be expressed as follows:

In the past, European and other immigrants decided what should be destroyed in African culture on the basis of what it was in their interests—that is, in effect, what it was in the interests of exploitation, plantation, mining companies and agricultural settlers to destroy. Everywhere the decision was solely in the interests of the European. Whether by military force, by taxation, by economic pressure or by legislation, the Natives were deprived of their land, taxed heavily to drive them into the labour market, forced to work at purely artificial rates of remuneration, or without remuneration at all, taught what the settlers thought was good for them to know, prevented from building up any personal resources which might make them in every way economically independent, and robbed of opportunities of developing new forms of self-government.

The new colonial philosophy rests on an entirely different assumption. It is based on the appreciation of the fact that only that must be destroyed in the primitive culture of indigenous peoples which hampers the development of that culture to a higher level of human personality, dignity and achievement. Only that must be destroyed which it is in the real interests of the societies of the indigenous peoples themselves to destroy, and they themselves must be harnessed voluntarily to the task of transformation.

It is the policy of achieving what Alfred Zimmern[1] has so happily named *the Principle of the International Cultural Minimum*—the

---

1 "The Cultural Causes of War" in *The Causes of War*, Edited by Arthur Porrit. Macmillan, 1932

principle, that is, of destroying those elements in the differently developed cultures of the world which prevent further growth to a higher synthesis of world cultures. It involves, therefore, the elimination of specific evils in less developed cultures, such as illiteracy, ignorance, superstition, animism, serfdom, slavery and caste, and not the attempt to exterminate those cultures themselves, even if such extermination were possible.

It is deeply significant that the Hilton Young Commission categorically recognized the principle that immigrant settlement in Africa, in so far as it is allowed free rein, must invariably enslave and destroy, instead of developing the cultures of primitive peoples, unless the rights of those peoples are safeguarded by every known device; for example, unless they retain possession of their land and can therefore bargain freely for the fair remuneration of any labour they are required by immigrant settlers to perform, and unless they are given the greatest possible opportunity of education to enable them to assert their individuality and to bring about the growth of their own social institutions in a manner in harmony with the development of the modern world.

It is equally significant that the British Government, in accepting the principle so emphatically enunciated by the Hilton Young Commission, laid it down that, quite apart from moral issues, "repression is not a possible course, not only because it is contrary to the declared policy of His Majesty's Government, but because conditions are such today that any attempt to persist in such a policy is doomed to failure."

These principles having been accepted, it was not possible to shirk the logical conclusion that the interests of the native peoples in British territories in East and Central Africa must be regarded as paramount.

The Hilton Young Commission defined paramountcy as follows:

"According to our view, the paramountcy of native interests is to be interpreted in the sense that the creation and preservation of a field for the full development of Native life is the first charge on any territory, and that the Government having created this field has a duty to devote all available resources to assisting the Natives to develop within it."

A later Joint Committee on Closer Union in East Africa stresses the great importance of "giving the fullest security to the legitimate interests of European settlers." It summed up the doctrine of paramountcy by saying "that the interests of the overwhelming majority of the indigenous population should not be subordinated to those of a minority belonging to another race, however important in itself."

We see thus in East and Central Africa the progress of a far-reaching experiment. The multitudinous practical and theoretical difficulties of that important experiment can be appreciated only by those who have followed the practical work that is being done in territories such as Tanganyika, and the bitter discussion between His Majesty's Government and the settlers in Kenya. In these territories the attempt is being made at last to put into practice those new principles concerning the development of backward peoples and the culture contacts between advanced and more primitive civilizations which inspired the clause in the covenant of the League of Nations that "to those colonies and territories ... which are inhabited by peoples not yet able to stand by themselves under the strenuous conditions of the modern world, there should be applied the principle that the wellbeing and development of such peoples form a sacred trust of civilization. . .."

But in that experiment, we must note that His Majesty's Government, like the Government of the Netherlands and of certain other Western Powers, at least has one very considerable advantage. These governments are in a position at any rate to endeavour to act impartially and to bring the full power of their national cultures to bear in holding the scales evenly, so as, in the words of the Hilton Young Commission, "to ensure that the contact of races produces no serious friction and that it does not lead to demoralization on either side."

In self-governing territories, as, for example, in Southern Rhodesia, with their strongly entrenched European civilization with vested interests, the problem of holding the scales evenly or of righting the injustices of the past becomes far more difficult, perhaps even impossible.

At any rate, in Southern Rhodesia there is hope that vested interests are not yet so strong as to prevent the adoption of those policies which will obviate the evils and excesses of culture contacts elsewhere. That this has been realized by the governments concerned is itself a good omen for the future.

What, then, is the position in the Union? Without doubt, the problem facing the people of this country is far more difficult than that confronting any other European power in Africa, and perhaps any colonizing power in the world. And this for three reasons:

First, because the Union of South Africa is a self-governing Dominion on the basis of adult franchise for all European men and women. This means that the democracy is placed in the position, although influenced as it is by the most far-reaching vested interests, of being the judge in its own cause. There is no strong impartial authority to hold the scales evenly between the different races and sectional interests.

Second, because in South Africa we are faced with problems which result from the fact that those who opened up the country after the gold and diamond discoveries and during the period of European capitalist expansion, were confronted, not only by primitive Native races as in the rest of Africa, but also by a European society which was still at a level of economic development at least two, and perhaps three, hundred years behind that of the new immigrants.

Economic imperialism in South Africa, therefore, exploited two civilizations weaker than its own, and it is well to remember that it was not only the Native who frequently sold his birthright for the then proverbial African standard of value—a bottle of gin. To this day South Africa is faced with the difficulty that it still harbours at least three levels of civilization—that of the Natives, that of those Europeans who have not yet emerged from the patriarchal traditions of the original settlers and are mainly pastoralists (or of those who have fallen below this stage), and, lastly, that of those who are definitely fitted for the modern European capitalistic society which South Africa strives to be. The struggle of these different levels of civilization continues to this day and provides the real clue to the bitterness of the backvelder against the European uitlander; for the uitlander destroyed and is further destroying his seventeenth-century civilization in a manner just as fatal to him as that in which the Voortrekkers uprooted the primitive society of the Native tribes.

Third, because the bearers of modern capitalist enterprise went to work in South Africa in the same way as elsewhere. They assumed that the country had not only mineral but also unbounded agricultural wealth. They assumed, as usual, that an unending stream of immigrants would follow them as a matter of course. They assumed that the land was blessed with inexhaustible Native labour resources which they had the right to use at negligible rates of remuneration and on the basis that the Native peoples were to be hewers of wood and drawers of water always, never to take a part in the determination of the future South African State. In their hurry, too, they naturally ignored the difference between those who still lived in the seventeenth century and those who were fitted for the twentieth.

The Native peoples in South Africa, as a result of the policy of the past, have in effect been reduced economically to that amorphous black proletariat which the Belgian authorities deliberately created in the Congo Free State. These people have no real bulwark against gross economic exploitation.

As the Native Economic Commission, 1930-32, has put on official record at last, the Reserves, instead of assisting the Native, are so overcrowded that farming in them in accordance with their present organization has become practically impossible. As a consequence, the poverty in these areas is so great that it leads to the periodic emigration of the larger part of the male population to seek work elsewhere and to provide ready cash for the heavy taxation it has to bear.

Let us be quite clear as to why this is so. The Native in South Africa is not allowed to own or lease land except in the inadequate Native reserves. He is forced by taxation and starvation into a labour market so overcrowded that he has to accept a wage which, in practically all occupations, is not sufficient to support a small Native family in the towns, and which is nothing but a subsistence wage, often in kind only, in the country. By law, by strict convention and by trade union restriction, he is prevented from doing skilled work or work that involves the handling of machinery. The breaking of his contract of service is a criminal offence. His existence in the country without his having attached himself to an employer has just been made a criminal offence also. Even his being unemployed in most urban areas is treated as a crime. The meagre educational facilities the State provides for the Native peoples is not enough to educate approximately one-fifth of the Native child population even up to Standards I and II.

"I deny," wrote Leonard Wolf, in his *Imperialism and Civilization*, "that any European government in the twentieth century can claim to be civilized if it spends 20 per cent. more on providing penal servitude and hard labour for its subjects than it does in providing them with education."

Yet the Union Government still spends more[1] on native prisons, reformatories and police than on native education.

In other words, no better example could be found of a European policy towards the subject race being framed solely in what is regarded as the interest of the European population than the policy of the democracy of the Union of South Africa. Let it not be thought that this is the will of only the propertied sections of the community. In 1916 the trade union and labour representatives of the European miners on the Witwatersrand gave the European workers of South Africa the unique distinction of suggesting publicly that it would be an advantage to let the State work the mines because then it could employ in them Native convict labour instead of recruited Native labourers. This, they alleged, would be much cheaper and would thus improve the position of the European miner.

We have pursued in the past and are still pursuing that policy of economic enslavement which stands condemned in the light of all modern economic development and the experience of every Western European colonizing power.

Stretched across the enormous area encompassed within the frontiers of the Union of South Africa, there lies a skeleton superstructure of twentieth-century civilization and economic activity. But the foundation is one of economic slavery and serfdom, illiteracy, ignorance and exploitation.

It cannot be urged too strongly that the hurried erection of the superstructure has caused not only Native but also European problems of culture contacts to be ignored. The European democracy in South Africa has refused even to face the need for passing those fundamental legislative measures, such as the alterations in land tenure and land ownership, which would protect and assist those Europeans in the country who have not yet found a foothold in the economic system of the twentieth century.

The prevention and punishment of Native crime cost the Union, not 20 per cent., but 147 per cent. more than Native education! It should be noted that Native crime in the Union is to the greatest extent merely a breach of restrictive statutes and regulations involving no moral offence whatever. This is clearly shown by an analysis of the criminal statistics referred to in the Commission's Report, for which see an article "Native Crime and Education," by Professor Edgar H. Brookes, *Rand Daily Mail*, September, 1932.

My purpose in referring to this matter, with which I have dealt fully elsewhere,[12] is to emphasize that the Poor White problem also is basically a problem of social and economic organization, differing only in degree from the so-called Native problem. There are some who think this problem can be solved by that form of scientific experimentation which is so dear to the hearts of pig and cattle breeders. But in my opinion there is no more hope of

---

1 Cf. *Coming of Age – Studies in South African Citizenship and Politics*, Section III, Chapter I, *"Problems of Economic Inequality."* Maskew Miller, Cape Town, 1930.

2 The Report of the Native Economic Commission contains very interesting statistics on this subject. The figures quoted are for 1929-30, the last completely audited set of figures available for the Commission.

The total expenditure on education for Natives in the Union was...	£591,698
The expenditure in the prevention and punishment of crime has been carefully investigated by the Commission and is as follows:	
Prisons and Reformatories	£528,468
Police...	800,000
Fines and Forfeitures	133,000
Total	£1,461,468

success in that direction than there would be if we attempted to deal with the Native peoples of Africa on the basis of a classification of their cranial capacity.

We are faced in this country with the enormous and ever more urgent task of developing and raising not one but two different cultures in order to prevent their demoralizing exploitation and to fit them into the economic organization which characterizes the Western world economy.

The high standard of life of the skilled European workers and the professional and businessmen in the present monopolistic European economy is a form of living on the fat of the land which may be possible when the European community is small or is not settling permanently and extending. But once this is no longer the case, even that standard of life will be affected for good or ill, and to an ever increasing degree, by the general level of productivity of the country as a whole. The larger the privileged section grows, the less becomes the possibility of maintaining an artificial relationship which assumes that South Africa can be divided into two separate economies, one primitive and poverty-stricken, the other yielding the highest standards of European civilization.

Notwithstanding the dreams of the imperialists who opened up South Africa, the truth is that this country is a land which is relatively poor agriculturally and which can be made to yield abundant riches only if wooed by the application of the most modern scientific knowledge and devices. From the pages of the Report of the Native Economic Commission there emerges an appalling picture of the results which are accruing from the failure to apply effort organized on modern lines to the land of this country.

The Commission found that the policy of the past under which the development of Native Reserves has been neglected in every way by European governments, has led to "a state of affairs in which, with the exception of a few favoured parts, the Native area can be distinguished at sight by its bareness, and which unless soon remedied will, within one or, at the outside two, decades, create in the Union an appalling problem of Native poverty."

The Commission came to the conclusion that "unless precautionary measures are taken against overstocking, the condition in the Transkei and the Native areas in the rest of the Union will be to-morrow what that of the Ciskei is today. The same causes are at work there, and they will inevitably produce the same effects in the near future—denudation, donga-erosion, deleterious plant succession, destruction of woods, drying-up of springs, robbing the soil of its reproductive properties—in short, the creation of desert conditions. . . . In agriculture the baneful effects of primitive subsistence economy show themselves in wholesale soil-robbery, which, save in a few localities where European agricultural methods have penetrated, seems to be the only kind of field husbandry known to the Native."

The Commission certainly realized the threat to the whole economic structure of the Union that is involved in this disastrous state of affairs. It even took its courage as far into its hands as can be expected from government officials and servants of a democracy like ours, and stated "that there need be no threat to the white community in the development of the Native, but that on the contrary this offers some hope of removing many of the economic maladjustments which exist today."

Some hope! In my opinion, in the economic development of the Native peoples lies the only hope for the future of this country. I think the question has long ceased to be one of halfhearted attempts at holding the scales a little more or a little less evenly as between white and black. It has become a question of the future standard of life of the whole population. It is a question of whether this country will advance economically or decline. We must not allow ourselves to be blinded by the artificial prosperity which we have obtained in the past from the intensive extraction of treasure—of gold and diamonds. We must ask what is being done to build up a sound modern structure for permanent economic production and development.

After presenting such a trenchant commentary on the underdeveloped nature of this country and the primitive organization of its economic efforts, one looks to the Commission for constructive suggestions for the future.

For the most part, however, I can find only a series of pious resolutions, so vaguely formulated that another Commission will be required to examine how they can be realized, unless, as is much more likely, the resolutions are ignored by South African politicians altogether. The following extracts are typical of the vague character of many of the statements which take the place of practical suggestions in the Report:

Par. 77: "It would be unwise to try to leave the Native in this fool's paradise. His light is insufficient for the new conditions of life. His mind must be freed from his animistic conceptions if he is to create worthy conditions for his descendants. He must learn to school his body to hard work, which is not only a condition to his advance in civilization, but of his final survival in a civilized environment."

Par. 79: "It is essential to put a stop to the ruination which is taking place on all sides, to introduce among the Natives a leaven of social education which will gradually, step by step, free the masses from their anti-progressive social heritage; and to create the economic conditions for their adjustment to the environment brought by civilization."

The Commissioners continually stress the fact that "in the economic development of the Reserves must inevitably be sought the main solution of the Native economic problem . . ." and that "unless this is undertaken soon and on a large scale the country must assuredly expect . . . the rapid extension of the process of ruination which is now almost everywhere in evidence."

Yet when we come to ask how this pressing need for development is to be brought about we are given only two fundamental suggestions. The first is the platitudinous hope, continuously repeated and continuously ignored both before and since Union, that more land will be provided by the European democracy for an extension of the Native Reserves. I do not think its practicability needs further comment. The second is the very startling and courageous suggestion that instead of the present 155 Native demonstrators at work in the Union there should, on the basis, we are told, of intricate statistical calculations of the Director of Native Agriculture, be a minimum of four hundred such demonstrators.

Apparently the additional 245 "shock troop" demonstrators will do all that is necessary in what the Commission calls "a race against time to prevent the destruction of large grazing areas, the erosion and denudation of the soil and the drying-up of springs."

These four hundred intensively trained demonstrators, if they use the Report of the Commission as a textbook, will have some very interesting things to say to their people.

They will make clear to the Native that he must fence his land, that he must not over-stock it, that he must repair dongas, that he must improve the water supply, that he must construct irrigation works, that he must reclaim many areas that are badly eroded, that afforestation is a very good thing and that "each location should have its plantation or plantations properly fenced and properly controlled as regards the right to cut wood."

They will tell him that each man should have larger areas of land to till—notwithstanding the fact that, for example, in the seven surveyed areas of the Transkei, there are already about eleven thousand married hut-owners who can get no arable plots at all. They will tell him also that he should educate himself, and, what I think he must have heard on many previous occasions from Europeans, that *he* at any rate should *work* harder!

At the same time, they will make clear to him that the "colour bar" in the towns is not to be removed, that he is still not to be allowed to purchase or lease land in European areas, that the Commission cannot recommend any alterations in the burdens of taxation that it lays upon him or in the negligible contributions that it makes from its revenues for undertakings that directly affect his welfare, that it does not favour any wage regulation to protect him in the towns, and holds out practically no hope of improvement in his terms of employment in the country.

What the four hundred demonstrators, however, will not be able to tell from the Report is where the capital for developing and improving the barren Native Reserves is to come from. It will be difficult even for them to explain where the mere labour for the carrying out of this paper Five-Year Plan in the Reserves is to be obtained in view of the fact that the greater part of the Native male working population is forced by taxation and starvation to work in European areas. As soon as the depression lifts the European economy is not likely, in any case, to want to spare these Native labourers.

The Commission, however, is good enough to make it clear where capital and other resources, such as those needed for education, will *not* come from. "Even if it were possible," they announce categorically, "it is manifestly undesirable for the European population to shoulder the burden."

The basic reason for the unsatisfactory nature of the proposals of this Commission is, in my opinion, quite clear. It is because the Commissioners in fact tried to square the circle.

They looked for ways and means of inaugurating a fundamental change in the economic structure of the Union—on one condition, that the change was not to inconvenience one single enfranchised citizen and was not to encroach on any of his vested rights. To endeavour to find ways of inaugurating change and at the same time to guarantee that everybody will remain in the same position as before is to attempt the impossible.

In my opinion, the solutions suggested by the Commission are useless in the form in which they are put forward. In reality, they are based on the fallacious assumption that it is possible to continue to ensure the European a standard of life based on the exploitation and definite restriction of Native development in about nine-tenths of the Union, and yet at the same time to enable the exploited to raise themselves in the economic scale in the remaining one-tenth, provided there is no burden upon, and the greatest possible measure of isolation from, the European economy.

The Commission has clothed this assumption in a mass of no doubt interesting and in part probably quite true anthropological wisdom concerning Native custom, folklore, superstition, mentality, marriage rites and what-not.

But it all does not avail to alter the basic fact that the Union cannot be developed in two separate water-tight compartments.

Whatever the development of the Native people along their own lines may mean, there is one thing that assuredly it does not, and in the Union cannot, mean. It cannot mean that we should create in the Union areas in which Natives will just be enabled to reach that stage of economic development which will support the largest Native population within the smallest compass and without migration to the European economy, and in which the main incentive to, and rate of, change will depend on a few hundred South African Government and Native officials, and on the resources the European democracy is willing to vote for this purpose.

Moreover, there is reason to believe that the only possibility of obtaining capital for a real measure of Native development and education in the Reserves lies in the possibility of attracting back to these areas savings which the Native is enabled to accumulate by being given the opportunity of more productive work, and a higher level of skill, in the European economy.

In all countries a large part of the capital needed for agriculture is raised from urban areas by the return migration of men and women with savings to invest in the land, who take the place of others that failed and left it.

In South Africa, owing to the artificial restrictions to which I have referred, the Native in practice is precluded from accumulating savings. The margin of savings is appropriated by the European population and a large part of it is dissipated in continuous consumption by those Europeans who are living at a higher standard of life than their real productivity warrants.

I do not wish to belittle the value of some of the general suggestions the Commission has made as to the crying need for almost every form of Native development that can be devised, and its arduous efforts to portray the present state of affairs accurately. But I believe that the Commission, nevertheless, has not gone to the root of the problem.

The fact is that poverty, soil erosion, drought, very low productivity, ignorance of modern methods and general economic under-development are not confined to the Native Reserves. They are found scattered all over South Africa. In fact, as I have shown in detail elsewhere[1] low productivity and inefficiency are a characteristic feature of the Union in agriculture and manufacturing industry in comparison with the other Dominions. They are the result mainly of the methods of serf and semi-slave labour that this country has adopted throughout its economic organization.

Unfortunately, it is useless, I think, to hope any longer that the European democracy will voluntarily and consciously subject itself to the inconveniences of change that are implied in a systematic alteration of this system. For this reason, the only alternative, that of allowing economic forces a greater degree of freedom to take

---

1 *Coming of Age, loc. Cit.*

their own course, must be adopted. We must—for that is apparently the only way we will get change at all—gradually remove the artificial restrictions on the labour, on the earning capacity, on the mobility from one occupation to another, and on the acquirement of skill, imposed upon the Native peoples in the European areas. The Europeans in this country must be prepared to shoulder the direct and indirect burdens and hardships of such changes in a higher direction or be subjected to changes in a lower. One thing is certain, it will be impossible for long to continue to maintain the present *status quo*. The Europeans in this country must either cease to be economic jailers or be dragged down to the level of the prisoners in the jail.

There are, as I have written elsewhere,[1] many who realize that the time for choosing which road South Africa must take is at hand. There is the artisan who can find no work for his son; there is the manufacturer who suffers from the restricted South African market; and there are the younger men at the University who watch with growing alarm the gradual ruination of both white and black on the land. They know the great potentialities of the Native worker, and know that the policy of restriction is preventing the development of South Africa's resources. But they cannot give practical shape to their ideals and hopes, for the mass of the voters of South Africa are still the landowners who desire no change and the Poor Whites who have not yet realized that the policy which keeps down the Native is the same policy as has been responsible for their own ruin.

A minority still hopes for the statesman with the courage to lead the country away from the traditions of the past. It realizes that South Africa must begin the construction of a State which is at least economically united, and which will not shirk its responsibility for the backward civilizations which it harbours; which stands as a co-partner with the other nations of the Western world, unafraid to move in step with the great changes which are taking place in the worldview of cultural relationships and the desire to base them on a higher appreciation of human dignity.

---

1 *International Affairs,* June, 1931.

Old Truths and New Discoveries

By
R. F. ALFRED HOERNLE
M.A., B.Sc.
Professor of Philosophy

Old Truths and New Discoveries

To speak on behalf of Philosophy to a modern audience is not easy. The man in the street often wonders what philosophy is about. The man of science generally is quite sure that it is about nothing. The easiest way of evoking a laugh from either is to repeat, as was done during this course of lectures by one of the proposers of a vote of thanks, the ancient tag that a philosopher is like a blind man in a dark room seeking for a black cat that is not there.

No wonder that my feelings are a little like those recently expressed by my old friend and former colleague at Harvard, Professor R. B. Perry, in his witty *Defence of Philosophy*: "There are many drawbacks to being a professor of philosophy, and one of the worst is that you cannot gossip lightly about your occupation. Picture yourself in that great American forum and social centre, the smoking compartment of a Pullman car. There has been an exchange of confidences about the boot and shoe industry in St. Louis, or the boot-legging industry in Detroit, when your neighbour turns to you and asks, amid a hush of expectancy, what *you* sell. To be as candid and optimistic as your neighbours, you would be compelled to say: 'My firm manufactures and distributes ultimate truth; our business is to discover the nature of the Universe, and apply it to the meaning of life.' Some sound instinct prevents you from saying it. You know that you would create a situation which neither you nor your neighbours would be able to support, much as though you were to say: '*I* am God.' So you hastily mumble something about being a teacher, hoping they won't insist on knowing the subject you teach—and then pass rapidly on to safer subjects, such as the hard winter we've been having or how late the train is."

I was tempted to ease the difficulty for myself by dealing with some special problem, such as the familiar question, again discussed by Sir Alfred Ewing before the British Association, whether we have developed the minds necessary to control the material civilization which we have created; or the present moral crisis, even graver than the economic one, in which humanity flounders.

However, had I yielded to this temptation, I should hardly have been true to my conviction that a philosopher should, above all else, strive to be "synoptic"; that his task is, so far as he may, "to see things together." Moreover, General Smuts, in his opening lecture on "Some Recent Scientific Advances in their Bearing on Philosophy," clearly means by "philosophy" our general worldview, and a general worldview, however fragmentary it may be in fact, none the less embodies an attempt at a synoptic grasp of things. In winding up our course of lectures, I feel myself, therefore, under an obligation to draw at least some of the many threads of the argument together. And I do not think I can do this better than by dealing with three topics from the previous lectures, viz., the breakdown of determinism in physical science; some philosophical aspects of evolution; and the economic paradox of a machine-age civilization. To these, I shall add a topic of my own which it has not been within the province of anyone else to touch on, viz., religion.

1.—*The Breakdown of Determinism.*

Both General Smuts and Professor Dalton have laid stress on the breakdown of determinism in physical science. They both have told us of "revolutionary" changes in the outlook of contemporary physics. They both have assured us that in the "microscopic" realm of electrons and protons, Nature is no longer thought to be deterministic. Needless to say, I accept the facts which they state concerning the changes of view among leading physicists of our day. But when they assert that these facts have revolutionary consequences for philosophy, then, as a philosopher, I have both the right and the duty to exercise my own judgment.

Before coming to details, let me make two general observations.

First, the influence which science, and changes in scientific opinion, can and ought to exercise upon philosophy is easily overrated. If a philosopher is, for example, a spiritual pluralist, like Berkeley or Leibniz, Lotze or McTaggart, no change in physical theories can possibly affect or upset his conclusions, simply because these are based on considerations to which no theories from the realm of physical science are relevant at all. If a philosopher holds that the physical realm is but the sensuous appearance of relations between spiritual beings, no revolutions in the way in which physical science, which limits itself to the study of these appearances, interprets the facts before it, can either conflict with, or support, a philosophical theory which moves on an altogether different plane. Similarly, if an Indian philosopher regards the whole world of the senses as *maya*, or illusion, he will maintain this view, and, from his standpoint, correctly, whatever theories may at any time prevail in physical science.

Moreover, secondly, this difference of plane applies even if one is not an adherent of either of the two philosophies mentioned. For, ever since Kant, the chief concern of philosophy in relation to science has been the twofold one of (*a*) leaving science entirely free on its own plane and within its own limits, and (*b*) insisting at the same time that there *are* limits; that there *are* other planes of thought. Science is a method of thinking about a certain field of experience. There it makes and unmakes its theories, develops and rejects its concepts, employs even deliberate fictions; in short, enjoys itself in whatever intellectual experiments promise to bring it nearer to its goal of understanding the facts it deals with. Philosophy enters only in order to remind the scientist of something which, in his eagerness, he is apt to forget, viz., that he does not exhaust the field of experience, and that there are other fields of it with their own methods of thinking. What, for example, can the student of "matter in motion" contribute to the man whose thoughts are engaged with our experience of beauty, or with moral ideals, or with God? Now, the philosopher, in pursuit of his synoptic ideal, surveys all these fields and methods, and claims thereby to become in some sort an expert in methods of thinking; in other words, a logician.

It is as a logician that I am interested in the breakdown of determinism.

Now, determinism is an ambiguous word, and the breakdown of determinism, consequently, can also mean more than one thing. It will help us to have a definite statement before us, and I quote the one which Professor Dalton gives in his lecture. He there says that classical mechanics rested on two principles, viz., "that every effect is due to some antecedent cause . . . and that the linkage between cause and effect is necessarily continuous." And he went on to say that the application of these principles to everything in the Universe depends on two assumptions, viz., that "we (*i.e.*, human beings with minds and wills) are but material systems, and that the material universe is itself deterministic." He added that "if either of these beliefs prove unsound, then determinism must seek its justification elsewhere."[1]

We must, I think, here make a distinction. The principle that every effect has an antecedent cause is completely general. There is nothing either said or implied in it which requires that every cause and every effect must be a material thing or event, or that the principle applies only in the material world. It is logically perfectly possible to have a "deterministic" psychology, without having also a "materialistic" psychology, *i.e.*, without saying that mind is really matter. Psychology may use the principle of cause and effect and still maintain that it deals with mind, not with matter.

But where Professor Dalton is right—it is, in fact, common ground between him and General Smuts and myself—is in saying that there is more in the universe, even for science, than material systems. In other words, the determinism which is also materialism has, we agree, broken down. Determinism, in this sense of the word, is usually called "mechanism," or the "mechanical theory of Nature," and its sting lies in its application to biology and, through extreme behaviourism, even to psychology, where it then means that every phenomenon exhibited by a living, and even by a conscious and intelligent, being can be exhaustively explained by purely physico-chemical laws. It is the claim that the laws of the inorganic suffice also for the organic, and that the phenomena of life and mind require no other concepts and laws for their explanation than those which suffice in physics and chemistry. On the necessity of discarding determinism in this sense we are agreed. But what we are discarding, I maintain, is the *materialistic* strain in this determinism, not the general principle of cause and effect, or, as I shall presently argue, the underlying principle of sufficient reason.

---

1 Lecture II, pp. 18, 19

We come, then, to the second of the assumptions which, according to Professor Dalton, underlie determinism, viz., that the material world is itself "deterministic," which can mean only "is subject to the law of causality." It is this assumption which has broken down, so we are assured, in contemporary physics.

In expounding this breakdown of determinism, General Smuts claims that the behaviour of the ultimate "microscopic" individuals in Nature is essentially indeterminate and unpredictable, but that on the "macroscopic" level of ordinary observation these individual uncertainties cancel out so as to yield the apparent regularities and uniformities which underlie our predictions and are formulated in our deterministic laws. But, really, these laws, the so-called "secondary laws," are "merely statistical." The "necessity" of physical happening is an "illusion created by the mass," hiding "the physical fact below it," viz., "the freedom or indetermination of the individual unit."[1]

It requires, as I am painfully aware, great boldness in a mere philosopher to challenge General Smuts on this point, especially when he can bring to his support so eminent an astronomer and physicist as Sir Arthur Eddington.

Still, the venture must be attempted. And the statements that "scientific prediction is of the same order as the expectation of an insurance company whose calculations are based on the law of averages and probability," and "in the individual case, complete uncertainty as to the date of death, and in the mass a very high degree of knowledge as to the incidence of that event,"[2] offer at least a point for logical attack.

Is this analogy between macroscopic events in Nature which are mass-effects because they are the results of the behaviour of incredibly large numbers of electrons and protons, and the sort of mass-effect with which we deal in insurance calculations, really valid?

I am not convinced that it is. We certainly can, if we like, describe the fact that over a number of years the average mortality in the population of a given area works out at, say, 60 per 1,000,

---

1   Lecture I, p. 9.
2   *Ib.*

as a "mass-effect." But this mass-effect has been discovered by the counting up of individual instances and establishing a ratio between the number of the population and the number of deaths within successive periods of twelve months. We certainly on this basis can calculate the probability of any one individual out of a random sample of 1,000 of that population dying within the next year, but just as certainly we do not assume that any one of the 60 deaths per 1,000 has happened without sufficient cause, or that, if the given individual does actually die within the year, his death will have no cause. In short, we are not dealing with uncaused events at all, *i.e.*, with events "uncaused" in the sense of being "free" and "essentially indeterminate." What analogy is there between human deaths, each of which we regard as duly caused when it occurs, though, to be sure, we have not enough knowledge to predict the moment of its occurrence in advance, and the behaviour of individual electrons and protons which, according to the theory offered, has no assignable cause at all? Granted that we use statistics in both cases; still this does not abolish the difference between events each of which we believe to be caused, and events none of which, according to the new view, is caused. Thus, General Smuts' appeal to statistics does not help to show what he, apparently, wants it to show, viz., that facts dealt with statistically are indeterminate, *i.e.*, uncaused, facts.

Moreover, there is a further point. Calling the macroscopic phenomena of ordinary observation "mass-effects" does not alter the fact that, as we perceive them, they are facts marked by a qualitative wholeness and individuality of their own. Take, for example, the mass-effect called the pressure of a gas on the walls of its container. This is a mass-effect because it is the resultant of the several pressures exercised by each of the thirty million million million molecules which, Professor Dalton tells us, are contained in one cubic centimetre of gas at ordinary pressure and temperature. Yet, when we measure it, we employ large-scale methods suitable to the phenomenon on its macroscopic plane, *i.e.*, we do not bother about the millions of molecules at all. Whatever complicated processes among the ultimate constituents of matter may lie behind the large-scale mass-effects with which we deal on the plane of ordinary observation, these latter phenomena have to be dealt with on their own plane by methods appropriate to them; and I do not see how it follows that these methods are invalidated in their own proper sphere because they are not applicable on the microscopic plane. Yet something like this seems to be General Smuts' argument concerning the "illusions" of the macroscopic plane.

I turn now to an argument which has been employed by both General Smuts and Professor Dalton, viz., the argument that determinism has broken down, because scientists have been compelled to resort to calculating probabilities. General Smuts bases his case exclusively on an appeal to Heisenberg's law of indeterminacy. Professor Dalton greatly strengthens the case by pointing out that, long before Heisenberg's quantum mechanics and Schroedinger's wave mechanics had been invented, statistical laws had already been introduced into the kinetic theory of gases, into the theory of radioactivity, and into the theory of light quanta.

I will take as a test case, as it were, what Professor Dalton tells us about the emission of an α particle from a radium atom whereby the radium atom disintegrates until it finally disappears as radium and becomes helium and lead. This disintegration, he says, "has proved to be absolutely beyond human control; neither heat, nor cold, nor chemical combination can interfere with this spontaneous disintegration, and it is subject to no deterministic law. Out of a large number of radium atoms, one in every two thousand ejects an α particle in the course of a year. The atoms are alike both in intrinsic properties and in external environment, and there is presumably no reason why one should die rather than another. Yet the call of Destiny inevitably comes, and that call must be answered, but none can say how the victim is selected. Our chain of causal connection is here definitely ruptured; we ascribe to each radium atom a certain chance of death. We deal again with probabilities, not because a deterministic scheme would be too laborious to work out, but because within the four corners of such a system there is no place to be found for the call of Fate."[1]

If I call attention to the paradox of speaking of this "death of the radium atom" at once as "spontaneous" and as governed by a

---

1   Lecture II, pp. 22, 23.

"Destiny" or "Fate" which we cannot unriddle, it is not in order to score by a cheap verbal quibble, but in order to draw attention to what seems a real difference between General Smuts and Professor Dalton, in that the former, if I am not mistaken, *does* infer from the lack of a cause an unpredictable "spontaneity" of the atom's behaviour, whereas the latter infers a "call of Fate" which leaves the atom no choice at all. I feel sure a Calvinistic theologian would feel much more at home in the company of Professor Dalton's atoms than in that of General Smuts's.

However, the logical point I wish to raise is this: the fact is that nothing has, so far, been found to account for one atom disintegrating when there is nothing to distinguish it from two thousand neighbouring atoms which do not disintegrate. But does this justify the confident conclusion that the principle of causation does not apply at all? Surely, such a negative is harder to prove than by saying: "No reason has been found; presumably there is none; therefore Nature at that level is not deterministic."

And when we come to the famous indeterminacy law of Heisenberg, with its equivalent in Schroedinger's wave mechanics, the case seems to me even clearer. I take Professor Dalton's formulation because it is briefer than that which General Smuts gives us. "If we know where an electron is going, we cannot say precisely where it is, and if we know precisely where it is, we cannot find out where it is going." How does this situation come about? Again I venture to quote Professor Dalton's admirably clear account: "We wish to determine the position of an electron; to do this, we must in some way 'see' it. Hence, we illuminate it with radiation of sufficiently short wavelength. The shorter the wavelength of the radiation we use, the greater is the energy of the quantum. When the radiation falls upon the electron the impact causes the electron to recoil, and we can tell only within certain limits of probability where the electron was going at the moment of impact. To reduce this uncertainty we must arrange for less vigorous collisions; we must, therefore, use radiations of longer wavelengths. But the long wave gives rise to a diffraction pattern, and all we can say is that it lies somewhere within that pattern."[1]

---

1   Lecture II, pp. 29, 30.

To me this means that the uncertainty to which the law draws attention is the "effect "—I apologize for the term—of what we do to the electron in the effort to observe it. We bring certain physical forces to bear on the thing we wish to observe, with the result that there is a disturbance which makes it impossible to find more than an approximate answer to our question. There is an effect of which, being ourselves responsible for its occurrence, we know the cause; but it is an effect which from the nature of the case we cannot determine by precise measurement. All we can do is to calculate the probability of its having a certain value, within a determinate range of possible values.

Is this situation fairly describable as revealing a fundamental indeterminacy or spontaneity at the very heart—or, rather, at the very basis—of Nature?

For the life of me, I cannot see it. And, curiously enough, Professor Dalton appears to agree with me or, at least, to abandon the claim to indeterminacy in the sense in which I am criticizing it. He says—and I heartily agree—that the theory of classical physics is abstract and hypothetical in that it postulates that a system, "whilst under observation, remains isolated from the rest of the physical universe."[1] In other words, the postulate demands, more particularly, that the physical processes involved in observing make no difference to what is being observed. This postulate of isolation has broken down in the observations on the behaviour of electrons and protons. In Professor Dalton's words: "In dealing with particles so minute as the electron or proton, the influence of the instrument of observation is no longer negligible, and the position and speed of a particle at any moment is not directly measurable."[2] Note "the influence of the instrument of observation," *i.e.*, of a physical thing involved in the nexus of physical processes. What is relevant is, say, that the instrument of observation is radiation of a certain wavelength. What is irrelevant is that the radiation happens to be brought to bear by a scientific enquirer, *i.e.*, by a mind expressing itself through a physical body and physical instruments. The same radiation, if it had come

---

1   *Ib.*, p. 29.
2   *Ib*

into play without any human agency, would have had the same effect. True, the effect, as observed, is such that we cannot assign to it a precise value by measurement. But from this, I suggest, we are entitled to infer, not its inherent indeterminacy as a fact, but merely its indeterminability by our methods.

What is common ground is that the fiction of isolation has broken down in this field. We can no longer assume that the object, which we are trying to observe or measure, remains unaffected by the physical processes involved in observing or measuring it. These processes affect the object, and affect it in such a way that, instead of precise, we get only probable, results. Two points are here in debate. First, whether this situation is rightly interpreted as involving an inherent indeterminateness, or spontaneity, in the fact itself; and, secondly, whether there is, in General Smuts' phrase, "an involvement of what we call mind or knowledge in purely physical facts."[1]

These seem to me far-reaching inferences to build on an uncertainty which "originates in the purely mechanical difficulty of observing a particle and keeping it isolated at the same time."[2] Arguing as a logician, not as a physicist, I say to the first inference: It is possible, but not proven. Nature may be inherently indeterminate, but the arguments adduced, though they permit of that conclusion, do not compel it. Logically, we must hold the door open.

And to the second inference I would reply in the words of Professor Dalton, whom I am glad to have on my side on this point, that "I cannot find in the principle of uncertainty any justification for assuming that the intervention of mind in an act of knowledge can modify in any way a physical situation."[3]

---

1   Lecture I, p. 11.
2   Lecture II, p. 31.
3   *Ib.*, p. 31, I would add here, because Professor Dalton has not put it into the text of his lecture, that by the breakdown of determinism he means that the phenomena under discussion cannot be accommodated in the differential equations of classical mechanics. This explanation, which I owe to a private communication from him, reduces even further the difference between our points of view.

In bringing this inevitably somewhat technical discussion to a close, I would add one further point. For the death of the radium atom, I do not see how the possibility can be ruled out that we may yet discover why some atoms die and not others. For Heisenberg's uncertainty phenomenon, the reason seems to lie in the experimental procedure which we cannot help adopting. But, whether or not I am right in my argument about these special cases, it would take more than the debatable evidence adduced to compel the surrender of the principle of sufficient reason of which the principle of cause and effect is a particular case. To give up that principle seems to me equivalent to giving up all attempt to understand the world we live in. The principle, as I understand it, admits of different sorts of reasons being sought and found for different sorts of phenomena. It is not limited to matter any more than to mind; it applies to anything and everything in which we can take a theoretic interest at all. And it is no infraction of the principle if in certain regions we cannot discover adequate reasons for a certain kind of event and must, for the present, be content with approximations, statistics, probabilities and other makeshifts.

2.—*Evolution.*

I stress this principle, because in an interesting way it applies again in the logic of evolution, where, once more, I find myself in the conservative position of defending the old against the exuberance of the new.

General Smuts did not refer in his lecture to evolution, except incidentally. But as it belongs—not least as the result of his own *Holism and Evolution*—to the changing worldview of much of contemporary philosophy, I make no apology for bringing his view of it into relation with the brilliant and stimulating discussion of the topic by Dr. Broom.

Dr. Broom kept carefully within the field of biology; he spoke only of the evolution of living forms on our earth. When General Smuts and certain modern philosophers, like Henri Bergson, S. Alexander, Lloyd Morgan, speak of evolution, they generalize the concept and apply it on a cosmic scale. They talk of the evolution of the Universe, not merely of the evolution of living forms in the

Universe. They offer us a philosophical extension of an originally scientific concept.

Yet there remains in this extension a recognizably identical feature: on either plane, biological or cosmic, evolution is a historical concept. It is such, not merely because it asserts a temporal sequence, but above all because it claims to discern a definite pattern in the sequence—a pattern which transforms the sequence from a random and chaotic into a directed and oriented one. Dr. Broom even speaks of a "directing power" which he infers from his pattern of evolution, a pattern of which the three main features are: (1) exhaustion of the evolutionary impulse in specialized forms, incapable of evolving further; (2) direction of the whole process of evolution towards the human species, itself now in respect of its physical structure an evolutionary full stop; (3) future evolution for man on the plane of mental achievement and social organization. Smuts' pattern is "holistic" and "emergent"; the Universe evolves wholes of ever higher and higher order, and in each higher order new qualities emerge which are not possessed by wholes of a lower order. For S. Alexander, cosmic evolution is from space-time to Deity, achieving ever higher degrees of perfection at each level. Even Bergson, though he refuses to acknowledge a pattern, yet cannot wholly escape it. Does he not contrast the upward lift of the *elan vital* with its downward slackening which yields apparently inanimate matter? Does he not assert a bifurcation of evolution along the lines of instinct and intelligence? Does he not hint at a possible fusion of these two divergent excellencies and dream of life's conquest over death?

However, be the detail of the pattern what it may, from the point of view of logic all these patterns have one common characteristic which is also their common flaw, viz., they not merely declare that in evolution something comes into being which was not there before, but also that the new (the "emergent") is bigger (more complex), higher (more organized), better (more perfect), than what went before. In short, every pattern reduces to this formula: *More out of less.* But, logically, this turns into *Something out of nothing.* Verily, a miracle; the stream rising beyond its source.

In *Holism and Evolution*, General Smuts saw the difficulty and thought to avoid it, partly by rejecting what he there calls "the hard physical concepts of cause and effect," viz., "that there can be nothing more in the effect than there was already in the cause," partly by taking refuge in the blessed word "creative"—"growth which becomes ever more and more in the process."[1] For myself, accepting evolution as a fact, I see only one way of dealing with this fact without doing violence to logic, and that is to go back to the old principle which was quite familiar to Descartes, and before him to the mediaeval thinkers, who inherited it from Plotinus and the Neo-Platonists, viz., the principle that there is *more in the cause than in the effect*.

I have no time to unfold this line of thought in detail, but there is one point I must emphasize before I pass on, viz., Dr. Broom argues from the direction exhibited in his pattern of evolution to a directive power and, judging from some letters of his which have appeared in the Press in reply to critics of his argument, he identifies this directive power with God. If so, again speaking as a logician, I feel bound to urge that this transition cannot be made on purely biological evidence. On that plane of thought, we can acknowledge only two authorities, viz., the general principles of logic and the special facts which fall within the biologist's province. By logic, more cannot come out of less; life cannot come out of the non-living, though it may well be communicated to our earth by an independent source of life. So, again, if there is a discernible direction in the evolutionary process toward greater perfection, once more the power (or whatever we may call it) which gives that direction must possess perfection antecedently in itself. But, admitting all this, it is still impossible to identify this source of life, or this directing power, with God on scientific evidence alone. In science alone, we cannot talk of God. If we want to trace God's hand in Nature, we must transcend science and supplement it by religion. To justify the transition to God we must appeal to religious experience, apart from which the word "God" is a meaningless noise, signifying nothing.

---

1 *Loc. cit.*, p. 9

3.—*The Machine Age.*

It is but natural that men should want to know what light, if any, scientific theories, and especially theories which, like the theory of evolution, deal with the origin and past history of man, throw on the future of mankind's existence on earth.

Evolution, as usually discussed, is purely retrospective; it is, as I said before, a historical concept. The ordinary student of evolution is concerned with tracing the steps, or stages, by which something has evolved to its present form of existence. He rarely tries to play the prophet and forecast the direction of future development from the past. He talks, in effect, as if evolution were finished.

Dr. Broom has told us that evolution *is* finished on the bodily plane. Living forms, including man, have attained to a degree of bodily specialization which makes further specialization inconceivable. We may grow physically bigger and better human specimens—healthier and, let us hope, more beautiful; but our superman will still in all essentials be a man, not a species different from man.

Only on the mental plane is there still room for evolution in man. Now, is it too bold a development of Dr. Broom's thought to claim that one direction, at any rate, of this mental development is to be found in the machines which human minds have evolved, and are still evolving, in ever new forms? A machine—the statement is not such a paradox as it sounds—is a biological phenomenon. It is an artefact. The making of it, no less than the art by which it is made; the use of it, no less than the skill required for its effective use, and the purpose to be realized by its use, are manifestations of life in human form. Machines are the most conspicuous field in which, through human minds and hands, the creativeness of the life-impulse, its inexhaustible fertility of invention, finds expression. No doubt, unlike organisms, machines have no life of their own; they cannot, in principle, be completely divorced from human control and supervision. But, though they are not themselves living beings, yet, in all their multiplicity of purpose and design, they exist only through living beings and to serve living beings. They are, I repeat, biological phenomena, or, at any rate, phenomena intelligible only in the context of the life of the organisms which have made them.

"To serve living beings," I said just now. Yes, that is the only intention, but is it also the only result? Or are machines not also reacting on the life which brought them into being, in ways which are unfavourable and disserviceable to, nay, perhaps even destructive of, that life?

The suggestion is not a new one, as readers of Samuel Butler's *Erewhon* well know. Again, in these lectures, Professor Greig has compelled us to ask ourselves the question whether art and literature and, in general, the things of the mind, can really flourish in a machine age.[1] And when we reflect on the economic troubles of our modern civilization, we can hardly help wondering, at times, whether some portion of the ills that afflict us may not be due to that very symbol and instrument of modern progress, the machine.

The most glaring paradox of our machine-age, brought home to all of us more or less painfully by the present depression, is surely this: that we are poor in the midst of actual and potential plenty. On the one side, people starve or barely subsist on charity; on the other, food actually available for consumption is destroyed or cannot be sold at a remunerative price. On the one side, a demand for goods which is ineffective for lack of the means of payment; on the other, a vast productive capacity which stands idle because its products cannot be paid for. Farmers go bankrupt and city populations are unemployed. The standard of life of millions of people is steadily going down, though our industrial plants, which could easily satisfy their wants, are working at far less than 50% of their maximum output. Sometimes one feels tempted to think that the only way to restore prosperity and give plenty of work at ample wages to all, even women and children, is another world war! A further paradox is that, in all industrial countries, the birth rate is steadily falling and the increase of population slowing down, even if few populations are as yet becoming actually stationary or dwindling. Yet the application of available scientific knowledge to agriculture, industry, trade, should enable us to sustain a far larger population than the surface

---

1   See Lecture VI.

of the earth now carries, and at a far higher average standard of life than now obtains.

What is the root of this paradox? May I draw attention to a line of thought which, though it is not likely to be the whole explanation, may well be more than a small part of it.[1]

Human civilization has developed *pari passu* with the invention of tools. A tool is, originally, nothing more than a prolongation of a bodily organ. It is wielded by human muscular power, and it enables man either to do what, with his bodily organs alone, he could not do at all, or to do it with much less expenditure of energy per unit of output. The machine is, in one sense, only a more highly developed tool, especially so long as it still requires human motive power, like a bicycle or an old-fashioned sewing machine driven with a treadle. Even when we invented machines which no longer used human muscles for their motive power, but were worked by wind, water, animals, and later by steam and electricity, for a long time the control and guidance of the machine in all the details of its use still demanded plenty of human labour. Man worked with the machine as with a more efficient tool, and every machine still required a man to look after it. Up to this point, the machine enlarged his efficiency in production and thereby raised his standard of life.

In recent years, however, a sad change has come over the spirit of man's dream. The machine is ever more rapidly displacing the man, in proportion as human muscle is being replaced on a large scale by the harnessing of natural forces as motive power. Even human supervision is being ever more extensively displaced by devices for self-regulation and automatic control in the machine itself. Every new invention throws men out of work. Man as a source of motive power cannot compete with steam and electricity. The original principle still survives in that the fewer men still required to tend machines have their productive efficiency enormously increased in relation to the time and energy they put into the work. One man with a machine is equal in productive capacity sometimes to hundreds of men without machines. But

---

1 See also the interesting book by Fred Henderson, *The Economic Consequences of Power Production*.

the redundant men are not only superfluous; they are sheer waste—unused and unusable, considered as sources of labour, *i.e.*, of power supply. There is no room for them in the system, for the only room they had was based on their labour, and their labour is no longer required.

But man is not only a producer; he is also a consumer for the satisfaction of whose needs production claims to exist. Now, originally, there was the closest connection between work and consumption. Especially in the days of pure hunting or agricultural subsistence economy, it was literally true that without work there would be no food. The curse laid upon Adam that he and his descendants should eat their daily bread in the sweat of their brows was literally verified in every man's life. It is perhaps because our religious mythology has invested work with the character of punishment for sin, that the moral tradition, even of those whose personal relation to the churches is of the loosest, is burdened with the over-valuation of what I may call the economic "virtues" of industry, hard work and thrift, and the corresponding over-condemnation of the economic "vices" of leisure, "idleness," amusement and play. But what we forget is that we cannot maintain this traditional morality and at the same time let the machine deprive the man who only works with his hands of his opportunity for doing so. Our economic system has ever less need of human labour in muscular form. Yet, when we see numbers of these "technological" unemployed, these victims of the competition of the machine, we tend to say: "Look at these loafers! They ought to be working! It would serve them right if they starved." And we condemn them for living on the dole or taking refuge in begging. We tend to apply to them the principle: if you do not produce, you shall not consume; forgetful of the fact that the wholesale elimination of men from the processes of production nowadays takes place without any moral fault of their own and often enough against their will. And thus the machine-age paradox takes on the grotesquely contradictory form: the more goods we produce by machines displacing men and preventing them from earning a living, the fewer men can afford to consume these goods. And so our machines lie idle or work only half-time, because there is no market for their products. There is no market because the potential consumers are debarred from consuming. They are debarred from consuming because they have done no work. And they have done no work because the machine has ousted them from doing it. Could bedlam itself be more mad?

We are at the parting of the ways. And we may define the two ways—the old one which we have been going and may continue to our destruction, and the new one which we shall have to try out if we are to survive—by comparing two senses in which the machine "saves labour."

At present it means that the machine *saves labourers* and their pay. That is, it reduces costs of production by reducing the number of wage earning workers. But, inevitably, it thereby swells the ranks of the unemployed and automatically diminishes the number of consumers of the product of the machine. Increase of products, decrease of population; enormous power of production with ever-shrinking power of consumption—that is why we live in an era of starvation in the midst of plenty and of depression in the midst of the greatest productive power which the world has ever seen.

The other meaning of "saving labour" through the machine is that machines *save labourers from labouring*, *i.e.*, they work for men in the literal sense of lifting the old curse from their shoulders, of releasing their energies and setting them free for other activities—for play, for self-cultivation, for study, for the pursuit of all sorts of hobbies, for that noble leisure which, Aristotle tells us, is the pre-condition of the highest mental activities. If, and in so far as, machines do the work for men, we must draw the logical consequence that a fixed quantity of work, say an eight-hour day or a forty-hour week, no longer constitutes the only moral and economic claim a man has to a share of the machine-produced goods. If the machine is thought of as working for, and in place of, the man, then it becomes absurd to deny to the man his share of the goods produced on the ground that he has done no work. I like to look at the dole in England from this point of view: it is a distribution of national income to non-workers which is made possible by the fact that the machines have been doing the work for them. Speculations among certain advanced thinkers concerning the possibility of reducing the hours of work per man per day or per week to a very small number seem to be inspired by the same logic.

No doubt, the way in which I have expressed these thoughts is crude, and they would need a lot of grooming and polishing to be made fit for reception in respectable economic society. I cannot but think, however, that there is in them an important element of truth.

The argument, however, always gives rise to a question which refuses to let itself be downed without an attempt at an answer. If a man no longer needs to work, or if he need work only very little, what will he do with his "spare" time? He will have abundant leisure which he will not know how to use. He will be idle; worse still, he will be bored. And idleness and boredom, we have been told from youth up, are the parents of wickedness and sin. Only the hard discipline of toil keeps man from the toils of the devil.

There is a problem here, I admit; the problem I referred to just now as that of the noble employment of leisure. Perhaps it is because I am a professor—though, indeed, my experiences with students have not always been encouraging—that I still believe that man is a rational being, that he has a mind which he can be trained to use in ways that only leisure makes possible. No doubt, this will mean an almost revolutionary re-orientation of our whole outlook—educational, moral, economic. But, like Dr. Broom, I look to the future with faith and hope. And Professor Greig's denunciation of the machine-age I would mitigate by urging that, for all its admitted drawbacks, the machine-age may yet justify itself by the leisure which it can provide for man, if only man will learn so to organize this leisure that it does not come to him as the economic disaster of unemployment and with the moral stigma of idleness, and if also he can learn how to make the best use of this leisure. I can imagine the leisured men of the future spending their day according to their taste and ability in countless wholesome and morally satisfying activities, which under the present system are threatened by a machine civilization, but which then will be not only compatible with it, but positively promoted by it. I can envisage a return of skilled handicrafts—not for the market, but for personal enjoyment in the exercise of skill and the making of things of beauty. I can imagine more people giving more time to music, wanting to learn to play for themselves music to which the wireless has first introduced them. I can imagine a renascence of the arts, just because those who have artistic gifts will be able to devote themselves to their cultivation, without having also to practise that other art which Plato calls the "art of wages," *i.e.*, without having to think of "making a living" either by their art or else by some bread-and-butter occupation which ultimately kills the artistic impulse within them. More people will have time to cultivate their gardens or to enjoy Nature, let alone penetrate her secrets by scientific research. The life of "theoria," said Aristotle, *i.e.*, the life devoted to the things of the mind, "is the happiest for man." Agreeing with him, I do not despair of machines making that life possible for all of us to a greater or less extent. For, whilst Aristotle thought his ideal realizable only for the superior few whose lives could be relieved from drudgery by the labour of slaves, we can make machines our slaves. Thus we shall all enter, in the measure of our mental powers, into the kingdom of free men, which is the kingdom of the mind. And in this country of ours it is not out of place to add that the kingdom of the mind is one into which, even as into the kingdom of God, all men may enter, without distinction of race, or colour, or creed.

4.—*Religion.*

A course of lectures on our changing worldview would be incomplete if no consideration were given in it to changes affecting religion. Perhaps, a philosopher who, like myself, believes that one of the tasks of philosophy is to be, if not a *defensor fidei*, at least a *defensor religionis*, may be forgiven if he attempts briefly to put down some reflections on the questions which are most likely to occur to persons brought up in the Christian faith when they observe and reflect on the impact of our changing worldview on the traditional teachings of the Christian Churches.

First, will religion, as such, die out with the further progress of human civilization?

No. Religion is man's emotional response to the Universe as a whole, or, at least, to something in the Universe through which the whole acquires supreme worth in his eyes, giving him an object of devotion and worship, in living for which his own little life acquires a value, a worthwhileness, which lifts it above the fluctuations of fortune and robs death itself of its sting.

More simply put, a man's religion is defined by whatever he is willing to live and, if need be, to die for; whatever he will suffer persecution for rather than abandon it; whatever he will himself fight and persecute for in order to make it prevail, or, at least, in order to prevent its annihilation.

This conception, it will be observed, is wider than the usual definitions, and it will, therefore, cover many things which are not ordinarily accounted religions. None the less, my procedure is deliberate and could, had I time for it, be philosophically justified. Here I must content myself with saying that we must recognize as a genuine religion everything which plays in human life the part played there by what we ordinarily recognize as a religion. Only, ordinarily in the concept of religion, we include organization in the form of a church; functionaries called priests, or ministers, or clergymen; and a definite ritual and ceremonial of worship. But these things are not of the essence of religion. And, if we omit them, we can then recognize many other religions—a religion of mammon, a religion of patriotism, a religion of nationalism, a religion of humanity, as well as a religion of Christ, a religion of Buddha, or a religion of Mohammed. Even Bolshevism is a religion; not otherwise can we understand the fanatical devotion of its adherents or the fanatical hatred of its enemies. Because it is a religion, it persecutes the Russian Church, its chief internal rival in the religious field. Because it is a religion, its enemies would, if they could, extirpate it with fire and sword, treating it as a heresy to be dealt with as orthodoxies have dealt, or, in their innermost hearts have wished to deal, with heresies all down the ages.

It follows, of course, that, if there are many religions, there are many Gods, or many different conceptions of God. For "God" is not the proper name of a particular being, but a descriptive term of invocation, which, like king or judge, names something according to its status or function; in this case, by the function of being the object of religious devotion, of answering to the demand of the religious soul for something that shall meet its craving for a soul-satisfying life. "God" is the name for anything that man worships in terms of the formulae given above.

This assertion does not, however, imply that all religions are equally good, or that all Gods are true Gods. On the contrary, there are poor religions and inadequate Gods—"false" religions and "false" Gods, if we like to say so; "false," because they play us false; because they do not really satisfy the need they claim to satisfy.

But this is an argument too long to pursue here. For my present purpose, the point is this: if religion is so understood, there is no human life—not even that of the so-called "atheist"—which is without religion, however poor that religion may be in itself, or however poor a thing a given individual may make of a religion which, in itself, is fine. Religion, in short, is rooted in human nature. It cannot, therefore, die out so long as human nature remains human nature. It will not die out until mankind itself disappears from off the face of the earth.

Next, will Christianity die out?

No, again. Churches may wax and wane; doctrines may be freshly interpreted or their traditional meaning may be revived; "fundamentalism" may disappear or, again, it may buttress itself even with philosophical arguments. If present tendencies continue, certain elements in the traditional creeds are likely to be even more widely dropped than they are now. But the spirit of Christianity will remain a permanent part of human civilization. The life of Christ, and his teaching as recorded in his own sayings in the New Testament, will remain a living fountain of inspiration to many, however much those who drink from this fountain differ from each other in their selection of what is significant in Christ's life or in their rendering of what is meant by his teaching. The traditional doctrines of Christianity took centuries to grow; there is no reason to think that there will not be further growth in the future. Christianity has changed in the course of its history; it must continue to change if it is to live. Assuredly it will both change and live.

Thirdly, will Christianity conquer the world and become the all-embracing world-religion?

No—and this denial is based, not only on the disunion of Christendom, which shows no signs of disappearing (at least, so far as Protestantism and Roman Catholicism are concerned), but even more on the fact that several non-Christian religions show much too vigorous a vitality to make it at all likely that Christianity will ever replace them. Unlike Christianity, most other religions, except Mohammedanism, are not—or, at any rate, are no longer—actively propagandist and proselytizing. Yet, against none of them has Christianity made any real progress in modern times. The successes of modern missionary effort have not been won among the adherents of the great Eastern religions which form part of civilizations sometimes older than, and always—except in science (a very modern development in the West)—as rich as, the civilization of Western Europe. They have been won against the primitive religions of uncivilized peoples where its conquests have been achieved, in part at least, by the prestige of the white man and of his material civilization, and not merely by the power of its own spiritual message. And, even here, its conquests have been incomplete, and this largely for the same reason which makes Christianity impotent against Eastern religions, viz., the unChristianness of Christians. The white man is nominally Christian, and wherever he has gone in his conquest and colonization of other continents, he has carried his Christian Churches with him as part of his civilization. But, in doing so, he has exposed to the whole world the startling fact that his civilization is divided against itself. Here, in South Africa, where the history of our native policy reflects the unresolved clash of the viewpoints of "colonist" and "missionary," and where economic interests and race-pride all too often triumph over the teaching of the New Testament, we know only too well how deep is the conflict between the Christian mind of our civilization and its White Supremacy mind. Where the voice of the Christian says, "My brother in God," the voice of the Nordic answers with "Lesser breeds without the law." An intelligent native may well be forgiven if, before the contradictory spectacle of one white man's preaching and another white man's action, he feels like the two tramps whom *Punch* pictured, some years ago, as confronted by a dog at a gate. "Look," says the first tramp, "he is wagging his tail." "Yes," replies the second, "but he is also showing his teeth. Which end are we to believe?" This, precisely, has been the dilemma of the non-European world throughout the centuries of the colonial expansion of Europe: which end to believe? The tail-wagging missionary end or the teeth-showing end of armed conquest and economic exploitation? It is the unsolved riddle still.

And yet, there is that in Christianity which, even though it be carried by an unChristian medium, may yet regenerate and save both the Christian and the non-Christian world alike. This is the conception of the infinite worth of the individual human soul. Whether or not we interpret this ideal in terms of a supernatural and other-worldly destiny of man, at any rate, so long as we also interpret it in terms of an effort for greater justice and humanity in the mutual relations of individuals, classes and races here on earth, it is an ideal in devotion to which all men of goodwill can unite. If everything else of Christianity were lost, but this ideal remained as an effective power in the lives of men and in their dealings with each other, the spirit of Christ would verily have triumphed in the end.